P9-CFA-854

The
PRESIDENT
WILL SEE YOU NOW

The

PRESIDENT

WILL SEE YOU NOW

My Stories and Lessons
from Ronald Reagan's Final Years

PEGGY GRANDE

BOOKS

NEW YORK   BOSTON

Hachette Books
Hachette Book Group
1290 Avenue of the Americas
New York, NY 10104
hachettebooks.com
twitter.com/hachettebooks

First Edition: February 2017

Hachette Books is a division of Hachette Book Group, Inc. The Hachette Books name and logo are trademarks of Hachette Book Group, Inc.

The publisher is not responsible for websites (or their content) that are not owned by the publisher.

The Hachette Speakers Bureau provides a wide range of authors for speaking events. To find out more, go to www.hachettespeakersbureau.com or call (866) 376-6591.

Photo credits listed on page 262.

Library of Congress Cataloging-in-Publication Data

Names: Grande, Peggy, author.
Title: The president will see you now : my stories and lessons from Ronald
    Reagan's final years / Peggy Grande.
Description: First edition. | New York : Hachette Books, 2017.
Identifiers: LCCN 2016044187| ISBN 9780316396455 (hardcover) | ISBN
    9781478967323 (audio download) | ISBN 9780316396462 (ebook)
Subjects: LCSH: Reagan, Ronald—Last years. | Presidents—United States—
    Biography. | Ex-presidents—United States—Biography. | Reagan, Ronald—
    Friends and associates. | Grande, Peggy. | Administrative assistants—
    United States—Biography.
Classification: LCC E877 .G73 2017 | DDC 973.927092 [B]—dc23 LC record
    available at https://lccn.loc.gov/2016044187

ISBNs: 978-0-316-39645-5 (hardcover), 978-0-316-39646-2 (ebook)

Printed in the United States of America

LSC-C

10 9 8 7 6 5 4 3 2 1

This book is dedicated to everyone who has ever wondered, "So what was Ronald Reagan really like?"

For his admirers, I hope this will add a new dimension to your respect— he was a true giant among greats.

For those who don't know much about him, may you get to know him as a person, respect him as a gentleman, and perhaps even develop a fondness for him by reading this book.

Whether or not you met Ronald Reagan in person during his lifetime, it's time for you to meet him now and I'm happy to introduce you. "The President Will See YOU Now…"

Contents

PART THREE

The
PRESIDENT
WILL SEE YOU NOW

Prologue

As the jet banked over Los Angeles International Airport, I felt happy to be coming home after an exhausting two-week, three-state business trip. When the plane was wheels down, I instinctively switched on my phone and it vibrated so frantically I feared it was broken. A steady stream of text messages and emails scrolled past—one at a time—not stopping long enough for me to read each in full. They continued one after the other: dozens of emails and nearly a hundred text messages. My pulse was racing as I caught key words and phrases that jumped off the screen: "Peggy, you must be heartbroken." "My thoughts are with you." "I'm sorry for your loss." "The world will never see another First Lady like her." "She will be missed." I put the phone down for a second to absorb the news. Mrs. Reagan had passed away while I was in the air. I had anticipated this day for years, but that did not lessen my shock and sorrow now that it had arrived.

At that moment—as the plane taxied to the terminal—I was transported back to that first day twenty-seven years ago. I had been a young woman still in college when I joined the president's staff. This was my dream job, one I held for a decade, from just a few months after he left the White House until he withdrew from public life. The experience transformed my life. Although it had been seventeen years since I worked for him full-time, my response to the news was automatic. I knew I would be going from the airport directly into action, to do whatever the former First Family needed from me.

My phone rang and I startled.

"Peggy, where have you been?" asked a former Office of Ronald Reagan colleague. "We have been trying to reach you for hours."

"My plane just landed," I said, gathering my things as quickly as I could. "I'm still on the plane. I can't really talk but I can listen. What do you need me to do?"

"We need you to go straight to Gates, Kingsley and Gates Moeller Murphy funeral home in Santa Monica. A Secret Service agent just arrived there. We will meet you there in about an hour."

"I'm on my way."

The people who had emailed, called, and texted me while I was in the air were colleagues in the years I worked for the Reagans, people who knew of my close personal connection, and friends who knew I would step back into action professionally but also would be personally grieving. They all assumed that I already knew. I was always in the know. Yet this was not like when President Reagan passed away and I was among the first to hear before it was released publicly. This time I felt as if I was the last to hear. It was devastating both ways. Knowing how quickly Reagan staffers leap into action, I assumed that the previously established funeral arrangements were well under way, and I would need to jump in with both feet at full speed.

Every death results in a wave of decisions and tasks that can overwhelm friends and family members. In the case of a former First Lady, the additional layers of logistics and complexity are enormous. Implementation would require an army, yet, as I would discover, none would manifest. A few dozen dedicated people would do as I had done—walk away from their lives, families, and other commitments to ensure that Mrs. Reagan was properly laid to rest and would be remembered in a way that was fitting.

As I waited for the other passengers to disembark the plane, I took out two stapled sheets of paper folded neatly into eighths that I had carefully and purposefully tucked in a secure pocket of my purse. I had transferred that now dog-eared document from purse to purse for three years, since my role in the plan for the First Lady's funeral was last updated. My husband, Greg, often teases me about my perpetual, and perhaps compulsive, state of readiness, but small things like this are part of my routine so that I am always prepared for a day just like the one that stretched before me. I unfolded the paper carefully, knowing that the creases made it fragile. On it was a list of people I had been assigned to call the moment that I knew Mrs. Reagan had died. As I walked through the airport to the baggage claim, I started making those calls.

The names on the list were people I knew well, part of the core group. We all had the honor of serving the Reagans, a high point in our lives. We were proud to be associated with them and were very much a family. There were a few people on my list who had preceded me working for the Reagans, and a few who had stayed on after I left. We had shared a unique experience and now, this loss.

As I glanced down the list, I pictured the president's stately offices in Century City and remembered the awestruck young woman who had arrived for a job interview twenty-seven years earlier. Many of the people I was about to call had helped guide me in my journey from naïve college student to someone who was comfortable in the world of motorcades and private jets, and could remain composed when surrounded by some of the most famous people on Earth. I knew when I called I'd be catching some of them in airports on their way to Los Angeles. All of us, the moment that we heard, would clear the week ahead to do what we could to ensure that everything came off perfectly, pulling together for one final event, our last time to collaborate as a fine-tuned machine.

Waiting at baggage claim, I thought of the last time I saw Mrs. Reagan—right before Christmas, visiting with the kids as we always did at the holidays. She was in her signature red, wearing a beautiful cashmere sweater, and had pulled up close to me, practically nose to nose, holding my arm as we spoke, as if she wanted to be able to see me and hear me and be reminded again of all that we had shared—because most of what we had shared involved her husband. I remember her looking intently at me as we reminisced about her beloved Ronnie. I told her again of my fondness for him, and for her, and how I still missed him. She said she did, too. We all do, but her most of all. Things were never the same since he left us. And never would be. She was gracious and hospitable, but I was afraid of staying too long, as she seemed tired. I didn't want to leave, though, not knowing when the next time was that I would see her—and I feared that I might not again.

Bag wheeling behind me, my heavy heart leapt when I came out of the terminal and saw my husband, Greg, with two of our four children, idling in our car at the curb in front of the baggage claim door. After twenty-five years of marriage Greg knew what he needed to do as soon as he heard that Mrs. Reagan had died. He canceled my car service, loaded the girls into the family car, and headed for the airport. He knew I would not be going home until late that night and that the family would not be seeing me much for the rest of that week.

My family got out of the car to greet me. Greg gave me a long and comforting hug, and sweet embraces from my two youngest daughters followed. I hopped in the front seat and reached back to touch the hands of my girls. The First Lady had been a big presence in their lives, and I knew they, too, were feeling this loss.

"Where to?" Greg asked.

"Kingsley Gates in Santa Monica, Twentieth and Arizona," I said. "Can we stop and get something for me to eat later? And I have to change my clothes." It was "game day."

We stopped at a nearby supermarket, where the girls dashed in to buy me snacks and a sandwich. In the front seat, with Greg shielding me from passersby, I wiggled into a dress I retrieved from my suitcase, changed back into heels, adding jewelry and a spritz of perfume. I smoothed a few wrinkles out of the dress, checked my makeup in the visor mirror, and was reapplying my lipstick when the girls returned. Within a few minutes, we were at the funeral home.

This was the same mortuary that had received the president's body twelve years earlier, and the physical sensation of grief from that memory washed over me as I entered the foyer. Right now, though, I had to put aside those feelings to focus. The specifics had not been assigned or defined, but a mental checklist immediately emerged as I introduced myself to the Secret Service agent who was waiting there.

I dove into the details. We did a quick walk-through to determine where the public would stand to observe and where they could place flowers. We chose spots for the media trucks that would broadcast live the arrival of the First Lady's body, established locations for stand-up live shots, and marked off a place from which the cameras could capture the arrival of the hearse. The hearse soon arrived. As employees of the funeral home gingerly unloaded the simple pewter-colored casket that held Mrs. Reagan's body, I greeted the staffers who had arrived with the motorcade. They were people I hadn't seen for a while and would have enjoyed reuniting with under different circumstances, yet I knew them so well and had worked with them for so many years that we did not even need to speak. We all understood our collective mission at that moment. Instinctively we moved in unison, silently, to protect her, as we always had done together in the past. We placed ourselves in a line to block some of the view of her casket from the media and the watching public.

From that Sunday of her passing through Wednesday, when the First Lady's body was transferred to the Ronald Reagan Presidential Library in Simi Valley, I was stationed at the funeral home helping to coordinate both the big, complex logistics and the small, simple ones of her funeral, from choreographing the departure ceremony to confirming who rides in which limousine in the motorcade. These were among the thousands of details we as a team arranged to ensure the world could grieve without the distraction of mishaps.

On Wednesday, before her body was moved to the presidential library, her family had some time with the First Lady in the chapel of the funeral home. Once the family had paid their respects privately, they stepped outside to watch eight of the United States Secret Service agents who had served on Mrs. Reagan's protective detail place her casket lovingly in the hearse. The motorcade departed at 10:00 a.m. exactly. Right on time.

I jumped into the last car in the motorcade, where I joined a longtime friend and Reagan staffer, along with the journalists from the Associated Press, a reporter and photographer who would capture the journey and share it with all other members of the media. The AP reporter sat directly behind me narrating what we witnessed, which lent a surreal quality to the drive. A steady click of the photographer's camera shutter punctuated his description.

"There are thousands of citizens lining every street and roadway, waving homemade signs and American flags along every part of our route...We're on the 405 freeway North now, and police and firefighters are saluting from the overpasses...some are standing at attention on top of their fire trucks or in front of their police motorcycles, large flags unfurled from the ladder trucks or draped over the highways," the reporter narrated. His words brought me back to the president's own funeral nearly twelve years earlier. Every mile along the way, just as they had for the president, the streets were thronged—only now everyone held up a smartphone to capture this last bit of the Reagan era, just as I was. All of us were reluctant to let it go.

As we took the Madera Road exit off the 118 Ronald Reagan Freeway and headed for the Reagan Library, my grief about the passing of the First Lady was magnified by the memory of how I mourned when President Reagan passed away. Mrs. Reagan left us in the middle of a tumultuous presidential election cycle where the campaign rhetoric was personal and bruising, and it seemed as though all of politics, everything that held the country together, was in disarray. President Reagan had come into office at a similar time, when our most cherished institutions were under threat and the country had fallen into a malaise, convinced that its best days were behind it. Yet Ronald Reagan took a fractured country that doubted itself and gave it something to believe in again. I could not help but wonder what he would say about our world if he were alive the day we brought the First Lady to be buried by his side. I wanted his warmth and charisma, wisdom and humor, to right this unsteady ship, return our country to its values, and revive its optimism, ingenuity, and patriotism, as he had done once before. Oh, how I missed him.

The outpouring of love and affection I saw mile after mile, from people who likely had never even met the Reagans, reminded me of all the ways they had touched lives across the nation. In the days after the First Lady's funeral, I knew I had a duty to tell the story of the Reagans as I had known them, not just because I cherish my memories but because I was an eyewitness to a piece of history that can give us hope in a confusing and contentious time. Ronald and Nancy Reagan were genuine people, not mythical characters. They lived the values they spoke of, the same when the cameras were rolling as when they were not. They saw people for who they were, but they also saw the best in them, and they always saw the best in our country and its unlimited potential.

In the decade I spent with President Reagan after he left office, I had unparalleled access to the man, his true self, and his values and how he expressed them in his daily life with his associates, local and distant friends, world leaders, and Mrs. Reagan. I want to bring you into his life, a life that I saw up close for ten years, to offer an intimate portrait of this icon who happened to be my boss. His is a celebrated story of patriotism and the confirmation that with vision and optimism anything is possible, especially here in America.

His also is the story of a real life—with the highest of highs and the lowest of lows, just like the rest of us. Yet he faced ordinary challenges with extraordinary confidence and faith to the very end. The emotion I felt that day of Mrs. Reagan's passing was in equal parts the loss of the Reagans personally, the bittersweet finale to their beautiful love story, along with a greater yearning for the certainty that President Reagan gave us, even as he gradually withdrew from public life, that our best days were still ahead.

Part One

1

To Serve the President

I grew up in a sleepy little town in the northern part of Orange County, California, back when Disneyland was still surrounded by strawberry fields. The view from my second-story bedroom window was nothing but orange groves, and behind my family's tract home in Brea, sheep and cattle grazed. The 1970s were rapidly approaching, and many Americans, including my parents, were eager to leave the troubling counterculture of the 1960s behind. I was the middle kid of three—an older sister, Carrie, and a younger brother, Paul, each of us perfectly spaced two years apart.

Carrie was always a hard act to follow—valedictorian of her class, an accomplished pianist, volleyball player, and member of a championship basketball team. Not surprisingly, she would go on to get her doctoral degree and become a college professor. My brother was a nonstop tornado of brilliance and creativity, always talking a mile a minute, saying "I have an idea," inventing things and making things that were functional—and often funny. He was part of the theater department, ran track and cross country, and used his straight-A brains to become a top doctor and leader in the arena of public health. We attended public schools; my parents had moved to Brea specifically because it had the top schools in the area, providing us with challenging coursework and opportunities for leadership roles and a variety of extracurricular activities. To get to high school, my siblings and I cut through a wash, ducked under a fence, and crossed railroad tracks flanked by a swamp thick with cattails. Life was good, and it was simple.

My parents, Terry and Susan Giboney, were both educators. My mother had been a high school home economics teacher before she became a full-time mom. She enjoyed teaching so much that she continued to teach Sunday school and adult night school classes to stay connected to the classroom, eventually going back for a master's degree and becoming a college professor. My father also was an educator, starting as an elementary school teacher, then principal, then personnel director for a school district, and eventually becoming superintendent of schools for a nearby community. The values my parents instilled in us were ones of faith, family, education, and gratitude. I deeply loved my family, my church, and my town. I was a good student and heavily involved in student government and leadership programs. When I graduated in 1986 from Brea-Olinda High School, I was voted "Most Likely to Succeed" for the yearbook. I was terrified by the pressure that brought. I had no idea what success would look like, so I hoped that it would somehow find me. Even so, I often found myself dreaming about what life might be like in a world much bigger than the one where I grew up.

Little did I know how perfectly my future would align with my childhood obsession. I was *that* kid, a precocious little girl whom no one really understood, in the grip of an unusual fascination. I read every book available in the library at William E. Fanning Elementary School about presidents of the United States, the White House, and Washington, DC. I couldn't understand why others didn't share the same intense interest. Perhaps since I was born right around election day I was destined to care about politics—and presidents. In fact, the newspaper headline on the day of my first birthday, November 6, 1968, was "Nixon Wins!" My mom prophetically clipped it out and tucked it into my baby book.

All through school, into high school, every paper I wrote or topic I researched led back to a president, a historical milestone, or a landmark in DC. Presidents and First Ladies were my alternate reality. In Washington, DC, important people made important decisions that affected us all, unlike in my small community, where it seemed that nothing historic had ever taken place. The office of the president fascinated me. This was an institution so strong and flexible that it could even withstand the mistakes of character and judgment of the almost four dozen individuals who had held the office. To someday see Washington, DC, and somehow walk the halls of the White House was my biggest dream.

In the summer of 1975, my family drove cross-country in our station wagon, visiting relatives all along the way, until we arrived in Washington, DC. When we finally reached the capital I was thrilled—and overwhelmed! The buildings were enormous, and everything seemed so important and historic. It was sensory overload. I looked at the men in suits and ties and the ladies in dresses and heels and wondered who they knew or what they had done to be so lucky as to work in the nation's capital. At that point in my life it had never even crossed my mind that an ordinary person like me could ever work in such an extraordinary place.

My parents accepted my strange obsession, but they didn't really know how to cultivate it. Other than opening our home as a polling place for every election, my parents were not involved with politics. They were Republicans, like everyone else we knew in Orange County, but not deeply passionate about their views or invested in issues or candidates. They thought DC might not be safe, especially for their daughter, and feared that if I entered politics it could corrupt me. In some ways they were right, because my obsession brought into my young mind worries that were very large for a little girl.

My interest in government and the presidency stoked my curiosity about the world and, when I was young, the state of it disturbed my idealism and my innocence. In the 1970s, when I was still in elementary school, I remember being frightened of nuclear war, upset by the gas crisis, worried about the weak economy and the inflation rate, even though I didn't truly understand what that meant. The history books I read told about great men who led our country, but I was scared of the weakness and pessimism I saw and felt all around me. I didn't understand why the country I loved and the institutions I revered could not solve these problems. The presidents of the past had overcome and endured and triumphed, and now I was paying attention to history playing out in real time, but the challenges were no longer abstract—they were tied to my nation, my community, my family, and me. All I knew was that people around me seemed worried and unhappy. The current president of the United States, Jimmy Carter, made me feel fearful, insecure, and pessimistic. Yet when I was in junior high, Ronald Reagan was elected president. I felt immediately he was a man who was worthy of the office.

When Ronald Reagan was sworn in as president of the United States in January 1981, there was widespread domestic malaise. The economy had slowed, jobs were scarce, taxes were high, and, worst of all, American morale was extremely low. On day one Ronald Reagan began to talk about it being "morning in America." He said that "America's best days are yet to come." He spoke of America as a "shining city on a hill" and made our nation believe that anything was possible—not only in the future, but that change was already taking place. In reality, the country was no different on Ronald Reagan's inauguration day than it had been the day before. Yet the perception had completely changed, and that made all the difference. I started looking at myself and my future through entirely new eyes. He championed a bold and ambitious plan of action that inspired me and made me want to be part of reinvigorating the nation.

The day President Reagan was inaugurated, January 20, 1981, I was only in seventh grade but felt like a weight had been lifted. As I watched highlights of his inauguration speech on the news that night, I was convinced he would keep me safe and always tell the truth. I had confidence he understood what was going on in America and in the world and would take care of it in a way that would benefit us all.

To me, Ronald Reagan was the perfect combination of everything I loved in a person: his values were strong, and he was optimistic and practical. His nickname, the Great Communicator, was well deserved. The way he explained the global economy and national security was not simplistic, yet was easy to understand. When he spoke on TV he always used *we*: *we* Americans, *we* the people, *we* as a nation. The personal connection I felt with him made me believe that I had to step up, too, because he was counting on me. We all had to do our best to restore America, and he would show us how.

My fascination with Ronald Reagan continued to grow as I followed him closely throughout high school. I not only was drawn to him personally but began paying attention to his policies as well, which were foundational in the forming of my own political ideology. Watching and listening to him helped me learn to articulate my point of view and influenced my worldview as it was taking shape.

Though politics, government, and President Reagan remained important fixtures in my life—a hobby of sorts—the practical side of me prevailed when it came to choosing a college and a major. I toyed with the idea of going to college in Washington, DC, but never seriously considered a career in politics back then. In addition, being a native Southern Californian, I don't just dislike cold weather, but I am actually terrified of it, avoid it at all costs, and couldn't imagine choosing to live someplace cold and snowy, even if it was just for four years. So warm and sunny SoCal was my choice for college—and a beautiful campus on the coast of the Pacific Ocean had captured my heart when I visited for the first time at the age of ten. Pepperdine University had everything I was looking for in a college: a small Christian school that offered a solid liberal arts education. It was far enough from my hometown to allow me to have a new life at school, and it was close to the beach, which I had adored since I was little. My dream of living on the ocean was about to come true, and I was ecstatic!

Beyond the beachfront property, I was there to learn and study, so I made a very mature decision to choose my major by process of elimination. I wasn't fond of science or math, so any major that required an abundance of those classes was removed from consideration. I wanted lots of options after graduation and saw marketing or PR as being too specific, potentially limiting my employment options. I was interested in journalism and broadcasting but, honestly, lacked the confidence at that time to be in front of a camera. I settled on an organizational communications major, which had elements of everything I thought I would enjoy without locking me into a narrow specialty. I hoped that it would prepare me for anything and everything—and I feel that it perfectly did.

I chose communications in part due to President Reagan's inspiring influence on my life. The Great Communicator was in the White House, and my affection for him drew me to communications personally as well as from a scholarly perspective. In my classes I analyzed Ronald Reagan's speeches, even writing an entire term paper on his remarks to the nation following the *Challenger* disaster.

In college I was involved in student government on campus and was a resident assistant in the dorms to help cover expenses, but unlike high school, where I was involved in anything and everything, in college I primarily focused on my studies. I was highly motivated to get on with the rest of my life and wanted to fast-track my college experience— and did.

During those brief college years, though, I met my husband, Greg. I was a little sister for his fraternity and briefly dated one of his roommates, so our paths had crossed periodically, but at first he did not spark my interest romantically. He was a senior and I was a freshman. He sported a big bushy 1980s mustache, so he seemed to be very old and mature, like a nice big brother, but not someone I would be interested in beyond that.

The summer after my freshman year, though, Greg and I got to know each other better on a Pepperdine semester abroad in Heidelberg, Germany. Many of our classmates were more interested in shopping, meeting Europeans, and exploring nightlife than seeing Germany and beyond. Greg and I, however, shared the goal of seeing as much of Europe as we could. He planned great weekend adventures, and I trusted that I would be safe in his group, so I asked if I could tag along on a weekend trip to Switzerland. He bristled, warning me that he would not wait for me if I was running late and he would not carry my bags. I proved his expectations wrong by being tolerant of dirty, crowded trains, resilient with schedule changes, and easygoing during travel snafus, with a deck of cards on hand—always ready to beat him in gin rummy. That became the first of our many travel adventures.

That semester, as we spent time together on trains and in cafes, we became close friends and confidants, even though we discovered that we were wired very differently. I wasn't the typical frivolous college fresh-man he had thought but instead was on pace to graduate a semester early. I had thought he was so mature and old, yet he said he was "try-ing to cram four years into five" as best as he could. He saw no reason to rush the fun and stuck around for an additional year at Pepperdine. After the summer abroad, when we returned to the States and started back to school that next year, it only took a few months for our new-found friendship to turn into a more serious relationship.

In January 1989, my senior year at Pepperdine, the university announced that Ronald Reagan would give his second post-presidency speech on our campus. I counted down the days until the moment when I would be able to see him in person. I planned to get to Firestone Fieldhouse very early so that I could get as close as possible, but the morning of the speech my alarm didn't go off. I woke up in a panic, hurriedly dressed, grabbed my camera, and ran down just in time to get a seat in the far-thest section from the stage. Nonetheless, I could hardly breathe from anticipation.

The former president was announced to thunderous applause, none louder than mine. There he was—Ronald Reagan—himself, in person, in the flesh, in the same room that I was. The utterly impossible had become possible. I snapped an entire roll of pictures. From my seat, with the weak zoom of my inexpensive film camera, my record of this historic moment looks more like *Where's Waldo?* I couldn't have cared less.

Never in my wildest dreams could I have imagined my *Where's Waldo?* experience with President Reagan would be the very beginning, not the end.

In the summer of 1989, I was acutely aware that graduation was nearing. I would be finishing a semester early, in December. I had an opportunity to pursue work experience in lieu of one additional course and was excited to find an internship for my final college semester. I made a list of ten places in Los Angeles where I would be interested in working. I knew Ronald Reagan had recently left the White House and had opened an office in West LA, so that, of course, would be my top choice. I didn't know if they had an internship program or hired students, but I had to find out. In fact, I wasn't really sure at that point what his office even did, but I knew that whatever it was, I wanted to be part of it. This seemed like an impossible-to-attain dream job, but my father always said, "Someone has to have the job you want, so it might as well be you." Thankfully, I believed him.

I sent letters to ten organizations asking for the opportunity to intern in their offices, describing my experience (which, though limited at that point, was supported by great enthusiasm), a tireless work ethic, and an internal drive to succeed and achieve. For several weeks I received no response to any of my letters, which was making for a very disappointing final semester ahead. Then one afternoon during summer school the phone rang in my dorm room.

"Is this Peggy Giboney?" said a woman's voice.

"Yes, it is."

"This is Selina Jackson, intern coordinator from the Office of Ronald Reagan," she continued.

I jumped up from my desk, eager with anticipation.

"We received your letter and are impressed with your previous work experience and appreciate your interest in our office," Ms. Jackson said. "Are you available to come in for an interview on Thursday morning at ten a.m.?"

"Yes, of course!" I practically screamed, trying hard to suppress my glee. "I am available then!"

"Oh good," Ms. Jackson said. "The office is in Fox Plaza, located at 2121 Avenue of the Stars in Century City. I'll leave your name at the security desk and they will escort you to the elevator to access our secure floor—the thirty-fourth floor. See you on Thursday at ten."

I hung up and stood staring at the phone, unable to comprehend my luck. I didn't have any political experience on my resume, so I wondered what had caused them to give me a call and give me a chance. I didn't dare tell anyone about the phone call and upcoming interview lest it jinx my good fortune. Besides, no one would believe me anyway—and it probably wouldn't ever pan out. Right?

Another thing that little girl in the library at Fanning Elementary School had dreamed of was a better wardrobe. I had studied the fashions of the First Ladies almost as carefully as I studied the actions of their husbands. I worked my way through college selling men's sportswear at Nordstrom, taking full advantage of my employee discount, and already had the perfect outfit for this job interview: a long knife-pleated classic Burberry plaid skirt, crisp white double-breasted blouse with covered buttons and a Peter Pan collar, and the ultimate Republican red blazer, complete with the compulsory shoulder pads of the era. Navy ballet flats with panty hose (of course—always back then), curled hair with teased big bangs, pearl earrings, colored eye shadow, and more makeup than my typical collegiate look.

The interview was twenty miles away, down Pacific Coast Highway from Pepperdine to the Century City area of West Los Angeles. Every drive to visit my parents in Brea began with this long, curvy stretch of road with breathtaking views of the Pacific to my right. This trip was different, though. Instead of staying on the 10 freeway, I took the 405 North and exited on Santa Monica Boulevard. The Office of Ronald Reagan was in Fox Plaza on Avenue of the Stars, a street I soon saw was worthy of its name. I'd never driven on such a wide, grand thoroughfare. The buildings were not crammed together, like the density of downtown LA or Beverly Hills. The tall office buildings and five-star hotels stood far apart, each an elegant statement. Driving down the broad boulevard gave me a good feeling, as though I had arrived in a place where I was destined to be. Then I pulled into the parking lot and saw how much it cost to park. I knew I wouldn't have enough cash on hand to get my car out of the garage after my interview. I'd figure that out later. I was expected at the president's office.

The president's office was on the top floor, the penthouse, but it was more like an impenetrable fortress, protected by the United States Secret Service and accessible only if you had a secure elevator key card. My ears popped as the elevator rocketed up thirty-four floors in a matter of seconds. I straightened my collar and blazer, and took a deep breath as I exited the elevator.

I had pictured an entry space that looked like the White House, but this reception area was much more California casual in its undeniable elegance. Jumbo glossy photos of President Reagan with world leaders, the president with Mrs. Reagan, the president with flags in the background, in the White House, and with the Statue of Liberty in the distance lined the walls. It all felt very patriotic and formal and important. The receptionist greeted me politely, and I asked for Selina Jackson, the intern coordinator and executive assistant to the chief of staff. I was asked to take a seat. I couldn't help but notice the heavy bulletproof doors on both ends of the reception area and guards positioned in the hallway. It felt very intimidating. I took a deep breath and decided that no matter how my interview went, I was grateful I had made it to the thirty-fourth floor, regardless of how brief or long my stay there might be.

Selina was much younger than I had imagined. She walked with the confidence of a woman who had worked in the White House during the Reagan administration, but that experience had not muffled her small-town Kansas charm. Her sparkling brown eyes, big bright smile, and welcoming manner immediately put me at ease. She led me past the Secret Service agents posted in the hallway and into the president's conference room, motioning that I take a seat in one of a dozen wood-and-leather armchairs that surrounded the massive polished conference table. I faced wall-to-wall windows that framed a sweeping view of Los Angeles, facing west toward Santa Monica. A majestic porcelain

eagle stood in front of the wall of glass, with smaller side tables display-
ing bronze sculptures of cowboys, saddles, and horses—a nice hint of
Western ranchero in the otherwise stately environment.

In spite of the butterflies in my stomach, Selina and I talked like old
friends. At first, she asked me the standard interview questions about
my background, my work experience, and my specific interest in the
office and the president. I tried to temper my enthusiasm a bit so as not
to seem too eager or too obsessed with Ronald Reagan, which I thought
would not appear very professional. Since I had not worked much in
an office or in politics, I instead chose to focus on my personal traits,
work ethic, and personality. I provided examples of projects I had coor-
dinated, shared previous successful roles, and demonstrated a sincere
willingness to learn from her and become a student of the office—its
priorities, its people, and its purpose. This personal approach seemed to
work, and soon we were talking warmly and comfortably. I was almost
surprised when the interview was over. Selina escorted me to the lobby,
promising she would be in touch soon, asking me to wait for a moment
while she validated my parking stub so I wouldn't have to pay. Whew—
I had completely forgotten about that.

Waiting for her in the lobby felt almost like a dream state. It was
so foreign to anything I had ever done or experienced, yet somehow
strangely familiar, as if this was all meant to be. The door nearest
me suddenly swung open and four Secret Service agents in suits and
ties, with earpieces, radios, and with guns holstered under their coats,
walked hurriedly toward me. Did they know who I was? Did they know
what I was doing there? Were they going to shoot me? Arrest me? And
then, behind the lead agent I saw two older gentlemen in golf attire.
Wait. Was it? Could it possibly be? It was. It was the president and his
golf buddy, Walter Annenberg.

In all of my interview prep and planning it had never occurred to
me that I might actually meet President Reagan. I didn't know what
to do, so I thought about what I would do if the flag were passing. I
stood up straight, placing my hand over my heart, not even looking at

him, staring off nobly into the distance. I'm certain I looked completely ridiculous.

Instead of walking past me, he walked right toward me, looked me in the eye, and extended his hand. I shook his hand and introduced myself.

"Well, hello, Peggy. It's nice to meet you," said the fortieth president of the United States of America.

I had imagined him as a ten-foot-tall giant; after all, he had been a movie star, a governor, and the president of the United States. He had tackled communism head-on, fixed the domestic economy, and solved many of the world's problems. Yet here he was, an ordinary man—just over six feet tall. His hair in pictures appeared jet black, but up close I saw touches of gray, evidence of his seventy-eight years. He was ruddy and rosy-cheeked, full of life, happiness, and vitality. His smile was more asymmetrical than I had noticed in photographs—and it was perfect in its imperfect way. And those eyes: a wonderful, bright, true blue and carrying so much joy.

He was gone as quickly as he appeared, taking all the people, the energy, and the aura of power and importance with him. The office was suddenly eerily still.

Selina then walked through the same door, grinning ear to ear, having witnessed my salute.

"It's pretty incredible, meeting him for the first time, isn't it?"

"You should have warned me," I said, still trembling inside.

"No, it's much better this way!"

And though I felt I had horribly embarrassed myself, I had to agree.

Selina then handed me parking validation stickers.

"I was going to wait to call you tomorrow and leave you hanging in suspense for at least a while, but I already know that I want you to work here with us. So can you start interning with us on Monday?"

Yes, I could.

I held it together until I was outside the building. I did not know whether to shout for joy, cry, or drop to my knees in prayers of thanksgiving. I was so overwhelmed by all that had just happened that I started laughing. Out loud. The preposterousness of it all. Me. Him. This office. Fox Plaza. Avenue of the Stars. We had met. He shook my hand. And now I work for him? I did not have any idea what Monday would hold, but I knew with confidence that my life would never be the same after that day. And in fact, it had already changed.

2

First Day at Work

On Monday, August 7, 1989, I drove down Avenue of the Stars toward my new job, feeling confident I had thought everything through. Over the weekend I spent considerable time contemplating my presentation for the first day at work. My hope was to blend in, yet distinguish myself in a way that would make me look more like a staff member than an intern. Wardrobe, I had decided, was key. I chose a purple double-breasted coatdress with shiny gold buttons, heels, hose, and matching gold jewelry—very East Coast preppy, just like the other women I had observed during my walk through the office with Selina. I knew that a proper appearance would buy me a little time. My personal goal for day 1 was simple: Do not make any stupid mistakes and ensure that there would be a day 2!

I would be working twenty hours a week as an intern in the Office of Public Affairs, to the right of the conference room where I had had my job interview. Although I wouldn't be receiving a paycheck, I knew the experience would be life changing and would allow me to get some work experience while also finishing my coursework at Pepperdine. Selina introduced me around the office and gave me a key card, which was both my parking pass and my access pass for the elevator. She showed me the back entrance for the staff and shared with me the code to open that door. Then she showed me to the intern desk, where she gave me an overview of my duties and quickly reviewed the phone system. She thanked me for being there (imagine that!), wished me luck, and headed back toward the president's office, to the left of the conference room.

The intern desk was bare: no personal mementos or photographs, as it was shared throughout the week by other interns. Our job was to answer the phones while we combed through current newspapers and magazines for articles that mentioned the president, and be available for projects and errands as needed. The inbox was stacked high with publications waiting to be reviewed.

Selina had acted nonchalant about my assigned duties, but I felt as if I had been given the keys to Fort Knox! I had secret intel—and backroom access. I was so excited I wondered if I would be able to recall the sequence of numbers to get into the office or remember what to say when the phone rang. I thought if others saw me grinning at my desk while such serious business was under way around me they might think I was too giddy, or maybe a bit too eager. I suppressed my grin and got to work.

I picked up a copy of the *Wall Street Journal* and started to flip the pages. The phone rang.

"Office of Ronald Reagan," I said brightly.

"Mark Weinberg, please," the man responded.

"May I tell him who is calling?"

"Ronald Reagan," the president laughingly replied.

Gulp.

"Why, yes! Yes, of course! Hold on for a moment. I'll be happy to connect you."

Think, Peggy, think. Don't mess up transferring the president's call! I succeeded but now I was 0-2 on interactions with my new boss. Why was I so surprised when I saw or heard the president? Of course the president comes to his office. Of course he calls his office.

Although the desk seemed a bit neglected, it was a great position from which to watch office life. I sat in front of the office of the press secretary, Mark Weinberg, and was part of an open-plan area of several desks for staff who assisted with scheduling, public affairs, events, and advance work. I was in a perfect location to observe the steady stream of people walking from office to office asking questions, getting answers, and returning to implement the tasks at hand. Staff members often stopped by the kitchen to microwave some popcorn, munch on treats sent in by fans or friends, or grab a Diet Pepsi or Fresca from the fridge.

I soon realized that the other members of the staff had not noticed my blunders because, as the weeks went on, they trusted me with more and more tasks. After interning for Mark in Public Affairs for a month or so, I was asked to assist Selina and the chief of staff, Fred Ryan. This brought me to work on the other side of the office, to the left of the conference room, what I saw as the inner sanctum, the "Holy of Holies." My desk was now mere feet from Ronald Reagan's. When I stood up at my desk I could look straight into his office and see him. Though I tried not to stare, stealing a glimpse of him at his desk reading, writing, or signing autographs never got old.

Though this side of the office was much quieter on the surface, the level of activity was equally adrenaline-producing. I had no idea when I started working there how busy the office would be and how active a life and demanding a schedule a former president would have. I never envisioned the amount of interest there would still be in his life now that he didn't have the power of the position or the pressure of facing another election. I knew how inspired I was by him and his presidency, but I couldn't have fathomed the number of other people worldwide who shared in my admiration. Nor did I understand yet how essential the team behind him was to implementing his vision and supporting his success.

In most other countries, when a head of state leaves office, they immediately become a private citizen, completely independent of the government they previously led. In the United States, though, former presidents are given a pension, funding for staff and office space, medical care through the military, and lifetime Secret Service protection. Yet even beyond the residual perks of their former role, there is an unspoken expectation from the American people that their former presidents will still be accessible and responsive personally, and visible on the political landscape, while not overstepping the authority of the current president.

It was evident from the sheer volume of mail and phone calls and requests that even though Ronald Reagan had left the White House, he hadn't left the hearts and minds of the American public. They still wanted to know how he was doing, his thoughts on current issues, and what he was involved in. People still wanted to attend events where he would be speaking, they asked for autographs, requested to meet him, and had an overall desire to be supportive of and connected to him and his life. The outpouring of interest and fondness was overwhelming to witness from both a sentimental standpoint as well as a logistical standpoint of just keeping up with the daily deluge.

Working on the other side of the office I saw firsthand how enormous the role of the chief of staff was. Fred Ryan oversaw all of the president's travel, speaking, writing, and events, in addition to his own portfolio of projects. Added to that was a massive international fundraising effort for the Ronald Reagan Presidential Library and Museum, which was scheduled to open the following year. Selina definitely needed another set of hands to assist in supporting Fred with this gigantic undertaking. We would write and send out letters to donors, follow up with thank-you notes and gifts, prepare proposals, create briefing papers, and gather background information on prospective major donors.

Putting together a fundraising trip for Fred, especially if it was an international trip, required weeks of forethought. Before the advent of the Internet, making travel arrangements and planning every detail and movement often involved staying late into the evening to call offices overseas, faxing and refaxing, praying that the intended recipient would indeed receive it—and then respond. We often used the international operator, "00," or would have the appropriate country desk at the State Department advise us, sometimes using a local consulate office or embassy to assist in reaching a particular person. Other times we just got lucky in getting through, but then often couldn't remember which way we had tried to call in order to duplicate it!

When our extensive preparations played out as smoothly as we had hoped, agendas could be covered, relationships could be advanced, and goals could be accomplished without distraction or error. We called it "organized spontaneity." We wanted everything the chief of staff and the president did to have an air of effortlessness and appropriateness, disguising the untold lengths we had gone to prior to the actual implementation day.

While all of this was taking place at a dizzying pace on this side of the office, we also had to be ready to jump off a call or stop a project at a moment's notice if the president needed something or if there were visitors in the office. The office was formal, and we were all conscious of maintaining that tone. Although the staff had warm, fun-loving friendships, office business was conducted in a polite, professional manner: hushed, respectful tones of conversation; no music playing during office hours; and no eating at your desk when visitors were on the floor. Desks needed to be kept tidy (or quickly made tidy) at all times. I often had to stash projects that were overflowing my desk to the "basement" under my desk until after the president left the office for the day. Then I would haul everything back up to my desktop to get through it all before I left.

I was about to graduate from Pepperdine and was planning my wedding to Greg for the spring, a busy time in a young life. I never thought I would get married right out of college. I envisioned working, traveling the world, and doing important things and did not see that aligning with a husband and eventually kids. At least not yet. Getting an "MRS" degree was not part of my college plan. Although I resisted marriage at first, it was hard to deny that Greg was the perfect partner for me. He asked me what I wanted to do with my life that I thought he wouldn't be supportive of. He wanted to help me pursue everything I wanted in life. And he wanted it to include him. I couldn't help but say yes to his marriage proposal. And he has been everything he promised, and more.

As graduation and the wedding approached quickly, I thought also about what an honor it was to hold my job and how much I wanted to be part of the permanent office staff. My internship was scheduled to end just as I was graduating and I was concerned I would have to find another job. Selina and I talked about my desire to stay, and she told me that some people in the office had come to LA as part of the transition staff but were eager to return to DC. She suspected a role might be available very soon. She arranged for a small stipend to keep me on staff until a job opened up. I was grateful and optimistic but couldn't afford my rent on a part-time salary, so Daddy to the rescue! He supplemented my income for just a few months until, as Selina had predicted, a full-time paid staff position opened up and was offered to me. I was both relieved and elated. It was early 1990, and I was now an official employee of the Office of Ronald Reagan, working in the chief of staff's office for Fred and Selina. I had a business card with my name on it, just beneath a gold-embossed presidential seal with Ronald Reagan's name on it. Life was good. Very good.

PEGGY GRANDE

OFFICE OF PRESIDENT RONALD REAGAN
2121 AVENUE OF THE STARS
LOS ANGELES, CALIFORNIA 90067

I hadn't been working with Selina and Fred very long when we began prepping for a lengthy international trip on which a majority of the staff would accompany the president. The Berlin Wall, which had separated the democratic and communist portions of Germany from 1961 to 1989, had come down less than a year after Ronald Reagan left office.

In June 1987, when President Reagan was still in office, he spoke at the Brandenburg Gate with the Berlin Wall as a backdrop, demanding that General Secretary Mikhail Gorbachev of the Soviet Union "tear down this wall." Shortly thereafter the citizens of East Germany demanded the same by voting with their feet: fleeing their homes for uncertain futures in Austria and Czechoslovakia to get away from the oppressive East German regime.

In September 1989 the pressure was building to tear down the wall as hundreds of thousands of brave East German citizens demonstrated in front of it, demanding their freedom. In November of that year, the wall did come down in dramatic fashion. Although Ronald Reagan had spoken with confidence just two years earlier about the ultimate demise of communism and the fall of the wall, I think even he was surprised at how quickly it happened.

Many of the senior members of the office staff had been with President Reagan when he originally made that memorable speech and were thrilled when German chancellor Helmut Kohl invited the president to travel back to Berlin in September 1990 to watch him take a hammer and chisel and personally chip away at the Berlin Wall. I volunteered to double my hours in the office while the rest of the staff was away.

I watched news clips on television from the office as President and Mrs. Reagan walked from West to East Berlin as thousands cheered "Danke, Herr Reagan!" It filled my heart with pride to see them stroll right through the remnants of the checkpoint that had kept so many Germans apart, yet was unmanned now that the wall had come down. The good feeling was short-lived, however. It seemed that everyone in the world also shared my pride in this moment, and immediately after President Reagan chipped a piece from the wall, the phones in the offices started to ring, and they did not stop for a full week. People called to share stories of their life behind the Berlin Wall and called to thank Ronald Reagan for their freedom, which they attributed directly to him. The media would call to ask for a quote from him about his emotions on such a return trip. They wanted a statement, a comment, or photos of this historic visit.

I thought back to my own visit to Berlin with a small group of friends from college, including Greg. We went to East Germany on one of the weekends during our semester abroad. It was 1987, just two years before the Berlin Wall fell. The city was still veiled in secrecy, suspicion, oppression, and fear. The train we boarded in Frankfurt was locked once we entered East Germany. East German passengers exited and entered other train compartments, but ours remained sealed, guarded by large gun-wielding soldiers. When I pulled out my camera to snap a picture out the window, the soldier pointed the barrel of his gun my way, incentive enough to immediately put the camera away! The East German train stations were nothing like those in the West. I felt like a time traveler, returning to a day where clothing was simple and drab, people were plain and hurried, with their burdens and worries clearly worn on their furrowed brows as they quietly and efficiently shuffled from place to place with little, if any, conversation or interaction.

We made our way to Checkpoint Charlie in West Berlin and had to read and sign documents that basically said we realized we were leaving a place where the United States had influence, diplomatic ties, and friendly relationships. By signing this document we were acknowledging that if we got into trouble or something happened to us in East Germany, we were on our own. The U.S. government could not help us and would not come and get us. The foolishness and beckoning adventures of youth far superseded any intelligent reasoning of maturity and adulthood, so as a group we signed our names, surrendered our passports, and ventured on to the other side...

The small room of entry on the East German side made the DMV look modern and luxurious by comparison. We were required to exchange a minimum amount of currency, which would prove to be far too much to ever spend there, and took our first steps into East Germany. Nothing could have prepared me for what I saw.

Massive government buildings rose side by side. Wide-open streets had very little pedestrian or vehicular traffic. There were few trees, no color, very little signage, and, upon closer inspection, bullet holes and pockmarks of damage were still visible on many of the buildings—remnants from World War II. Locals who saw us put their heads down and hurriedly walked around us, avoiding eye contact and diverting their path so as not to intersect ours. The senses were dulled and confused. The silence was oddly deafening and distracting, like walking around with earplugs in. The city looked as if it were in black and white, stripped of anything bright or colorful. The air was still and devoid of scent. The group I was with visited a few of the made-for-tourist museums and sights, and paid next to nothing for a tasteless lunch at a diner, depriving even the olfactory sense of anything satisfying. After several hours with nothing else to see or do or buy, we started heading back toward Checkpoint Charlie, taking a route off the beaten path through a residential neighborhood. The few people we saw ducked inside, pulled drapes, and avoided any sort of acknowledgment. At one point we looked up and saw an armed guard watching us out the window of a tall building. No wonder the residents were so cautious.

We couldn't get back to the border fast enough and were forced to surrender any remaining currency we had (though I smuggled a bit out as a souvenir in a location they did not check!). I also smuggled out some East German toilet paper, fascinated by the fact that it was closer to cardboard than to Charmin! As we finally returned to West Berlin, it was as if our time-machine bubble had burst and we were back in the 1980s. Bright lights, neon signs, shops, music, restaurants, and bars flooded the senses with sights and sounds that were familiar, even though the language was not. A bit like New York's Times Square with a hint of Vegas—opulent and sleazy at the same time—almost as if to flaunt its freedom in the face of its unfortunate neighbor. Safely back in the West, we were shell-shocked and speechless. We just sat silently as a group, trying to absorb what we had just experienced. To this day I'm not sure it's fully digestible or can be made sense of.

I digress in telling this story because taking the trip had given me a very brief, yet firsthand view into the world of communism that Ronald Reagan hated so deeply, vehemently spoke out against, and ultimately would play a pivotal role in ending in portions of the world. That personal insight and experience is something that I never could have gotten from a book, absorbed through stories, or shared a passion for without experiencing it for myself firsthand, even briefly. Although it's a trip I didn't tell my parents about for quite some time (for obvious reasons), it is one I look back on with gratitude for having taken the risk and satisfied my curiosity about what it was really like behind the Iron Curtain. As I sat alone in the office in Los Angeles, I thought back on that trip to Germany just a few years before and appreciated the exhilaration the Germans on both sides felt in tearing down that wall and understood why they wanted to honor the president. It was an honor to be even a small part of their celebration.

Following the trip to Germany, the traveling party also went to visit the shipyard in Gdansk, Poland, where Lech Walesa, an electrician by trade and also a labor activist, started the Solidarity movement that ultimately led to the overthrow of the communist regime in Poland. Lech Walesa, who had been inspired by Ronald Reagan, became the first president of a newly free Poland and was influential in leading his country away from the former rule under communism and helping to build a new government more reflective of and responsive to the people of his country.

This trip was a Ronald Reagan "victory lap" of sorts, though the president would be the first person to give credit to the people of both former East Germany and Poland, not to himself. Nonetheless, the press wanted to interview the president or get a statement from his spokesperson, and many of his longtime friends and associates wanted to speak with him and congratulate him on this triumph. The phone rang at night, too, with the staff calling to get their messages, share notes, and leave instructions for me to follow up on and take care of the next day. They needed schedules adjusted, phone calls made, speech cards revised, inquiries answered. I didn't want to be just a message taker and have everyone arrive back to a mountain of call slips; I wanted to move the office business forward, not just stay afloat. Although the rest of the staff didn't say it outright, instinctively I knew this was a test.

I suppose I passed, because not long after this trip, Selina told me she was leaving the office to go back to the East Coast to attend graduate school. I was devastated that she would be leaving but was eternally grateful for all she taught me. I am forever indebted to her for hiring me, training me, and ultimately asking me to replace her when she left.

I assumed all of her duties and overnight, at the age of twenty-four, became the executive assistant to the chief of staff, the internship program coordinator, and President Reagan's primary photographer. Even though I had no experience with photography, Selina had asked me early on, when I was still an intern, if I could step in for her and take photos of one of the president's quick meetings with a visitor. That one chance to say yes was the starting point for a role that gave me the unparalleled opportunity for the next decade to be the ultimate "fly on the wall" for so many of President Reagan's appointments, visitors, events, and travels. When everyone else leaves the room, the photographer gets to stay, observing the president's private meetings with VIPs, interactions with friends, and getting glimpses of this man behind the scenes.

Being the president's photographer also allowed me to become a familiar face to him, even though I didn't start out as such. In fact, the first time I was asked to take photos of his appointment, I walked into his office to tell him his next appointment had arrived and that I would be bringing them in shortly—and I had to reintroduce myself to him.

"Hi, Mr. President. I'm Peggy—one of your interns. Selina asked me if I would take photos of your next appointment, which I am happy to do if that's all right with you."

"That's just fine. Thank you, Peggy."

"Thank you, Mr. President," I replied, and walked out to retrieve his guests.

Since I had watched Selina handle these appointments in the past, I knew how things were supposed to be done. The more intimidating part was due to my inexperience with anything other than a point-and-shoot camera. I wasn't sure how my photos turned out (or even if they turned out at all) until a week later when we got them back from the lab. (Yes, these were the "olden days" of film cameras—pre-digital.)

Thankfully that first set of images looked great, which allowed me more opportunities to take photographs. And I did go back and actually read the manual when it seemed I would have a second and third chance to snap pictures. Most of the success of these images was due to Ronald Reagan's incredible poise in front of a camera. He never took a bad photo. Thanks to my having a good eye for framing and lighting, a steady hand, and finding the Auto setting on the camera, he made my photos look terrific!

Slowly but surely the photography duties were transferred exclusively to me, which I loved. Being in and out of the president's office several times a day, I enjoyed small opportunities to talk with him briefly before and after each meeting. These grew into longer opportunities as I began to interact with him with greater confidence and authority, stepping up to keep the appointments on time and managing the photo ops with greater command. Soon I was allowed to run these meet-and-greet visits on my own. There was no better feeling in the world than walking into the president's office and having him look up at me and flash that sparkling smile—no more introduction necessary. After a few months of being in the outer circle, I was finally entering the inner one.

An essential component of staying in that inner circle appeared to be getting to know Mrs. Reagan and developing a relationship with her as well. I first met Nancy Reagan briefly in the office one day when she joined the staff in the conference room for a birthday celebration. She was as petite as I imagined, perfectly coiffed and polished—the consummate hostess. She was warm and gracious, welcoming me to the office when I introduced myself to her as one of the new interns. I would see her several times in passing in the office over the next few months, but first cemented a connection with her at the office Christmas party she and the president hosted for the staff at the Century Plaza Hotel adjacent to the office.

Greg met both her and the president for the first time that evening, and we had a picture taken of the four of us in front of the Christmas tree. After the formalities of the photos and the celebratory toasts, it was time for casual conversation. I was talking to several of my office colleagues and turned to look for Greg, and I discovered he was deep in conversation with Mrs. Reagan. They were chatting like old friends, having a great time laughing and thoroughly enjoying each other's company. I heard later from a woman on her staff who said that Mrs. Reagan thought he looked a bit like Tom Selleck, since back in the day Greg sported that same bushy *Magnum, P.I.* mustache. Whatever the reasons, their immediate and unlikely friendship gave me a strong foundation on which to build my future relationship with Mrs. Reagan, too. Her instincts about people were astute, and her husband trusted her intuition. Over time I grew to have a strong alliance with Mrs. Reagan as she recognized that I shared her goal of wanting what was best for her husband and discovered that my loyalty to him ran deep and pure.

Aside from my semester abroad, I hadn't really done very much traveling before working for the president, but I was thrilled that my job would involve some—especially with him. Within the first few months of working for the chief of staff, I was invited on my first trip. Private air travel was completely foreign to me, and it was surreal having Greg drive out onto the tarmac and pull over next to the plane to park and drop me off (pre-9/11, things were very different at airports). We would chat with the other staff and the Secret Service agents until the president arrived. Once he did, he would walk over to say hello to Greg before he boarded the plane.

Walking onto a private plane for the first time was amazing. The aircraft we used was always beautifully appointed, though fairly small compared to a large commercial plane. We made sure the president took good care of the pilot and the flight attendants, bringing little gifts of thanks and taking pictures with them. I would choose a seat near the back—it was better to be invited forward, where the president sat, than to be asked to move to the back. I always brought work to do but also enjoyed the casual time with staff to just be together, which was a novelty. I paid close attention and took my cues from the other staff members who were more experienced and accustomed to this life. It was a good life—and didn't take much getting used to! The planes were spacious and comfortable, and the most incredible part of all was that once you boarded, they shut the door and you were off. No waiting around, no delays—just get on and go. No ID required, no ticket. Since I was known to the Secret Service I was simply allowed on. The food was delicious and freshly prepared and served on fine china and in real glasses. No plastic packages to open or stale bread to ignore. Such luxurious travel "ruined" and spoiled me. Still now, every time I fly, I long for those days again.

One of the first big advance trips I was sent on for the president was to Iowa in 1991. He was making a speech at a convention center and there weren't very many moving parts, so it seemed fairly straightforward and simple—a good first solo trip for me. The purpose of an advance trip was to go ahead of the president and confirm that the event logistics and details were finalized in a way that was not only safe from a security standpoint but also ensured that every step and movement and event element had been perfectly planned, choreographed, approved, and rehearsed. With a president, even a former one, nothing was ever left to chance or ad-libbed. Every step and route and location and interaction and photograph and camera angle and toe marking and timing cue was planned, agreed upon (often even argued about), and ultimately perfectly executed, making it appear as if it all just happened seamlessly.

Yet one thing you can count on is that there is always going to be something that comes up that you didn't count on. On this trip it was my car. I landed in Cedar Rapids, Iowa, and went to the car rental counter as indicated by the travel agent who did all of our bookings. I gave them my confirmation number and my ID and was told that I couldn't rent a car because I wasn't old enough! I was only twenty-four and needed to be twenty-five.

Undeterred, I pulled out my gold-embossed business card bearing the seal of the former president, along with my official government ID, trying to convince the woman behind the counter that she should ignore her protocols, override her system, and rent me a car. What would I do without one? How would I get around? I couldn't possibly call the office and tell them that I was having any issues on my first solo trip. But she would not budge, so I took a cab from the airport to the event venue, thankful that my hotel was within walking distance. I ate all my meals from wherever I could walk to, and then made sure to delegate any of the running around that needed to be done before the event to our host group. No one on either end ever knew that I didn't have a car, and it actually worked out in my favor since when the event was over I just caught a ride with the president to the next event—no need to return a rental car!

After three years on the job and three years of marriage, I was overjoyed to be expecting our first child in 1993. However, I wasn't yet sure how my pregnancy would align with my expanding work responsibilities. I had shared the news with the office staff, but I hadn't yet told the president. It was March 1993 and we were flying to Mexico, where the president would give a speech. I knew we would have travel time together, so I planned to tell him my big news then.

We boarded the plane, which had an overwhelming fresh-paint smell, and I secretly worried about the paint fumes being dangerous for the baby. In Mexico our motorcade consisted of very old Suburbans. I jumped into the staff one and realized there were no seat belts. So, bouncing around, I clutched my stomach as we endured potholes and bumps and erratic driving, trying to evade the persistent and invasive press on our way to the event. (In fact, the press was so bold in their attempts to get photos of the president in his car that they would go onto the shoulder of the road to try to get around and ahead of him. It was the only time I saw the agents from our Secret Service detail jump out of their vehicles at red lights with guns drawn!)

After the president's speech and before a scheduled photo op, we were in the holding room with the rest of the staff and the president's Secret Service agents when I started to tell him about my pregnancy.

"Mr. President, I have some happy news to share with you," I began.

He looked at me with a broad smile and curiosity.

"What's the good news?" he asked.

Just then, the doors to the holding room flew open and Secret Service charged into the room, declaring there was a bomb threat at the venue. They moved quickly and precisely, surrounding the president to usher him out. He stopped the agents briefly, grabbing me by the arm, making sure I moved out with them. Within moments we all were safely out of the building and in the motorcade on our way back to the airport. Talk about a memorable moment! Fortunately, no bomb was ever found at the venue, but unfortunately for the guests there would be no photo op.

I hadn't gotten the words out of my mouth yet in the greenroom, but back on that private plane with those unsettling paint fumes, I waited until we were at cruising elevation. As soon as the seat in the front of the plane next to the president's was empty, I hopped up into it. He smiled at me, waiting, again, for my happy news.

"As I was saying…" I started again, laughingly, "I wanted you to be among the first to know that my husband, Greg, and I are expecting our first child."

"That is wonderful news," he replied. "Nancy will be thrilled to know, too. We look forward to meeting and welcoming your little one in a few months."

I was relieved when everyone finally knew, as my work clothes were starting to get a bit too tight to hide it much longer!

At the time I didn't think my pregnancy would directly affect the president very much. Yet fast-forward just a few months. I was now about six months pregnant and the president's longtime executive assistant decided to retire. She had served President Reagan in a variety of capacities, going back to when he was governor of California.

Hers would be incredibly big shoes to fill, and I had no idea whom they would find to replace her.

Imagine my shock when the phone rang one evening at home and President and Mrs. Reagan were both on the phone. They were calling to ask *me* to serve as President Reagan's new executive assistant. My mind was racing as I thought about what an honor it was and how fortunate I was to have this opportunity. I felt humbled that they had decided I was worthy of this important job and delighted by the prospect of an incredible challenge, yet I was also grounded in the reality of my current condition and was worried that maybe they had forgotten about it.

"I would be so honored to serve you in that capacity, Mr. President, and I want to accept your kind and generous offer, but I have to remind you that I am six months pregnant," I said. "I will need some time off when the baby is born, and I haven't really established yet when I will return."

"We know," said Mrs. Reagan, jumping in. "It's obvious [alluding to my unmistakable pregnant belly]. Of course we're willing to wait. We will make it work. We want you to take this role."

I had always embraced and rarely avoided any challenge, and am at my best and most efficient when required to make the seemingly impossible happen while making it look simple. This, however, was far beyond that. The woman I would replace had traveled the world with the president of the United States, had been his face and voice for eight years as his executive assistant in the White House. She had the experience, connections, expertise, and gravitas of a seasoned professional with relationships and perspective that I did not have. How on earth would I replace her? And how could I serve him in the manner to which he was accustomed? Was it possible? I would never be able to duplicate her, so I determined that I couldn't—and wouldn't try. Instead, I would have to be myself, the best version of myself. And that would have to be enough.

I was about to become a mother for the first time and was also facing the immense responsibility of serving President Ronald Reagan personally every day. As with everything in life, I wondered how it would all work out, but I pressed forward, trusting that if it was meant to be, then it would be possible.

3

Getting to Know the Boss

Every day when I walked through the lobby of Fox Plaza to make my way up to the thirty-fourth floor, I entered the world of politics—the politics of the elevator. The other passengers in the elevator to the top floors were some of the most powerful and influential CEOs, attorneys, and financial advisors in Southern California. As we crowded in, my Nordstrom-trained senses would often detect the scent of expensive cologne on the men, spot the Chanel suits or handbags on the women, notice the turn of an Armani cuff on a shirt or the artfully constructed vents in the back of a bespoke jacket. Elevator politics played like poker. We sized each other up, daring someone to go all in. One man stepped forward, swiped his key card, and pushed the twenty-eighth floor, an impressive opening. The next slowly extracted the card from his jacket pocket, waiting to make sure everyone was looking, and raised him to thirty-one. Then I stepped forward and played my thirty-four, the equivalent of an elevator royal flush. My well-clad companions would take a second look at me, a young woman who looked much younger than her age, and would wonder, *What is that kid doing with a keycard to the top floor—the president's floor?*

Often, in the beginning, I wondered that, too.

Yet as time went on I found my footing. I was responsible for keeping President Reagan on time, on schedule, on task, and on point. I not only had to keep pace with the president, but I was expected to be three steps ahead of him. And those steps had better be in the right direction since the United States Secret Service was also following along. I was young, yet I had to present myself as a voice of authority, even when I wasn't always completely confident myself. The pace of life and business didn't allow for the luxury of second-guessing, so it meant that I had to make many quick decisions and learn to trust my instincts. While my formal schooling ended with a bachelor's degree in organizational communications and a minor in business, my informal schooling was ongoing, with a pace and intensity far greater than even that of my college years. From my prime observation point, I wasn't just watching President Reagan but other leaders, too—of countries, of industries, and of companies—the best of the best.

I made it a habit to arrive at the office every day at eight thirty a.m., half an hour before the office officially opened, and ninety minutes before the president arrived. My desk faced the conference room, a formal seating area, and the doorway to the president's half of the office. From there I could see everyone who entered that side. To the right was the chief of staff's office and his assistant's desk, and just ahead of me on the left was the president's office. To the side and behind me were huge corner windows showcasing the sweeping beauty west and south. I always wished I had more time to simply enjoy these incredible views, as they were truly spectacular!

When I arrived I would put my purse and bag down behind my desk and wrangle the pile of newspapers that waited there. The president liked to read the funnies first—his "dessert" before he got to the "main course" of his daily reading—so I would take that section out of the *Los Angeles Times* and refold it with the comics on top. Then I'd review his work folders. I had several legal-size folders I used to organize his workday: schedule, correspondence, signatures required, and other items requiring his review or follow-up. The folders were deep blue, embossed in gold with the presidential seal. I'd check to see that the items in the folders were in order and ready for him and would stagger them on my desk with titles visible, awaiting his attention. I would gather up his schedule folder, along with the folded funnies and the other newspapers, then turn to unlock the door to his office.

He liked a well-organized workspace, and I wanted his office free of clutter, so I did not put very much on his desk. I placed his schedule folder, containing his schedule for the day and the briefing papers in the order the events would be taking place that day, along with the folded comics section, in the middle of his desk. The rest of the papers were placed to the side of his desk, with titles showing—*Los Angeles Times, Washington Post, New York Times, USA Today*, and *Wall Street Journal*.

Then I filled his carafe with fresh water and replaced his glass with a clean one. When I opened the sheer pleated curtains to let the glorious Southern California morning sunlight bathe the room, it always was a happy moment. In the new light I'd assess the room, fluffing the cushions and pillows on his couch, straightening any pictures or items on his shelves or behind his desk that were out of place, and feeding the fish in his aquarium. I turned on all the lamps and overhead lights before I walked out, including the one in the fish tank, always checking to make sure that all the fish had made it through the night.

The staff had given the president a saltwater fish tank as a birthday present thinking it would make for a beautiful visual, as well as give him "company" when he was working in there alone. We also knew that his littlest visitors would thoroughly enjoy it. The evening before his birthday we had it installed in his office. The fish in the tank were named Gorbachev, Thatcher, Mulroney, and such. He thought it was a wonderful gift. Well, this lovely gesture for him turned into a bit more of a headache for me than anticipated.

Nearly every Monday when I came into the office there were one or more fish floating—not swimming—in the tank. I would call my friend Erik Felten, who worked on specialty projects on the other side of the office, and ask him to scoop the carcasses out of the tank. Erik and I would make a mock processional over to the president's personal bathroom in his office and give the fish a royal flushing down the presidential commode. We would have to explain to the president each Monday why there were so few fish in the tank. I would then call the aquarium maintenance company to send over some replacements ASAP.

The case of the dead fish would remain a mystery until we figured out that the air conditioning in the office would shut off over the weekend if no one was in there. The tank was getting too warm on Saturday and Sunday, which is why the dreaded results ensued on Mondays. We eventually switched from a saltwater tank to a freshwater tank that allowed us to acquire hardier fish. They maybe weren't as pretty as the saltwater fish, but they lived a lot longer and our Monday morning processionals could cease. Still, I never lost the habit of checking the tank every morning to make sure that the successors of Thatcher and Gorbachev were still happily swimming.

At about nine thirty each morning the staff would gather in the chief of staff's office to review the day and plan ahead. Around the time we were wrapping up our meeting, a Secret Service agent would arrive to tell me that the president was on his way to the office, giving me just enough time to set my things back at my desk, grab my keycard and some business cards, and head downstairs with the agent to await the president's arrival.

His black Town Car would pull up to the elevator in the parking garage with a Secret Service vehicle in the lead and another one behind. When the cars stopped, the agents from both would jump out. If things were clear, the president's lead agent, who rode in the front passenger seat of the president's car, would get out and open the back door for the president. (Even when I was a passenger in his car, I was never allowed to touch the door. It was opened and closed for me, and I would await instructions as to when I was clear to enter or exit.)

As the president exited the car, he always had a huge smile on his face. He was happy to be there, happy to be starting another day, and happy to present me with the canvas White House bag from his "roommate" (his quip for Mrs. Reagan), which I would take from him to carry upstairs. His lead agent, along with a few other agents, would escort him as he rode the escalator up from the parking garage and walked into the building.

The lobby of Fox Plaza was always bustling with people who hoped to catch a glimpse of the president heading into his office. Plus, Bruce Willis's first *Die Hard* movie was filmed there. Bruce Willis fans seemed just as happy to see Ronald Reagan.

As he walked through the lobby on his way to the elevator, people would wave hello, run up to shake his hand, ask for a quick picture or autograph, or just want to say something to him. While Secret Service made sure the president was safe, their job was not to run interference with the public, which is why staff always accompanied him. I usually gave people who approached him my business card and asked them to contact me to set up an appointment or send in a request.

For security reasons, we tried to keep the president moving along toward his office as quickly as possible. Periodically there would be a photographer or camera crew who knew his routine and waited for him in the lobby, trying to get a picture or a statement, so sometimes he was captured on camera entering the building, which meant that I often was, too. In the office we had a rule that if you were seen on television or in print in the shadow of the president you owed the office breakfast. (It was done in jest, but was also meant to incentivize staff to keep a low profile.) But sometimes it was unavoidable—so I bought a lot of breakfasts over the years! Once we got upstairs, agents held the locked doors open so the president could walk straight in and directly to his office to begin his day.

Whether he was in the office or not, the main phone line was a public number (which appropriately ended in -1980) that was listed in the phone book and available through the information operator, so the phones rang all the time. Most of it was legitimate business. Some of it was not. It was as if people all over the world believed that Ronald Reagan was sitting in his office twenty-four hours a day and would be happy to speak to anyone who called at any time—and boy did we get some strange calls! For one reason or another they had been thinking about the president and had something urgent they couldn't wait to bring to his attention: a conspiracy theory, an alien sighting, or a suspicion that the CIA was bugging their phone. I was never quite sure what they expected President Reagan to do with any of this information. Over time I learned the names of the regulars who would call and knew how to assure them that they had been heard and I understood their point, but the president was a very busy man and couldn't talk to them personally right now. However, he would be happy to have them send him a letter.

I never had seen anything like the mail Ronald Reagan received daily—and the gifts, particularly on his birthday! The mail first was x-rayed at the federal building across town before being delivered to our floor in Fox Plaza. Our correspondence staff then undertook the colossal task of sorting it when it arrived. At the holidays, or on the president's birthday, or on his wedding anniversary, the mail was seemingly without end. Whether the letter was from a head of state, a patriotic American, or a total lunatic, nothing ever got thrown away or ignored. Everything received a reply. That was very important to the president.

The majority of the mail consisted of notes to him, thank-you cards, or heartfelt expressions of fondness, admiration, and respect. I loved seeing the faces, houses, and children of so many happy Americans— and the president did, too. Pictures of their baby—or their dog they had named Reagan, or even a boat named *Reagan*. There were also Reagan tattoos in surprising locations (enough said). When people sent photos of themselves in various states of undress, I would pause for a moment to consider the thought process of someone who staged such a photograph, had it printed, and, after taking a good long look at their image, decided, "You know what? I think President Reagan needs to see this!"

The president had staff, including me, write much of his correspondence, yet often he took pen to paper himself to thank people from the heart. Emily Post would have been proud. It's estimated that over the course of his lifetime he wrote more than ten thousand pieces of personal correspondence (and that doesn't count all the mass mailings that were sent out under his name). As such, it seems highly appropriate that the U.S. Postal Service has issued a stamp in his honor three times, more than any other person. It was important to the president to acknowledge people, thank people, and not take their kindnesses for granted.

As his executive assistant, I saw how this played out in his written correspondence. In his signature folder would be a stack of photos to be signed. I typically put a Post-it note on the picture with the person's name written out and would make a suggestion of what to write, from something as simple as WBW, RR (With best wishes, Ronald Reagan) to something longer like "Thank you for dropping by the office. I enjoyed seeing you again and meeting your family, RR." The president would often add something personal and clever, like to a friend who had golfed with him: "We may not be ready for the PGA, but we sure had a lot of fun! RR." One day when he had a particularly large stack of photos and letters he had been signing, he brought the completed folder back to me shaking his hand as if it ached from signing his long name so many times. "Some days I wish my name was Bob Hope," he joked.

Other times he would handwrite a long personal letter and would bring it to me asking if I could type it up for him and send, though I knew the recipient would much prefer the handwritten version to my typed version. The president had always been a bit self-conscious about his penmanship since he was born left-handed back in the day when teachers required everyone to write right-handed. I assured him that the recipient would not be critical of his penmanship. I'm sure there are many recipients of these personally handwritten letters who are grateful for my intervention.

I especially loved the old-fashioned aspects of his personality, his adherence to protocols, and his humble nature. He didn't like using the phone to "buzz" me from his office. If he needed something, he got up and walked out to my desk to ask. Seated with my back to his office, if I happened to be on the phone and on my computer simultaneously, it might take me a few moments to sense he was standing there, and I would startle when I did. He always apologized for interrupting me. I responded that nothing and no one was more important than him and what he needed. Each day, after he had finished his lunch, he would push out his own lunch cart rather than calling me in to do so. And when we would walk up and down stairs he would reach over and hold my elbow to steady me—keep in mind I was in my twenties and he was in his eighties!

I remember one occasion when I helped prepare the president's office for a small press conference. We took in extra chairs and set up lighting. After the event, I was walking in and out of his office carrying the extra chairs one at a time back to the conference room. During one of these trips, I sensed that someone was following me. I turned around to see President Reagan behind me, carrying one of the chairs.

I stopped and said, "Mr. President—don't worry about that—I can come back and get it."

He firmly set the chair down and looked at me, saying, "What makes you think you can carry a chair any better than I can?"

I was momentarily speechless, then replied, "Okay, follow me!"

The gentlemanly side of him never liked women doing heavy lifting—literally—but the professional side of him deeply believed that men and women were equally qualified to do any job. After all, he was the first president to put a woman, Sandra Day O'Connor, on the Supreme Court. This was not a gratuitous appointment, but one that was done because he absolutely was convinced she was well qualified and the right person for the job, and he felt strongly it was time for a woman to serve in this capacity.

President Reagan lived a life of gratitude, never taking for granted the people around him or the great lengths to which people went on his behalf. That gratitude extended even to me.

My most cherished possession is a doodle of a cowboy he surprised me with the first Christmas I worked for him as his executive assistant. The doodle looks a lot like a self-portrait of him in a cowboy hat. He signed it and had Mrs. Reagan sign it as well: "Merry Christmas to Peggy—Nancy and Ronald Reagan." When he presented it to me, he was a little apologetic. He said he wished he could have done more, but since I was usually the one that did his shopping for him, he wasn't quite sure what he could give me without getting me involved. (As a former president he couldn't exactly run out to the mall very easily—and Amazon Prime didn't yet exist.) This gift was from his pen, from his heart, and there is nothing that I could possibly treasure more.

4

Invitation to the Office of Ronald Reagan

During the post-presidency years, I was given a firsthand view of what diplomacy—the Reagan way—really looks like. To Ronald Reagan it looked like relationships, not rhetoric. Diplomacy was personal, not political. World leaders and political figures came to visit him because they wanted to and felt personally connected to him, not because they had to. After he left the White House they didn't come visit for protocol or diplomatic reasons; they genuinely liked him and treasured his personal friendship and wanted it to continue even beyond his presidency.

In addition to VIPs with global stature, a surprising number of everyday Americans were also able to fulfill their dream of having a private meeting with Ronald Reagan in the years after he left office. Of course we screened requests rigorously, but people who wrote inspiring letters that made a good case for meeting with him often were granted an appointment. Some of the letters were so well written they made it very hard for us to turn down the request. Besides, nothing brought the president greater joy than to meet with those who had given him the opportunity to serve as their president.

One such request came from a Pacific Northwest family whose son had Asperger's syndrome, a form of autism, who was fixated on Ronald Reagan. The six-year-old boy had read dozens of books about the president, memorizing every fact and detail of his life. The letter from his family described how he talked about little else apart from when he was going to get the chance to meet his hero. This family's request got an immediate and unanimous yes. I think the president was as excited to meet the boy as the boy was to meet the president.

When I went to the lobby to greet the family, I could see the anticipation on the little boy's face and the excitement in his jumpy movements. He started talking as soon as he entered the office, only pausing for a moment when the president bent down to shake his hand. He was talking *about* the president, not necessarily *to* him. Every now and then he would look at his hero, as if to quiz him on his own life story.

"Did you know that you played football in high school?"

"Why, yes, I did. I played right guard and tackle."

"Did you know that you were a lifeguard and saved seventy-seven lives?"

"Well, yes, I was, and yes, I did," the president replied with a grin.

On and on the little boy went, and the president loved it! Sometimes the president was surprised that he got the answer "wrong."

"Did you ride horses at the White House when you were president?"

"While I was president, yes, but at the White House, no," President Reagan said. "I rode horses at Camp David and at my ranch in California, but not at the White House itself."

"No, that's not right," the boy said, "correcting" the president on his reply. "Ronald Reagan did ride horses when he was president and lived at the White House."

And the president just smiled. We all did.

"And you like jelly beans—especially the black licorice ones, right?" the boy asked.

"Yes, I do, and I hope that you do, too." And with that the president presented the elated little boy with a jar of Jelly Belly jelly beans to take home. You could see from the look on his face how thrilled he was to receive this gift.

This entertaining and endearing appointment would not have taken place had the family not summoned up the courage to write and ask. I often thought of all the people who would have loved to meet the president but never thought it would be possible, so they didn't even try. A lesson for all of us: you can't get something if you don't ask for it.

One of the best parts of my job was calling people to tell them that the president wanted to schedule them for an office visit. I heard the shock in their voices and remembered how I felt when my own life-changing call came from the Office of Ronald Reagan. I often imagined what would happen after we hung up. I pictured the person calling and telling everyone they knew, trying to figure out what to wear, scheduling a haircut, maybe a manicure, thinking about if they should bring a gift. And if so, what on earth do they bring to the former president of the United States, who likely already has everything? And then panic would set in. What am I going to say? What should I *not* say? Are there certain protocols? Will Secret Service be watching? The excitement of anticipation was a wonderful part of the experience itself.

As the president's assistant, I escorted visitors in to meet him. I saw part of my job as putting his visitors at ease so they would not find themselves either mute or babbling on this day, likely to be one of the most memorable days of their lives. I wanted them to savor every moment. I found it amusing that even a famous celebrity, top sports figure, or other high-profile individual would sometimes be anxious about meeting President Reagan for the first time. Often they would grab my arm and say, "Peggy, I'm so nervous. Please don't let me embarrass myself in front of him." Didn't they realize that most people felt that way about meeting them?

So whether it was someone rich and famous, the janitor of the building, or a patriotic American, I didn't want anyone to "miss the moment" and look back regretting that they had squandered this opportunity.

I talked with visitors for a few minutes in the lobby before I walked them in to ask if there was anything in particular they wanted to share with the president. In a blink, this visit would be over, and they would wish they could capture the moment again so that they could relive every detail whenever they wanted. I recommended that they take a good look around the office. Enjoy it—relax, smile, and take it all in.

Before we entered his office, I had them stop to sign the guest book. As they did, I would look in to see if the president was standing at the front corner of his desk ready to receive his visitors. He always was. I walked the guests in and introduced them to the president. After brief greetings, I asked everyone to pose for a picture. I remained in the room while they visited, usually snapping a few candid photos as well. If the guests froze and didn't know what to say, I would jump in and say, "Mr. President, they were just telling me out in the lobby that..." and save the conversation, preventing things from being awkward or uncomfortable for anyone.

I would tell the visitors that they would have "just a few minutes" with the president, even if they were on the schedule for a ten-minute appointment. I never specified the number of minutes because I wanted to reserve the right to cut the meeting short if things weren't going well. Some people became overwhelmed and exhibited strange behaviors when they were in his presence. Some would walk in, say hello, shake the president's hand, snap one quick picture, thank him, and walk toward the door as if they were visiting the Ronald Reagan Wax Museum. When that happened, I would stop them and insist that they stay and visit for a few minutes.

In spite of our best efforts to screen visitors, a couple times a year we would still be surprised by an odd or uncomfortable visit. Some guests would squander their time by asking him something strange about UFOs or aliens or go on and on and on with excitement, never even letting him get a word in. In those cases I would decide that the appointment didn't need to last the full ten minutes. I would say, "Thank you so much for coming in today. The president has another appointment in just a few minutes that he needs to prepare for..." as I motioned to the door. As they exited I would steal a glance back at the president and see him smile a knowing smile or see a raised eyebrow that said it all. While he never seemed truly annoyed with any of his visitors (I was the one who would sometimes get annoyed), there were some visits he didn't mind that I cut short.

Other appointments were extended because both the president and his guests were enjoying each other's company so much. I told all of his guests before they met him that they would be surprised to find how approachable he was and how interested in them he would be. What I did not tell them was how carefully I had prepared the president for this meeting, regardless of how long or short it went.

Before people walked in the door, the president knew who they were, why they were there, and how long they were scheduled to stay. In the packet that went home with him every evening was his schedule for the next day, including copies of the briefing papers on every appointment, the same ones I placed in a folder on his desk every morning. The briefing paper would provide background information on the visitor and their connection to the president, if any, and the reason for the visit. Sometimes I quoted language from the letter they had written to him so the president knew what had resonated with them about him or his presidency. Gifts had to be approved in advance, so I would tell him what they were bringing, allowing him to accept it appropriately.

Prepared in this way, the president was free to greet each guest as a friend. When I entered his office with a first-time visitor it was wonderful to experience him as if for the first time again and again. I remembered how it felt when he approached me, looked me in the eye, and shook my hand that first day in the lobby. This legend, who had loomed so huge in my imagination, was suddenly before me. Over the course of the years I met hundreds of famous people, and many were just what I expected. Others, based on their public image, I assumed would have a larger-than-life presence but didn't quite live up to that in person. Ronald Reagan was one of the few who did not seem smaller than his image, which was enormous to most. He was even more charming, more handsome, and more gracious than imagined. He was a man who genuinely delighted in meeting new people and had a way of making everyone feel as though they were important to him—because they were.

If a visitor was tongue-tied, the president had a number of ways of making them feel more comfortable, usually by telling a story. Sometimes he would talk about upcoming travel he had, or places he had just been, or would share a story about a current event or about the person's hometown. I was always amazed that he knew so much about so many cities and places. He often used funny accents when telling a story or a joke, especially his Irish accent, which you knew he had heard his Irish father, Jack, use many times.

On one of his walls, the president had a painting of the banks of the Rock River near his hometown of Dixon, Illinois, which often caught the eye of guests and would inspire him to talk of his early years in the Midwest or tell stories from college. He often used self-deprecating humor to connect with his guests, joking that although he officially majored in economics at Eureka College, he actually majored in extracurricular activities. He would also make light of his post-presidency visit when he returned to the Eureka College campus and received an honorary degree—laughingly offering up that he always suspected that perhaps his original degree was honorary, too.

One of his favorite stories, which he could tell in incredible detail, came from when he was in his early twenties, working as a sports announcer for radio station WHO in Des Moines, Iowa. He gave play-by-play broadcasts of the Chicago Cubs games from an offsite studio using only the teletype wire and his imagination to describe the game for the local audience that was outside the signal reach of the Chicago station. He would describe the crowd, the stadium atmosphere, and how the batters looked as they approached home plate for the at-bat, taking practice swings and adjusting their stances, even though he wasn't actually there.

One time, midgame, the wire went silent and, while waiting for it to come back up, he filled the air time by calling multiple foul balls, describing the crowd, inventing a scuffle between two boys in the stands, the batter asking for time and stepping out of the batter's box, another foul ball, and another one, fabricating the elongated color commentary, while he waited nervously for the wire transmission to start up again. This went on so long that it eventually wound up in the *Guinness Book of World Records* for the longest at-bat (though it hadn't really been). Then the president would grin widely and laugh to himself as he told his visitor he was surprised to learn when the wire came back up that the batter had actually popped out on the first ball pitched!

As the president's elbow-holding chivalry would suggest, he was always respectful in the presence of a woman and would not tell any jokes or stories that could be seen as inappropriate, including in front of me. His standards were very conservative as to what he thought was risqué or inappropriate in mixed company. If the meeting was exclusively men and he had something to say that he thought was a little edgy, he would motion for them huddle up with him and give me a glance indicating that I needed to step back for a second. Although I could still hear the joke he was telling them, I appreciated that he didn't want to offend me, though nothing he ever said in my presence was even remotely offensive.

Just when I thought I had heard his entire repertoire of jokes, the president would tell one that I had never heard before. Depending on the items you commented on in his office, you may get a story about some of his favorite horses, like El Alamein or Little Man, or the painting in his office called *Cocktails on the White House Lawn*, which amusingly depicted all of the presidents of the United States and their wives outside the White House having a cocktail party together. He would also offer up an explanation for the satirical wooden "Executive Decision Maker" on his desk, which, when spun, stopped to land on either YES, NO, MAYBE, or SCRAM! He would laugh about this gift, which he enjoyed immensely, and then made sure to always turn it and leave it saying YES. There also were beautiful oversized scrapbooks of his presidency years that had been painstakingly assembled by a group of volunteers in the White House. We used them as reference material at times, but they also made wonderful conversation pieces, especially when the visitor had worked for his administration.

One of the appointments that truly stands out is the visit of U.S. Air Force fighter pilot Captain Scott O'Grady, who was shot down in 1995 behind enemy lines in Bosnia where he was enforcing a no-fly zone. He ejected from the plane when it was hit by a surface-to-air missile and survived in hiding by eating bugs and grass and leaves, evading capture for nearly a week until he was rescued by a group of Marines.

President and Mrs. Reagan had followed the entire story, from the shooting down of his plane to the uncertainty of his circumstances and prospects for survival, but remained hopeful, along with the rest of America, praying for his safe and expedient return. They were overjoyed when he returned to U.S. soil and reached out to contact him, asking for the opportunity to meet him. A calligrapher created a beautifully ornate, gold-lettered certificate to present to him, along with a medal designed specifically for him to honor his service, his bravery, and his sacrifice. Captain O'Grady was clearly in awe of the Reagans, and although he was trying to pay tribute to the two of them and thank them for all they had done for the nation, it was clear that the honor was intended to go the other way on this day.

As their appointment ended, the president stood tall and straight at the front of his desk and asked if Captain O'Grady thought it would be all right for him to salute the captain, even though he was no longer the commander in chief. The captain replied that he hoped so, because he wanted to salute his former commander in chief as well. To see these two men, one with much of life still ahead of him and one who had seen much of life already, both of whom had made sacrifices in service to their country, sincere and dignified in saluting the other, was powerful and touching. Although I was caught up in the moment, as was everyone in the room, thankfully I remembered to snap some pictures of that salute and was grateful that they turned out clearly. I was sure they would look blurry due to the trouble I had focusing the camera with tears welling up in my eyes. American heroes do that to me!

The president also honored duty and service that did not play out on the battlefield, including the United States Secret Service agent who had stood outside the president's bedroom window at the White House as he slept. Although he had stood at this post for eight years during the Reagan presidency, he had never officially met the president. When he was retiring from the Secret Service, the man and his wife planned a trip to California to celebrate. They wrote asking for the opportunity to stop in for a quick meeting—of course the answer was yes. I watched President Reagan thank this man for allowing him to sleep soundly and safely at night. The agent replied that it was his honor and privilege to do so because he realized that the president was often called upon to make monumental decisions during the day and he took pride in the fact that he had helped the president be well rested and clear of mind to make those important choices. Again, it was a mutual admiration club.

We had many powerful and important people come to visit the president from all walks of life and a variety of faiths. The president always looked for commonality, not differences, finding that there was always more to agree on than to disagree on, regardless of the visitor. Such was the case when we invited Mother Teresa into the office. Mother Teresa was a nun and a missionary (and now a canonized saint) who worked primarily on the streets of Calcutta, India, serving the poorest of the poor. She also founded the Missionaries of Charity, which was active worldwide running hospices and homes for people with AIDS, leprosy, and tuberculosis. She was known globally for her kindness, compassion, and full commitment to those in need. Although the president wasn't Catholic, he shared her faith in God and her desire to serve God and the people of this earth in whatever capacity he was called to do so.

As you can imagine, the staff was all abuzz the day Mother Teresa visited President and Mrs. Reagan in December 1991. We heard her before we saw her. The blue-trimmed white saris of the Sisters of Charity who surrounded her, dressed identically to Mother Teresa, but walking a few paces behind her in unison, swooshed. The women were respectful and attentive, quiet and observant, not worshiping her, but rather showing reverence for a woman they knew walked very closely with God.

I had never seen Mrs. Reagan tower over anyone, yet she dwarfed

Mother Teresa. And the contrast between Mother Teresa and Ronald Reagan was staggering. Though she was born a mere six months before Ronald Reagan, the years had taken a very different toll on each of them, bearing witness to the lives they had lived. Ronald Reagan's life had had its struggles and he had faced many pressures, yet had remained optimistic. He was a magnetic leader whom people looked to for his strength, vitality, and broad shoulders on which to hang their hopes and dreams. Even at the age of eighty he stood tall, with sun-kissed rosy cheeks and the naturally tanned skin of those who are fortunate enough to call Southern California home.

By contrast, Mother Teresa showed every one of her eighty-one years. Her smile and eyes were ringed with the sadness of having seen sorrow, tragedy, destitution, and utter despair. I looked at the lines in her face, like age rings in a tree, recounting the years not in decades but in moments of tenderness and sacrifice, discomfort and service in the filth of India's streets, which had been the hallmarks of her life's work.

She and President Reagan shook hands, and then she reached her left hand over to clasp his hand in both of hers, a sign of endearment, the kind of intimacy reserved for friends and a tribute to their shared bond of faith. The president's hands were well manicured, yet toughened from working at the ranch. Hers were large and strong-looking for a woman with such a petite frame—rough and leathery, clear evidence of a life that was often personally demanding and physically damaging. Her gnarled, dry feet in crude sandals also belied all the places they had walked—on the dusty streets, in the trash piles where people lived, through the sewage that filled the streets of the poorest parts of Calcutta, and into the water where people and livestock bathed side by side because there was no alternative. The pristine white of her garment stood in stark contrast to the small portions of skin that were visible. Those were worn and tired and had been sacrificed fully so that others could feel seen and acknowledged and loved.

They smiled broadly at each other and spoke quietly, though words were not really necessary. Clearly there was respect and shared values between them. Each had authority and influence: one on dusty forgotten streets who spoke primarily through her deeds, the other from an exalted place where the world listened to his every word. Yet for all their differences, together there was a peacefulness, a gentleness, a warmth and kindness, and a shared heart to improve the lives of others, each in their own way.

In watching these two very unlikely icons stand together, I knew that each had succeeded in advancing their primary goals from their own places in the world—a wonderful convergence of humility, power, optimism, and peace.

Yet there is one office visitor who was not known on the world stage but stands out for me as being more memorable than any other. She was a frail, elderly Romanian woman who came into the office in late 1993 looking very much the part of a Russian babushka, sans the headscarf. She was dressed traditionally in a vintage wool suit with thick stockings, chunky-heeled shoes, and matching handbag. She was severely stooped not only with age but from carrying the burdens of a life marked by oppression. The pain and sadness etched in her face reflected the hardship she and her family had endured. Her suffering was one thing, but to watch the suffering of her family, feeling that her life circumstances and those of her family would never change, is something that had been heart-wrenching for her. Then along came Ronald Reagan, who started a domino effect of freedom globally, specifically in the Soviet Union and in Eastern Bloc countries such as this woman's home country of Romania. She personally saw and felt positive changes directly during the Reagan years. In her eyes, no one had played a greater role or been more influential than President Reagan in the newfound freedom she and her family now enjoyed.

When she entered his office and saw President Reagan, she instantly dropped to her knees and bowed at his feet. She started sobbing loudly and uncontrollably, kissing the president's feet—literally kissing them—with tears falling on his shoes. He was overwhelmed by this expression of emotion, as was I, just observing it.

After a moment, he reached down to thank her for her humbling gesture of gratitude and helped her to her feet. As she stood before him, looking intently into his eyes, she took a moment to pull herself together. She then, very slowly and in broken English, thanked him for freeing her, freeing her family, and freeing her people from oppression. As I watched her standing there, very small in stature but bold in expression, I thought about the millions of people this one woman represented who shared her experience and shared her emotion and most certainly would have shared in her touching gesture if given the opportunity.

In all of these meetings there was a common thread. One life, the president's, had made an overwhelming, positive impact and had changed the course of each of their lives forever. Likewise, for each one of us, while our decisions may not topple communism or free entire groups of people, we can—and do—have a lasting impact on others through our words, our actions, and our kindness. Some we may be fortunate enough to know about. Others will serve as our legacy regardless.

5

Communicating Greatness

I was one of millions of people who were glued to the television in a state of shock in January 1986 after the Space Shuttle *Challenger* exploded only seventy-three seconds after it took off. I was in my AP history class, a senior in high school, and we all sat motionless, not knowing how to absorb what we had just seen. This reaction was revived continually as the networks played again and again that horrible moment when the spaceship caught fire and disintegrated midair. It was a flash, a matter of mere seconds, but one that never lost its impact no matter how many times we saw it. Those bright lives, now lost, who had carried the hopes of our country and our yearning for exploration and adventure, ended in an instant while much of the nation watched in disbelief.

If ever there was a singular moment when we needed a leader to help us understand our feelings, this was it. As vividly as I remember the tragedy, I equally recall how President Reagan addressed the nation from the Oval Office that evening, canceling the previously scheduled State of the Union Address to console the nation in mourning. Amid his own shock and grief he somehow found the words to help the nation find a way to accept this loss. We grieved and grew together as a nation that night.

A year later as a college freshman, my communications class assignment was to deconstruct a speech of my choosing. I was asked to analyze how the speech was structured and why it had been so effective.

Although many of my fellow students chose long-ago speeches made by historic figures, the one that still moved my heart was President Reagan's *Challenger* address from the year prior. In analyzing his speech, I wanted to better understand how he pulled this off.

When I sat down with a printout of the president's *Challenger* address in front of me, I appreciated the structure right away. Human nature places the speaker in the middle of every story, but a great communicator, like Ronald Reagan, puts his audience at the center. He began by connecting to the audience in their feelings of loss, making each of the people who were listening believe that their grief mattered and was being heard and understood. Although mourning is a very private emotion, Reagan soothed the audience by saying that personal pain was something we now shared and was a way we were now connected to our fellow countrymen. His speech went far beyond words that day, joining us all in a place of deep emotion and collective sorrow.

In delivering all of his speeches, Reagan's background as an actor was incredibly helpful because much of communication is performance— not in an insincere or showy way, but as a way that someone who knows how to capture an emotion, evoke a memory, or touch a heart can connect words to people. Ronald Reagan was once asked, "How can you be an actor and be president?" He quickly replied, "I don't know how you can be *president* without being an *actor*."

Classic Ronald Reagan—skillfully turning an insult into an asset and not taking himself too seriously, while still taking the role extremely seriously. Ronald Reagan was not role-playing the presidency, though his experience in Hollywood certainly enhanced his ability to communicate and connect with his audiences, and do so with style. He left Hollywood long before he first ran for public office, but Hollywood never left him.

Actors, in essence, are storytellers creating a scene that captures the imagination of the audience. Hollywood's influence on Washington's leading man, Ronald Reagan, took his ability to tell a compelling and engaging story and used that skill to persuade, convince, and even entertain. Politically, the left traditionally does this very well, using stories to convey a greater truth, tugging at the heartstrings and connecting principles and traits to real-life examples. On the right, however, the tendency is often to use facts and figures to compel, influence, or persuade people intellectually instead. Ronald Reagan came along and married the two, using stories to convey the underlying truths grounded in facts and figures, and he did so with great effectiveness. He brought statistics to life in descriptive language with personal application masterfully.

When he spoke to the nation that night of the *Challenger* disaster, I remember how his face reflected the agony he felt. His voice was soft and low and he spoke with minimal inflection. As he looked into the camera, he seemed to embody what we all felt, saying, "Today is a day for mourning and remembering. Nancy and I are pained to the core by the tragedy of the shuttle *Challenger*. We know we share this pain with all of the people of our country. This is truly a national loss."

As the president mentioned each of the fallen by name, the personal connection, along with the warmth of his kind words and the dignity of his expression, was an invitation for all of us to acknowledge and then release the pain we carried. That was something else I admired about this speech: simplicity. He did not need any grand rhetorical flourishes or soaring language. In the restrained language he chose, he invited us not to admire him but rather to come forward, to fill in a simple structure with feelings of our own.

He spoke of the way that tragedy can unify us as a country, rather than driving us apart. He reminded us simultaneously of what we had collectively lost and what we still collectively shared: our values, our sacrifices, and the true heart of our ideals. Then, like all great speeches, there was a call to action. He pledged that the space program would continue and that we as a nation would never forget these seven heroes. When I watched him deliver these words, I was moved by the tenderness in his voice. As I wrote in my paper for that class (amazingly, I still have it): "By making himself vulnerable through disclosing his emotion,

President Reagan brought himself into oneness with the citizens of America." The greatest orators connect with the audience and, through that, connect the audience to each other. In that simple and effective way, he helped the nation begin to heal.

After studying the Great Communicator in college, it was a privilege to then watch firsthand in the office how his words came together as a speech.

The president was constantly being asked for a statement, a comment, a public service announcement, a videotaped message, an op-ed, or invited to deliver a speech. The majority of speeches were written in-house, though professional speechwriters were brought in periodically for a major address. Although he was no longer president and didn't have an entire full-time speechwriting team, his post-presidency remarks continued to live up to his Great Communicator reputation thanks to Mark Weinberg's quick wit, skillful writing, and close personal connection to President and Mrs. Reagan. Mark, who ran the public affairs office where I first started out, had worked as deputy press secretary in the Reagan White House. He knew how to write in the president's voice, had years of experience working with him, and could anticipate the angle the president wanted to take on a subject. Mark's deputy director, Cathy (Goldberg) Busch would polish the remarks, making them as impeccably put together as she always was.

I was given opportunities to review press releases and do background research, but was most excited whenever they asked me to edit the final drafts of his speeches. In a small staff it was especially important to have the most eyes possible on the text before it was finalized to avoid errors or misstatements. As I worked on the speeches, I noticed how the language choices were positive ones. Instead of saying "never forget" he favored "always remember" or instead of "I do not want" he would use "I am pleased to."

The remarks would typically start from a standard stump speech with talking points that were current and reflected what the president thought was important to emphasize. With those as a foundation, the staff would customize a draft for the president to review and revise. He liked his speeches to be printed out on half sheets, as well as handwritten in his own version of shorthand on index cards that he would write and mark up himself to revise and study and practice.

The president was very involved in the speechwriting process, typically knowing exactly what he wanted to say and how he wanted to say it. Regardless of how good the draft speech was, Ronald Reagan always improved it and found a way to better connect to the audience and put them at ease. He once told me he wanted those who heard him to feel as if he was having a conversation with them and hoped they were enjoying it as much as he intended.

He inevitably would add a perfect quote or story to suit the occasion or the audience. His inventory seemed limitless, and I never knew how he did it until one day, after he had left for the day, I was looking for something in his office and opened up his desk. There I came across several tall, thin black cardholders stuffed to overflowing with handwritten lined index cards.

I had seen him looking through these folders before but never really knew why—until that moment. The cards were filled with quotes. Some in blue pen, some in black pen, some in cursive, some in all caps, some written up along the sides when there wasn't enough room on the last line. Many of the cards were old and worn, as if they had been written years ago and had been referred to often. The quotes ran the spectrum from jokes to politics, policy to marriage and family, character to patriotism—just as you would expect.

Then there were other quotes that seemed oddly out of place: quotes about communism or socialism or liberal ideologies that were in direct opposition to his views. Why would he collect those quotes, too, when he didn't believe any of that? Then the genius of the man became crystal clear to me. He studied the frame of mind of those whose ideology he opposed in order to understand them, hear their point of view, and then better formulate an argument against it from his own point of view. I would roll my eyes when I heard critics dismiss him as an "amiable dunce." Far from it—he was so bright, well read, and astute at synthesizing information that those who opposed or demeaned him often didn't even know what hit them. Ronald Reagan would deliver the perfect line to make his point and do so brilliantly, tactfully, and memorably. Just ask Walter Mondale, who, in essence, lost his election to Ronald Reagan during one of their debates. The moderator asked Reagan about concerns over his advanced age being a factor in the election. Without missing a beat, Reagan replied that he wouldn't exploit, for political purposes, his opponent's youth and inexperience. Mondale laughed so hard that if the election wasn't already won, Ronald Reagan won it right then with that one line.

The president was the master of going off script. He could read an audience and his timing was astonishing, knowing just when he'd reached a pause in the speech that could benefit from an extemporaneous addition. During events I always held a copy of his printed remarks that was identical to the one he had at the podium. When his remarks took a little detour off script, ever the master, he would wind up perfectly back where he left off. Unless the audience had a copy of the speech in front of them, they would never have known that he had made a freestyle inclusion. Not surprisingly, what he said off the cuff was typically the most quoted, most remembered line of the entire speech. No one did it better, and I saw it time and time again.

When speaking to a group of car salesmen, talking about their latest car models, he bemoaned, "If only I had my driver's license still..." He started speaking to a group of restaurant owners by saying he was eating in a restaurant recently and the waiter came up to him and said, "My name is Joe and I'm going to be your server." He replied, "My name is Ron and I'm going to be your customer...but then I realized that he probably already knew that." Or one of my personal favorites: he would get up to make brief remarks rather than a full address and he would start by saying, "I'll say to you what Henry the Eighth said to each of his six wives...I won't keep you long." When on a college campus he would refer to the most popular student hangout or reference a current event at the school or a local issue. He wanted to connect with his audience and be relevant to them.

But words on paper or an inscription on a photograph were just a two-dimensional representation of his thoughts. Black letters on white paper could never predict the impact of their presentation once the president communicated them aloud masterfully. I recall being in the recording studio listening to President Reagan read aloud from his autobiography, *An American Life,* for the audiobook and getting chills thinking about how powerful his story being read by him would be for future generations to hear and embrace. Even now when I call the Reagan Foundation and get put on hold, the president's voice comes through with excerpts from his speeches and I get to hear his voice again. It's the only time I ever wish to be left on hold!

In typical humble fashion, in his farewell address to the American people, Ronald Reagan stated, "I won a nickname the Great Communicator, but I never thought it was my style or the words I used that made a difference: it was the content. I wasn't a great communicator, but I communicated great things, and they didn't spring full bloom from my brow, they came from the heart of a great nation—from our experience, our wisdom, and our belief in the principles that have guided us for two centuries."

6

The Perfect Gentleman

W hen then President-Elect Ronald Reagan was three days out from his January 1981 inauguration, the *New York Times* made a big fuss about the country's eagerness for a new era of glamor in the White House, fawning over the future First Lady and her ability to be elegant without being gaudy. Yet the fashion tastemakers were less than optimistic about the impact Ronald Reagan would have on the national style. When men's fashion designer John Weitz was asked about the future president, he was droll in his assessment. "Reagan is a result of men's fashion—not a fashion maker," Weitz said. "He is a very normal-looking businessman—he could be the chairman of the board of any major company—and wears the same clothes as most other businessmen in the country."

Well, I would say to Weitz, you had to be in the room with Ronald Reagan to know that he wore a suit like no chairman of the board I've ever met.

What Ronald Reagan taught me about style is that it comes from within. I worked for Nordstrom in college and saw many wealthy people who spent thousands of dollars on clothes and still would not turn a head when they entered a room. They may have dressed up their exterior, but their interior was not in sync. When someone says, "He wears clothes well," I learned from observing the president what that truly meant—he wore the clothes, the clothes did not wear him. Not only was President Reagan's public image one of elegance, style, and classic, timeless choices, but his personal actions mirrored and reinforced his confident, warm, and gentlemanly appearance.

The president had a style that arose naturally from his good looks and his personal charisma. His ability to be comfortable in his own skin formed the foundation of his style: a strong sense of what he valued and a confidence that created a strong, positive impression no matter what room he was in or what he was wearing. Ronald Reagan knew that substance was imperative but style mattered, too, because it helped a leader earn respect and gain support. People wanted to be part of something that was polished, important, and bigger than themselves. They found that in the substance and the style of President Reagan.

His strong, athletic body stayed fit and trim well into his eighties as he continued to clear brush and ride horses at his ranch and work out with a personal trainer when he was at home. If you were in a room with him, you sensed a masculine elegance, a surefootedness that formed the basis of his ability to interact with the world. He came across as a man who knew himself, knew his mind, and was confident in his abilities. That, more than any garment he could don, was the essence of his style. For formal occasions, the president always looked especially handsome, adding just a little bit of flair to his tuxedo by wearing a custom-designed shirt with wide horizontal pleats instead of the tiny, more traditional vertical ones. On other days, he would dress like a man's man, either in dress slacks with a polo and cardigan sweater to play a round of golf, or in well-worn blue jeans and T-shirts or plaid flannel up at the ranch; he'd found his style when he came to Hollywood in the 1950s and hadn't changed it very much in forty years.

His clothes really were timeless. One day he walked into the office wearing a plaid sport coat I hadn't seen before.

"I really like that coat, Mr. President," I said. "Is it new?"

He shook his head and laughed, unbuttoning his blazer and holding it open so that I could see the label inside.

"This coat was made by Mr. Mariani in the 1960s. My dear, this coat is older than you are!"

And looking at the photos from his presidency, I realized that many of the items he wore to the office regularly during the post-presidency really were from the 1980s. While he originally paid more to have his clothes custom tailored, he certainly got his money's worth. His suits and dress shirts were custom made and monogramed by Frank Mariani, his Beverly Hills tailor who worked with him for more than fifty years. Frank also was the tailor for Bob Hope, Jimmy Stewart, and other high-profile Hollywood celebrities. The custom dress shirts for Ronald Reagan dropped slightly in the front collar to elongate the look of his neck (something the movie studios started doing for him back in his Hollywood days). He was a trendsetter without being trendy, relying typically on traditional basics, and had a few signature pieces that stood out—like his brown suits. No one could pull off a brown suit like Ronald Reagan. From a lighter brown in spring and summer to a deep chestnut brown in fall and winter, he wore brown well and often, sometimes causing comments in the press because, well, brown suits were not thought of as fashionable until he started to wear them. He paired his brown suits with matching brown shoes, which made it necessary to think ahead schedule-wise.

The son of a shoe salesman, he knew the protocol of not wearing brown shoes after six p.m. (did you know that?) and he followed it rigorously. If he had an event in the late afternoon or evening following his time in the office and he wouldn't be going home first, we would put on his schedule that went home with him the night before "Dark Suit Only" for the next day, which meant he would be wearing black shoes with his dark suit and wouldn't have to go home and change his shoes, wouldn't be late to his event, and wouldn't be frustrated by the detour. Thinking ahead and planning ahead was vital—in big things and in little things like this one. Like insurance, you don't always appreciate the forethought until one of those days when it pays off.

On days when the president was heading out late morning for lunch and to play nine holes of golf, he came to the office dressed casually instead of wearing a suit. One morning when he was going to be headed to Los Angeles Country Club, we got a last-minute call from a VIP who was in LA only one day and wanted a quick meeting. The scheduling office added it to the president's calendar and Secret Service was notified. A few minutes prior to the meeting, I went to the closet to retrieve the navy blue blazer we kept there for just such occasions and brought it into his office, reminding him that his appointment would be arriving soon.

I walked behind his desk to help him into his coat. He put one arm in, then the other, and as I went to pull it over his shoulders I realized that it had pulled his arms back much farther than usual. The coat was much too small to cover his shoulders. I now had the president, in essence, stuck in a straitjacket, but with both arms locked behind him. I apologized and removed the coat, realizing that one of our male staffers must have hung his own blazer in the president's closet and failed to mention it to me. The president was a good sport about it but did jokingly ask to check the label before agreeing to try on the next coat I brought him.

While his appearance was always impeccable, you never felt like he was judgmental toward you if your appearance was less so. I didn't have a budget for custom clothing as a low-level government employee, yet I often attended star-studded black tie events where I had to at least fit in. Having worked at Nordstrom for years, I had an eye for style but thankfully I also had my father's ability to find a great deal. Numerous events I attended with the president I was wearing a black tie–worthy black dress that had cost me less than twenty dollars! The goal was always to look like a million bucks without spending much. The ladies in the office called our black tie dresses our "uniforms" because we wore them so often. My priority was always to blend in, to not be too noticeable as overdressed or underdressed—just right and not really noticed at all—good or bad. But I certainly noticed the other attendees and treasure moments of meeting and talking with old and new

Hollywood—people like Jimmy Stewart, Charlton Heston, Merv Griffin, Eva Gabor, Goldie Hawn, Kurt Russell, Bo Derek, and my personal favorite, longtime friend and supporter of the Reagans, Tom Selleck.

No matter what Ronald Reagan wore, the camera loved him, and he never took a bad photograph. He always stood up straight and tall, arms to his side, feet planted, pants breaking perfectly over his slip-on style leather loafers, a pleasant smile and bright eyes, which never erroneously blinked, and shirt cuffs perfectly peeking out a half inch from his coat sleeve. He was a true pro.

He knew that a perfect photo wasn't entirely about luck but also about preparation—and a little bit of strategy—which he shared with me, and sometimes would share with his guests. When he was in Hollywood and fellow actors and actresses were lining up to take a photo, he told me that he would always defer to the A-list stars who insisted on jumping into the middle of the photo. While they may have thought he was just being polite, in actuality he said that although most people vie for the middle spot of honor, when the photo gets printed in the newspaper or a magazine, the caption always lists the people in the picture from left to right. So by standing to the left, instead of in the middle, his was the first and most prominent name in the caption. I think of it every time I line up for a photo—and now you probably will, too!

His manners were impeccable, which actually became a bit of an issue at times. He never was comfortable walking in front of a woman. On one occasion we were backstage at an event when the booming "voice of God" announced "Ladies and gentlemen, the fortieth president of the United States." Since I was standing right there, Ronald Reagan motioned toward the stage and insisted that I precede him. I insisted that they weren't there to see me, but rather were waiting to see him. He replied firmly, not moving, "Then they will have to wait." I reluctantly took a quick step out and to the side of the curtain, motioning him past me. The look of confusion on the faces in the audience was something I will always remember and didn't ever wish to repeat. So in future events

I remembered to wish the president good luck backstage and walk away right before he was announced, so that when the drapes parted, he had no choice but to walk onto the stage alone.

When I told the president I was engaged to be married, he gave me his best wishes but didn't congratulate me, saying he would congratulate my future husband the next time he saw him. In the moment I thought that was a bit odd, but later when I looked it up I realized that traditional wedding etiquette states that telling a bride "congratulations" insinuates that it was not a given that she would succeed at getting married or that she didn't have her choice of suitors. Instead, as he knew, you're supposed to tell the bride "best wishes" and reserve "congratulations" for the groom. Old-school, maybe, but polite, definitely.

He was disciplined and consistent in the way he thanked people, too. On the way home from Washington, DC, where he had just received from President George H. W. Bush the Presidential Medal of Freedom, the highest honor that can be bestowed upon a civilian in peacetime, we were on the *Forbes Capitalist Tool* airplane, which had been graciously loaned to him for this historic trip. As it was a long trip, the president had taken off his suit jacket but left on his tie—and his medal, wearing it all the way home. (I secretly wondered if he planned on sleeping in it.) To me, this symbolized the great appreciation he truly felt not only in receiving the honor of the medal but for the honor of having been elected to serve as president of the United States. He always was aware of and grateful for that privilege and was mindful of all the people who had entrusted him with that honor.

I snapped a picture of him on the plane wearing that medal and have always loved that photo for the way it captured his humility and genuine pride. Yet recently I looked at that same photo more closely and realized what he was doing when I snapped the photo. He was writing his thank-you notes! Of course he had an assistant—me—who would have been happy to prepare his follow-up correspondence. Yet he wanted to express his heartfelt gratitude to President Bush personally, so he took pen to paper himself—and did so extremely promptly, before we even got home.

He modeled a gracious appreciation toward others in everything he did. From the way he dressed to the way he treated others, he was the epitome of class, a consummate gentleman, and a wonderful role model. Always.

7

Mrs. Reagan's Ally

I'm not exactly sure when or how Mrs. Reagan and I started collabo-
rating behind the scenes a bit or when our more friendly relationship began. Greg takes full credit, saying that Mrs. Reagan adored him
first—which is probably true. The essence of my connection to Mrs.
Reagan was her need for truth and transparency. Mrs. Reagan had
a reputation for being a very perceptive judge of character and read-
ily showed her appreciation and support for those who faithfully surrounded her husband. She wanted to know that everyone at the office
had his best interests in mind, and, over time, she grew to trust me and
understand that I shared her goals.

My strong relationship with Mrs. Reagan didn't happen overnight.
It doesn't for anyone. The Reagans had so many people work for them
over the years that I'm sure they learned to hesitate before immediately
trusting someone new and waited for opportunities that showed this
person was someone with whom they could have more than a formal
relationship. So in time—through seeing her around the office, dropping things off at the house, talking with her on the phone—steadily
and surely a relationship was forged.

Once I started working as the president's executive assistant, naturally I spoke with Mrs. Reagan much more often, and I would continue
to do so even more frequently in the years to come. I learned a lot from
her and a lot about her over the years.

When she would call from her private phone line at the residence, she usually didn't identify herself but would say immediately whatever was on her mind, jumping right into the conversation, practically mid-sentence. Sometimes it took a second to catch up to *what* she was talking about. Of course there was no confusion over *who* was calling. Her voice was rich and smooth, mature and polished, without sounding old or stuffy. She spoke deliberately and carefully. Her questions were often pointed, yet delivered with a warm tone. That warm tone was part of her disarming charm, at least for me. I think that many people misinterpreted her direct questions as being confrontational when, in fact, she was just focused on getting things done and getting answers. She respected you if you talked with her openly and honestly. If you were dodgy, she would know, and she wouldn't appreciate it.

I learned in those conversations with her the power and importance of listening and of patience. She was a very busy woman, always doing several things at once, and when you called her at the residence you never knew what exactly she was in the middle of, but it was safe to assume that she was multitasking. In some of our earlier calls when there was a lull in the conversation, I would jump in to finish her sentence or try to move on, trying to be helpful. But I soon learned that was not helpful and that it was better to wait until she resumed the conversation and not try to guess what she was going to say. Just wait. Patiently. And I learned to multitask on my end as well while we talked.

As we grew more familiar with each other, if there was something going on at the office I thought she needed to be made aware of, I told her. I didn't try to sugarcoat it or try to explain it or fix it, I just shared it with her and left it to her as to whether or not it was something she needed to concern herself with. And though my loyalties were always first to the president, there was never anything that he would have wanted to keep from her. He wasn't interested in office politics or the minutia of behind-the-scenes planning. For that reason, I never felt in speaking with the First Lady that I was betraying the president's trust. Rather, I was looking out for his best interests, as she was. Usually she didn't get involved in the office business, but I thought in fairness to her that sometimes there was something she needed to know.

I would call and talk to her about anything I thought might affect her husband directly or personally or anything I saw coming down the pipeline that I wanted her to have a heads-up on—like suggesting to her that she ask the president about his appointment today with a particular visitor who had brought in a gift for her. Other times, after a particularly humorous appointment, I would call to tell her about how things had played out. She would laugh and say she could picture the entire scenario. I also would call her regarding things I saw on the news, read in the newspaper or magazines, or was hearing from people on calls or around the office. This was the pre–Drudge Report era, so news didn't travel nearly as quickly as it does now, but the office certainly had its sources and seemed to get wind of news before everyone else. I wanted her to hear it from me first. She was always appreciative and never breached confidence of anything I shared with her.

One of my favorite "Mrs. Reaganisms" was what she said the first time I called her to convey something confidential.

"Hi, Mrs. Reagan—it's Peggy. I need to tell you something, but you didn't hear it from me..."

It was as if I could hear her body language over the phone, leaning in, because she loved to be fully in the know.

"You know, Peggy, I'm a well, not a fountain [of information]," she said.

That was true. She always kept confidences, but also wanted to be looped in, even when it was something small, like an orange sherbet–colored sweater.

Although President Reagan was known for his style and classic taste, even the best sometimes have an off day. Fortunately his weren't the catastrophic 1970s pea-green leisure suit type of missteps, but just a choice or two that perhaps weren't the very best look for him—or maybe for anyone.

He wore a few suits on which the windowpane pattern was a bit too bold and photographed poorly. One day he walked into the office wearing bright white shoes, looking like Bert's Jolly Holiday costume in the movie *Mary Poppins*! This was in June, after Memorial Day, so it was technically appropriate according to etiquette, but the women in the office were unified in their criticism and made him promise to never wear them to the office again.

Then there was the day he came strolling in to the office ready to play golf that afternoon—in golf slacks, a golf shirt, and a cardigan sweater. Sounds benign enough, but you had to see this cardigan sweater to believe it.

Picture orange sherbet—that was the color of the sweater. Not bad if you're a retiree in Miami, but not the type of sweater you would expect to see Ronald Reagan wear to his office. He needed an emergency fashion correction, yet he had a busy morning scheduled, so there was not a moment to pause. His early visitors that day would have to have their once-in-a-lifetime appointment and keepsake photograph with President Orange Sherbet. Not awful, but not exactly presidential.

When there was a lull in the action, I knew what I had to do. I picked up the phone at my desk and dialed the residence. Over the years Mrs. Reagan and I had formed an alliance based on our shared goal of making sure that the president always looked distinguished and polished. This allowed for us to have frank discussions about everything from diet to wardrobe to schedule, which laid the foundation for more difficult and personal conversations that were yet to come.

"Hi, Mrs. Reagan, it's Peggy. Did you see your husband this morning before he left the house...?"

"No," she replied. "Why...?"

"You will know as soon as he gets home," I responded.

"Oh dear. Do I need to make something disappear?" she inquired.

"I'll leave that up to you, but my vote would be yes. And I don't think you'll have any trouble determining which item I'm voting on."

A few hours later my line rang. It was Mrs. Reagan.

"It's done," she replied in hushed tones.

We laughed at our covert success. I smiled, thinking about the lucky (if fashion-challenged) person who might unknowingly pick up the president's orange sherbet sweater at the secondhand shop.

Many years later I was proud to work as a consultant alongside Stewart McLaurin, who served as the executive director of the Ronald Reagan Centennial Celebration. When we were introduced he seemed very familiar but I couldn't place exactly where we had first met—until I visited his office and looked at his vanity wall. Then I knew. There he was, pictured alongside President Reagan, who was wearing that orange sherbet sweater the one and only day it ever made an appearance at the office. Stewart treasures that photo regardless, bright cardigan and all.

Mrs. Reagan and I also conspired behind the scenes to ensure that the president's waistline didn't increase as his age did. You see, the president loved dessert—especially chocolate. In fact, if I served his lunch all at once, I knew without a doubt he would rearrange his table so that lunch began with dessert—and then he would eat whatever else he had an appetite for. I wasn't about to tell the president he needed to eat his veggies first, but I did decide I could play this situation to my advantage. And I did.

Instead of bringing his lunch in to him in his office all at once, I would take in everything except his dessert and wait until he was finished eating the rest of his meal. Then, I would present his dessert with great flourish. There was nothing like seeing his face light up when he saw it was time for dessert.

The great dessert presentations were short-lived, however, as soon the president's coats and pants began getting a little snug. So a few dietary changes were made at home and aligned at work as well. Sorry, Mr. President, no more dessert for a while.

And though Mrs. Reagan stayed very slim herself, she was known to sneak a cookie or two periodically, even if they were off limits for the president.

We were on a plane once and the president approached me, thinking he had smelled cookies. Mrs. Reagan was mid-bite into a big, delicious one and saw him walking her way. She quickly turned toward me, mouth full, handed me the contraband cookie, and motioned for me to talk to the president and keep him occupied while she tried to swallow it all down. I hid the rest of the cookie behind my back and made small talk with the president until she finished and could walk back to their seats together, sneaking me a sly knowing glance on her way.

The president's staff saw Mrs. Reagan as an ally and an asset to everything we did. Quite often she would be accompanying the president, so it was necessary to work together closely with her and her staff. Events and trips she would be participating in were naturally of greater interest to her, and she was more involved in the planning and conversations surrounding those. The president's travel schedule was of interest to her primarily in knowing when he would be gone and how long he would be away. They never liked to be apart longer than necessary.

Most of the time when I called her I was simply bringing up a practical matter that needed her attention. The president loved being the "Pony Express," as he called himself, the messenger who delivered a canvas bag with an image of the White House on it back and forth to the residence to Mrs. Reagan every day as he left the office and returned it in the morning. In this canvas bag was information for Mrs. Reagan to review, upcoming schedules, books or photos to sign, and mail that had come through the office for her.

Often there was something in the bag that needed an explanation, like a signature request that required use of one particular type or color of pen, or if I had drafted two versions of a letter to the same person so that she could pick the one she preferred to sign and send it back for mailing. I wanted her to know I hadn't lost my mind in duplicating these letters—the double drafts were intentional and both would not be sent. I would take the initiative to answer a question before it arose, sending hundreds of Post-it Notes back and forth between the two of us over the years, so that having a conversation wasn't even necessary much of the time. She would send the bag back to the office the next morning with the president and would call if there was something in there that needed special instructions.

Over the years I learned so much from watching Mrs. Reagan, and, in trying to emulate her style, it became hard not to think like her. I would approach every event, even casual ones in my own home, as if I was the advance person and would walk and think through every motion. Though Mrs. Reagan never worked from a set checklist, I did watch and listen with interest to the questions she would ask about an event, the things she would notice and comment on when she walked through a venue or an event space, and I tried to think like she did, which was with great attention to detail, even to the smallest nuances, from room temperature to lighting to floral arrangements to seating to staging. She had an eye for the way things should be and knew how to arrange things so her guests would feel as if everything had been thought about ahead of time especially for their arrival. Because it all had been.

So for me at home, whether it was a backyard birthday party for one of my kids or dinner for a few friends, I was always thinking through my "Mrs. Reagan checklist." What would catch the eye of the guests as they arrived? A flag or balloons or something festive? Was the front door area clean with fresh plants or flowers surrounding it? When they arrived inside, what would they first see and smell in the house? What would be available to them immediately to eat or drink? How and where would that be served? Seating would be purposeful, with place cards when appropriate, to ensure the guests were surrounded by interesting conversation.

I would think through each guest. Did an elderly guest need to pull all the way into our driveway? If so, let's move our own cars up the street and out of the way. Do young kids need something to keep them entertained? Crayons and fun printouts to color or crafts and games would be provided. Was the food served on time? Freshly prepared and tasting great? Mrs. Reagan taught me that it was better to have something simple, well prepared, and properly served than a fussy gourmet menu that delayed the meal time. In the president's honor, dessert was extremely important, and thought was given to after-dessert coffee or hot tea, as well as making sure to conclude everything on or before the anticipated departure time. I would think about every aspect of entertaining, even at home, so thoroughly (and unnecessarily for the type of entertaining we do as a family) that finally my husband would say to me, "Peggy, you know the president is not coming for dinner, right?"

8

Rawhide's Ranch

We were flying back from Houston, Texas, where President Reagan had just given a speech, and he was in an especially good mood. This was not simply because the audience had received his remarks with laughter and thunderous applause, but because we were not flying back to Van Nuys, California, where the flight had originated earlier that morning, but to Santa Barbara. When the plane landed he would join Mrs. Reagan, who was waiting for him up at their ranch. Knowing how much he loved his ranch—and Mrs. Reagan—it was easy to see why he was so happy.

Although President Reagan was not particularly superstitious, he was a man of routine and tradition. As a young adult, Ronald Reagan didn't like to fly, and as he got older, he never liked being away from Mrs. Reagan. I noticed that every time we traveled he wore the same cufflinks: gold rectangles featuring the calendar for the month of March with a small stone on the square for the fourth, the day that he and Mrs. Reagan were married in 1952. These cufflinks were an anniversary gift from Mrs. Reagan, and wearing them was his way of taking her with him when he traveled. We referred to them as his "lucky cufflinks."

Midway through our flight from Houston to Santa Barbara, the pilot warned us there was rough weather ahead. Soon we were bouncing and tossing, dropping and rising, and teetering from side to side. Though all of us were seasoned travelers, we began to wonder where they kept the motion sickness bags on this small aircraft. The flight attendant made sure we found them, though thankfully none of us had to use them.

In the midst of this bumping about, we looked at the president and said, "At least you have your lucky cufflinks on, Mr. President."

He smiled in reply as if yes, those magic cufflinks would be enough to get us safely to Santa Barbara. Wanting to be the hero of the moment and calm our fears, he reached down and tugged up the sleeve of his suitcoat to proudly reveal his cufflinks...and we realized, with horror, that they were *not* his lucky ones.

He mouthed, "Oops. Sorry!" as he pulled his coat sleeve down to completely cover the imposter cufflinks.

"Ahhhhhhh..." we all started to pretend scream, though we were only half kidding.

I was certain that was the end, but we managed to land safely in Santa Barbara and, as we said goodbye to the president, he promised to not make that mistake again. And though it never officially went on his schedule, from then on, before a travel day, I would remind him about his lucky cufflinks. And thankfully, after that day, he never forgot them again.

Though no staff, only Secret Service, accompanied Rawhide (the Secret Service code name for President Reagan) on this particular trip to the ranch, there were other times when staff went up with him, primarily when he was entertaining a prominent visitor. We never stayed overnight at the ranch—there was no room for staff—so we would either drive the two hours each way up and down from LA on the same day, or stay at a local hotel in Santa Barbara. There was a small guesthouse next to the main house where family or close friends would stay, along with a caretaker on property who lived there year-round to tend to the dogs and horses. We also had to either pack a lunch or bring some snacks since the accommodations were fairly rustic and catering had to be ordered in for even the smallest of meals if the Reagans were hosting guests. While there occasionally were provisions made for the staff, it was easier to come up there self-contained, just in case.

*   *   *

I will always remember the first time I went to the ranch how surprised I was by the difficult route.

A Secret Service escort met the staff just north of Santa Barbara, where Refugio Road climbed up from a picturesque section of US 101 along the beautiful coastline. I had heard the road to Rancho del Cielo was fairly rough and winding, especially in inclement weather, but I found it challenging to navigate even when the day was dry and clear.

The road started out wide and well paved, but the more we climbed to the top of the ridge, the narrower and rougher it became. We first passed the Circle Bar B Guest Ranch Stables, then a long row of brightly colored mailboxes. Proceeding up the switchbacks we crossed over two cattle grids until we reached a yellow gate. Without a guide, we definitely would have driven right past the gate, unmarked other than a number written on the rock pillar to the side of the gate. The security system was a simple padlock. We stopped as the agent got out of the car, unlocked the padlock, swung the gate open, got back into the car, pulled the car beyond the gate, parked again, and returned to lock the gate behind us.

Much of the ranch road cut across the land of several other property owners, the road deteriorating further as we went along, eventually becoming a rutted dirt road, changing later to gravel. The president had an easement through each of these properties along the route so he could reach his ranch, and most of the time we didn't see any evidence of the people who lived along the road. On other parts it seemed as though we were driving through someone's backyard—because we were. One of the homes that was visible from the road had a yard filled with old cars, abandoned appliances, trash, and vegetation growing over discarded household items—a shocking sight on the way to the presidential retreat!

I wondered if the neighbors knew when the president was at his ranch or not. Or knew of all the special visitors who had driven through their overgrown and unkempt backyard—including the queen of England!

During the Reagan presidency, even the queen had taken this treacherous road to visit President Reagan at his ranch. I heard that it had rained heavily before her visit, leaving the road rain-soaked, muddy, and nearly impassable. The queen kept with her commitment to visit and proceeded up Refugio Road anyway—until her limousine got stuck in the mud. Completely stuck. It couldn't move forward or backward—at all. So she stepped out of her limo and got into the SUV security vehicle that had been ahead of her and rode the rest of the way up to the ranch in that. She was a very good sport.

She was not the only one who had to truly be determined to make it up to the ranch to visit President Reagan. Such was the case similarly on a very foggy morning in February 1993 when the former British prime minister Margaret Thatcher braved the rough and winding road for a visit with the Reagans post-presidency. Though she didn't get stuck in the mud, the fog was so thick she could barely see out of her window as they made their way up to the ranch. She must have felt like she was in the middle of a cloud. Undeterred, she arrived at the appointed time, stepping out of her car in a subtle plaid-skirted business suit with matching scarf and handbag, wearing heels and panty hose that were very out of place for the ranch but "proper" for her nonetheless.

The Reagans were in their typical ranch attire. The president was in well-worn blue jeans, a plaid flannel shirt, large cowboy belt buckle, and boots. Mrs. Reagan, also in denim, had a fisherman's sweater and bandanna-type scarf tied around her neck and was comfortable in her tennis shoes. They definitely were an odd-looking trio, due to the contrasting range and styles of attire, but there were warm greetings all around as the Reagans welcomed her into their modest ranch home.

Now, I don't know what you think about when you picture a president's second home, but I guarantee you don't picture the little house at Rancho del Cielo—unless you know Ronald Reagan, in which case you can picture him nowhere else. It was love at first sight when the Reagans first saw it back in 1974, near the end of his second term as governor of

California. This mountaintop ranch, dotted with oak trees surrounding a beautiful green meadow, overshadowed by rugged hills on one side and views of the Pacific Ocean on the other, was a place of beauty and serenity. Ronald Reagan returned to his love of horseback riding and physical work there, renovating much of the existing home, building fences, and clearing trails on the property himself.

The charm of Rancho del Cielo was not the décor but the views and the isolation that this "Ranch in the Sky" offered them. Leaders in other countries have palatial mansions as their retreats, but the Reagans' ranch home was a small adobe cottage, only about 1,500 square feet. It was originally built in 1871, and though it had been through several renovations since then, it still had only one fireplace to keep it warm in the winter and only its windows to cool it in the summer. The Reagans decorated it in the 1970s and had seen no reason to change it. The home and furnishings were special to them, representing years of memories there, but were surprisingly modest by anyone else's standards.

The eclectic mix was primarily Western, Southwestern, and Native American. There were bronzes of horses and buffalo to paintings of cowboys or cattle on the plains—some detailed and intricate, others very rustic and simplistic (almost like a paint-by-number). This was a cowboy's paradise, Ronald Reagan's happy place. There were some funny items that reflected his sense of humor, like indoor wind chimes, a presidential seal made of tack nails mounted on a piece of wood, and a pair of mounted heads of his-and-hers jackalopes (jack rabbits with antlers and fangs added to them), which a friend jokingly claimed that he had hunted on the ranch property and had stuffed and mounted for the president.

The colors were the rust and red hues Mrs. Reagan always favored. Several stuffed chairs featured Southwestern-patterned cushions, paired with wicker and bamboo frames. A large, worn wool rug warmed the sitting area in the living room, though the furnishings and personal items throughout were hardly unified in theme or color palette. The living areas were much more fitting of a ranch than the Reagans' bedroom, which was a shocking sunshine yellow, very different from the rest of the ranch house and in extreme contrast to the traditional, muted, formal décor that graced their Bel Air home.

The front room was in a space that had originally been a screened-in porch. Although it was now part of the main house, somehow it always still felt like an add-on. If you walked into the home not knowing to whom it belonged, you would think it could have been anyone's casual weekend home and likely would never have guessed it belonged to a former president—and certainly not to the Reagans. The bookshelves were filled to overflowing with family scrapbooks, picture books about horses and the West, and an eclectic mix of titles from fiction to politics, California to dogs, travel to home.

The Reagans found great peace and contentment at Rancho del Cielo any time they were able to visit. After the White House they tried to find a few days each month for an extended stay. Most often it was just the two of them. They would ride horses together, row out in their canoe on Lake Lucky, take walks, enjoy their ranch dogs, read, and cherish their unscheduled time together.

Though they loved being up there by themselves, they also enjoyed hosting Margaret Thatcher on that cool and foggy Saturday morning. Tea was served (of course) and they spoke of the lovely event the night before that they had attended together, commemorating President Reagan's eighty-second birthday.

With the formalities and greetings behind them, the president turned to talk about the history of their little adobe home and pulled a photo album off the shelf to show her how the house looked when they bought it. He showed her pictures of family and friends that had visited, and talked about the horses he had ridden there over the years. Of course it was not surprising to see how at home the president was up at the ranch. He was never trying to impress anyone; he just loved sharing his home and his ranch, which, in essence, was sharing his heart.

The Thatcher visit was exclusively held in the house due to the poor weather that morning, which never fully cleared. They couldn't go on a Jeep ride in the thick, misty fog, nor could they walk over to the tack barn in poor weather. It was clear by Margaret Thatcher's attire that she did not come with an intention to go horseback riding, either. Nonetheless, they enjoyed each other's company, lingering at departure time, not knowing the next time their paths would cross.

When Brian Mulroney, the former prime minister of Canada, came to visit a few months later with his wife, Mila, however, he was ready to rough it. On that April 1993 day the weather was clear, so he was able to see the landscape from the backseat of a dated blue Suburban the Secret Service used to get around the ranch.

Ronald Reagan and Brian Mulroney were great friends who enjoyed each other's company and would tell jokes and laugh heartily. Both had the gift of storytelling and credited their Irish ancestry for their ability to tell a tall tale. Former prime minister Mulroney and Ronald Reagan were alike in several ways. The same height at six foot one, they stood straight and confidently. They both had a story or joke for every occasion, no one laughing louder than the two of them at their own cleverness or sense of humor. They often commented to each other that for two Irishmen, they sure had married up, which was especially true since both men had lovely, attractive wives.

The prime minister's wife, Mila, was tall, thin, very fashionable, and strikingly beautiful. She not only had a sense of personal style but also a comfortable presence about her. She was a mother of four, and I could picture her handling anything thrown her way and doing so with a smile on her face. She and Mrs. Reagan were wonderfully poised and polished, supportive and gracious partners for their husbands and also were down-to-earth regular women. I laughed when I overheard Mrs. Mulroney talking to Mrs. Reagan during their ranch visit. She said, "Nancy, aren't you stylish in your trendy boot-cut jeans?!" Mrs. Reagan replied, "These old things? I've been wearing these since *the last time* they were in fashion!"

Watching President Reagan show Brian Mulroney around his tack room was like watching a professional chef give a tour of his kitchen. Each piece of equipment had a place and a purpose. Everything was well worn yet lovingly maintained, and his eyes danced as he talked about the trails he had cleared with his chain saw, the post rail he had to repair, or his current favorite horse. His soul was there, and he felt closely connected to the things that filled the ranch. And to the creatures there, both great and small. One of the most special and personal locations on the ranch property is his pet cemetery, where all of the Reagans' dogs are buried, along with Old Duke, a one-ton longhorn steer, and several of the president's beloved horses. He personally carved all of their headstones as a way of honoring those animals who had been so loyal to him. When you think of all the pressing issues facing a president, it means even more that he would take the time to do so.

As President Reagan's health began to decline, a decision was made to sell Rancho del Cielo. Although it was heartbreaking to let it go, the sale to the Young America's Foundation in April 1998 meant it would be preserved as a living monument to Ronald Reagan's legacy and would stand as an ongoing place of learning, encouragement, and inspiration for generations to come. Thankfully, the beauty and serenity of Rancho del Cielo, formerly known as the "Western White House," lives on, and the spirit of Ronald Reagan endures there. I have visited there several times since the Reagans sold it, and to me the ranch remains a special place where I can still go to feel connected to him through that place he loved so dearly.

9

A Stetson for Gorbachev

Mikhail Gorbachev was coming to town in May 1992, and the staff was swirling over preparations for the events being held in his honor. In the midst of large-scale logistics, there was one small yet vital task assigned to me. It sounded straightforward and easy enough—find a cowboy hat for President Reagan to give as a gift to President Gorbachev at the ranch.

Gorbachev was coming to California to receive the first Ronald Reagan Freedom Award, an honor the Ronald Reagan Presidential Foundation bestowed on "those who have made monumental and lasting contributions to the cause of freedom worldwide." It was telling that when asked who should be the first recipient, President Reagan chose Gorbachev. The work they did together reduced the world's nuclear arsenal and opened the Soviet Union and many surrounding countries to the West, ultimately leading to the downfall of communism in much of that region. The final symbolic collapse came with the literal fall of the Berlin Wall shortly after Ronald Reagan left office.

Although they had met only a few times, in those brief meetings Reagan and Gorbachev had formed an unlikely alliance that ultimately became a genuine friendship. This visit would be purely personal, not political or diplomatic. Plans included a formal airport arrival ceremony, a black tie dinner, and an informal visit to the president's beloved Rancho del Cielo, all culminating with the Freedom Award ceremony. Amid all the planning and preparations, when asked what personal gift he would like to present to him, the president said without hesitation: "A cowboy hat, a nice Stetson."

This got a hearty laugh from everyone at our staff meeting. How were we supposed to find a cowboy hat that would fit President Gorbachev? From the photos we had of him it appeared that he had a very big head, but it might just appear that way because he was bald. One staffer joked that his head may have swelled even bigger after winning the Nobel Peace Prize and being named *Time*'s Man of the Decade. That also got a laugh. So ha-ha-ha, everyone was laughing except me— knowing the job of finding a Stetson hat that would fit Gorbachev's head was falling to me.

Although this seemed like a little thing, the consequences of getting it wrong were very large. This was the first Ronald Reagan Freedom Award, and President Gorbachev's visit to Southern California was expected to receive extensive press coverage. If I got a hat that was too small for him and he was photographed with a tiny little hat perched high on his head, he would look ridiculous, the president would be embarrassed, and I would feel terrible, too. But it would be no better if it was too big and he put it on and it sank down, covering up his eyes. In order to get it right, I needed to call his office.

The time difference between Los Angeles and Moscow is ten hours, which meant if I placed my first call at ten p.m. California time it would be eight a.m. there. Not wanting a call from LA to Moscow on my personal phone bill, I made the call from the office. I was always swamped with work, so I decided that I would just work on through until then.

After office hours, when the rest of the staff left and the phones stopped ringing, it was easy to work. It's amazing what can be accomplished when there are no interruptions! Besides, the sunset view from the thirty-fourth-floor windows facing west was spectacular. Once the sun had set, though, the office felt eerie—and the fluorescent lights inside were a harsh contrast to the darkness outside. There was nothing to do but work. At ten p.m. promptly I placed my call to Moscow. Hours of waiting, just for the chance to try to get someone on the line.

I dialed the first number I had in my Rolodex, but wasn't sure if I should I start with a 1, a 0, or 00. I tried them all to see what worked. After multiple tries each way I finally heard ringing. And ringing. And ringing. They must not be open yet. Back to work on other things—try again in a few minutes. Thirty minutes later I called again. More ringing. And ringing. And an answer. In Russian.

"Hello. English?" I replied.

More Russian in reply.

I heard the phone being set down roughly and I waited. And waited.

I pictured a Russian bureaucrat walking the hallways looking for someone who speaks English. Or maybe they had gone to make a pot of coffee. Or stepped into a meeting and forgotten about me entirely. I continued to wait. Eventually I heard footsteps approaching and a thickly accented male voice.

"Hallo." Now we were getting somewhere. I thought.

I tried in the simplest of terms I could conjure up to introduce myself and explain why I was calling. I was not entirely sure that I was being understood or that I would receive the answer to my question. I asked for his name and fax number so I could follow up. I gave him my contact information, still unsure if I had made any progress on this call. I thanked him and hung up, wondering what my plan B could be, as this didn't appear to be promising. Before I left the office I drafted a fax that featured a crude drawing of a cowboy hat with an arrow pointing to the band of the hat and a question mark. Perhaps a visual aid would assist in breaking the communication barrier. Maybe. Hopefully. I finally headed for home—fifteen hours after I had arrived at the office.

With that part of the quest under way I considered the challenge of where to purchase a cowboy hat in the San Fernando Valley, where I lived. Texas—no problem. Los Angeles—big problem. I had noticed a Western wear store not far from my house. I popped in one day after work. They had hats, but nothing like what I was looking for. I asked them for a recommendation of the next place I should try. So another visit, another day, on the great Gorbachev hat quest. Again, no luck.

I stayed late at the office another night. Called Moscow again. Found my new best friend again and reminded him I still needed that hat size. He promised he would send it. I was cautiously optimistic. Miracle of miracles, I arrived the next morning to a fax from Moscow with a hat size—I think. It was 60-something. That did sound very big. I hoped it wasn't his Russian shoe size or coat size. I prayed it was his hat size. That next Sunday I went across the street from our church to the Los Angeles Equestrian Center. No luck there with a hat, either, but they were able to help me do the conversion from a Russian hat size to a Western hat size, and they seemed fairly confident they had gotten the conversion right. Now we were making progress, but still no hat, and Gorbachev would be arriving in a few weeks. In a last-ditch effort, I walked into a feed store nearby. They only had a few hats, but one at the top in the back in a box covered with dust was a Stetson, and it was Gorbachev's size, and it looked different from the president's. It was perfect. Victory! That little feed store had no idea that the dusty forgotten hat on a back shelf would soon be presented from one world leader to sit atop the head of another. I wondered whether or not I should tell the store owner, but knew the truth would sound implausible.

Gorbachev flew into the Santa Barbara Airport, and after the arrival ceremony there was a formal dinner hosted in honor of him and his wife, Raisa. President and Mrs. Reagan stayed overnight at their ranch, which was where they would welcome their guests and present the Stetson. As we waited the next morning for the Gorbachevs to drive up the gravel road to Rancho del Cielo, I thought about what an unlikely friendship this was.

They had met first as adversaries. Ronald Reagan despised communism and boldly referred to the Soviet Union as an "evil empire," "destined for the ash heap of history." Two countries, sworn enemies, had thwarted and vilified each other for decades, led by a confident capitalist and a dogged communist, and now those leaders were supposed to suddenly shake hands and get along? Yet when you look at footage from their meetings, even from the first one, there was an ease about the way they stood together. (Reagan "won" right then, just based on first impressions at that initial meeting—standing taller on an upper step, in coat and tie, without the heavy overcoat, hat, and scarf President Gorbachev wore, and appearing full of vitality, though he was twenty years older than his Soviet counterpart.) That meeting was in November 1985. Two years and three meetings later they met in Washington, DC, to sign a treaty that eliminated mid-range nuclear missiles, the first such reduction in the nuclear arsenal, a proud moment for both leaders that would have been unthinkable only three years earlier.

I wonder how much those personal meetings with Ronald Reagan influenced Gorbachev's desire to open his country to the West. The year after they signed the Intermediate-Range Nuclear Forces (INF) Treaty, Gorbachev's policy of *perestroika* reorganized the economy to promote initiative and creativity. The next year came *glasnost*, which allowed for greater freedom of the press and freer speech—nothing like we enjoy in the United States, but still an unprecedented loosening of control by the state in a totalitarian regime. I couldn't help but think that the same way Ronald Reagan inspired America to believe in itself and tackle difficult challenges head-on, perhaps Mikhail Gorbachev was also inspired by President Reagan to boldly do what needed to be done for his country and its people. Whether out of fear of imminent collapse or out of fear of force from opposing countries, or both, the actions he took certainly changed the landscape of the Soviet Union, the surrounding Soviet Bloc countries, and ultimately the world. Though an unlikely pair and through an unlikely chain of events, a friendship was built up. And a wall had come down.

The motorcade arrived, and I watched the two men greet each other with an embrace—one that history could never have predicted. Their personal bond was evident, the sparkle in Gorbachev's eyes as he watched what he probably considered to be a crazy California cowboy who had believed that anything was possible. And amazingly, it was.

And though they spoke primarily through a translator, there was an air of comfort and confidence, an ability to look each other squarely in the eyes and communicate far more than the words themselves.

The president took great pride in showing off his ranch, especially to someone like President Gorbachev, who had grown up on a farm and had driven a combine across his family's land. What different lives they had had, and yet they shared a love for the land and were experienced in working on it with their hands and comfortable doing manual labor.

The two former world leaders joined their wives for some refreshments outside and then it was the moment of truth: gift time. Press was gathered. Staff was watching. President Reagan stood to make brief remarks of thanks and friendship and then handed President Gorbachev his gift...the hat. I watched nervously, remembering the men behind the counter at the equestrian center who had been so confident they had converted the hat size correctly. What if they had not? Gorbachev opened the box, looked at the hat, smiled broadly, reached down, and put it on...and it fit perfectly—whew! All the work and effort and drama that had led to this one moment had been worth it. Photos were taken, gratitude was expressed, and shared smiles were abundant, none bigger than mine.

They proceeded over to the president's Jeep to take a drive on some of the trails. The president was like a little kid getting behind the wheel. He hadn't driven much during his eight years as president, so he always showed great excitement when he got to drive, though I'm not so sure the head of his Secret Service detail, who had to ride in the back of the Jeep, shared his enthusiasm. The rest of the ranch visit went off without a hitch, setting the stage for an equally successful Freedom Award ceremony.

Far from the peaceful solitude of Rancho del Cielo that week, Los Angeles was in flames—literally. We were in the midst of the Los Angeles riots following the Rodney King verdict, which went on for five days, but at that point we had no idea when they would end. There were discussions of canceling or postponing the awards ceremony, but Santa

Barbara is far removed from LA, and even the Reagan Library in Simi Valley was deemed far enough away to safely proceed with the events as scheduled, though additional security was added. From the windows of the office, though, you could see plumes of black smoke all over the city—a truly sobering sight. Everyone was on edge. My husband was particularly nervous about my driving home late at night by myself, so he drove to Century City and followed me home to ensure I made it safely. One night when he was unable to drive down himself he even sent a friend to tail me home. Though it might have been unnecessary or seen as overkill, it was appreciated and did make me feel much more secure. My own private security detail!

We had another small problem for the upcoming Freedom Award ceremony, which was about to become a large one. The custom-designed medal, made by Tiffany & Co., had not yet arrived. We called to track when it left New York, were told that it had arrived in LA, and then panicked when, on the day it was supposed to arrive, the message said "delivery delayed." Due to the unrest in the city, the main LA warehouse was closed and all deliveries were canceled. I pleaded my case to the poor woman at the call center, who said there was nothing she could do. I thanked her and hung up, but I was determined that there wouldn't be a medal-less medal ceremony! Straight to the top was the way I always did things. If the operator at the call center couldn't help me, certainly the president of FedEx could. So I hunted him down, called his office, spoke with his executive assistant, and told her of my dilemma. She wasn't sure anything could be done, but I had great faith that it would happen. It's an unwritten code among executive assistants that you help each other out, make each other look good, and do anything and everything you possibly can to pull off the impossible—and do so without ever letting anyone see you sweat.

As I had predicted, his assistant called back a while later and gave me the contact information for the person onsite at the LA warehouse who had confirmed they had the package and gave me a two-hour time frame to pick it up. One of our staff members lived close to the warehouse, which was down near LAX, so off she went, leaving for home early, hopes high. She arrived at a warehouse she described as looking like the final scene of *Raiders of the Lost Ark*, where the Ark of the Covenant had been hidden in a massive depository that appeared to go on for miles. Nonetheless, in typical FedEx efficiency, within minutes she was holding the coveted package. Thank goodness!

With the drama of the medal crisis successfully averted, and the riots in the city finally calming, the first Ronald Reagan Medal of Freedom ceremony unfolded beautifully, culminating in the special presentation of the medal. Just like seeing President Gorbachev put the Stetson on his head, I smiled inside with pride as I watched him receive the medal from President Reagan, knowing that the impossible had been made possible through sheer grit, creative determination, and an all-star team in our office.

Back at my desk the day after the medal ceremony, the staff was talking about how everything had gone extremely well. We were proud of our team for the extraordinary effort required to orchestrate this important visit flawlessly, especially under such extreme conditions. But our back-patting was cut short when a representative from Stetson called the office to say they had seen the pictures of President Gorbachev's ranch visit and were pleased to be so prominently featured, but there was one small problem: President Gorbachev had put the Stetson on backward! So much for the best-laid plans...

10

Rock River Painting

Although the Reagan family moved many times during the president's childhood, the town of Dixon, Illinois, is the place his heart called home. He was born in nearby Tampico, Illinois, to parents John and Nelle Reagan. John Reagan was known to everyone as Jack. Nelle was a homemaker who worked periodically as a seamstress. They lived in a five-room apartment on the main street of town that, like most homes in central Illinois in the early 1900s, did not have running water or an indoor toilet. When he was born, Ronald joined his older brother, Neil, who was two years old. The Reagan family was then complete.

Jack had the Irish "gift of blarney and the charm of a leprechaun." No one could tell a story better than Jack Reagan. Though lacking in formal education, Jack was restless in his willingness to seek out a better life for his family anytime an opportunity presented itself. As a result, the Reagan family moved across central Illinois five times in seven years—from Tampico to Chicago to Galesburg to Monmouth and then back to Tampico, where Ronald Reagan was born and where Jack returned to his old job. Jack's boss had promised to help him become part owner of a shoe store, and, in about a year, the Reagans moved again—to Dixon, Illinois, where Jack helped open a shoe store called the Fashion Boot Shop.

Ronald Reagan was nine when the family arrived in this small town of ten thousand on the banks of the Rock River, the bustling hub for the dairy farms that dotted the landscape. It was at Dixon High School where Ronald Reagan's many talents began to emerge. He starred in his first play, was captain of the football team and swim team, and was elected president of the student body, his first leadership experience. Despite coming from a poor family, the president often said that in Dixon he never felt disadvantaged, as there was always someone worse off than he was. Among all his pleasant memories of home were his summers as a lifeguard for the swimming hole in Lowell Park on the Rock River.

When he described his summers there, a smile rose slowly at the corners of his mouth, as if just the name Rock River brought him back to that beautiful and calm time in his young life. Over the course of seven summers, he saved seventy-seven lives, a number he kept track of by cutting a notch in a log on the river's edge each time he pulled someone out of the water. Ronald Reagan loved helping people, working outdoors, and swimming. He considered himself blessed to have work every summer in the midst of the Great Depression, particularly work that allowed him to spend his days on this tributary of the Mississippi. All of his dreams began in Dixon, his love of America was nurtured there, and life in Dixon helped shape this young boy into the man he would later become.

When I saw on the president's calendar one day in 1994 that his first appointment was with a gentleman from Dixon, I was glad he had nothing scheduled immediately afterward. When someone from central Illinois came to visit, the meetings always went longer than planned. The briefing paper indicated the visitor was an artist who was going to present the president with a painting he had made of the Rock River. This, I knew, would take much longer than the allocated ten minutes.

The front desk called me to announce that the president's visitor had arrived. When I went out to greet him, he proudly showed me his painting. Not being an artist myself or even an art connoisseur, I do not consider myself to be a particularly good judge of artistic quality or talent. This painting, while lovingly done, was definitely not a Michelangelo. That I knew. I also knew that the president would love it.

After the introductions and handshakes and a pause for me to snap a commemorative photo, the visitor produced a photograph from his pocket. The gentleman said he had watched with interest the president's 1992 visit to Dixon and loved one particular photo of President Reagan, in coat and tie, standing on the riverbank, pointing toward the Rock River. For this man that was an important connection: one of small-town America touching the world stage. As an artist, he decided to render the photo he was showing him in a painting. He then with a great flourish unveiled the painting he was clearly proud of.

I took photos as the visitor handed his Rock River painting to the president. The president smiled broadly, laughing in recognition of that special place in his past.

"This means a lot to me," President Reagan told the man as he held the painting out before him. "I appreciate your taking the time to paint this place which is so special to me."

The president placed the painting on his desk so the two men could admire it together. Soon they were deep into their stories of Dixon, the president sharing tales about the swimming hole, his years as a lifeguard, horseback riding along the river banks, and memories about the Lodge. The Lodge in Lowell Park was a grand hotel where many wealthy families spent their summers when the president was young. He told the visitor how the manager of the Lodge let him borrow his big gray horse to ride when there weren't any swimmers on the beach.

Through the generosity of that one man, the president grew to love riding horses. Young Reagan made some friends who also liked to ride, and when there was a free afternoon, they would often go to a local stable and rent horses for an hour or so. As he looked at the painting, he said to his visitor that Lowell Park was where he came to believe that "Nothing is so good for the inside of a man as the outside of a horse." Ronald Reagan was in so many ways still the same boy from Dixon. He never had seen being from a small town as something he needed to overcome, but rather saw it as the very foundation for all that he would later become.

The ten-minute appointment stretched to fifteen before I politely interjected myself and reminded the president of the other appointments he had coming up on his schedule. The president again thanked the man for his visit and for the lovely painting. I escorted the president's guest out, planning to return to the office and take the painting to be recorded, cataloged, and eventually sent to the Reagan Library as part of the permanent collection, per usual.

When I returned to his office I discovered that the president had an entirely different plan. As I rounded the corner I saw him casually carrying a priceless Southern California mountain landscape, called *Desert Below Julian* by Charles Reiffel, which was on loan to his office from the Los Angeles County Natural History Museum. He had removed it from the wall behind his desk and looked at me wide-eyed, still holding it, like a child who had been caught with his hand in the forbidden cookie jar.

"I won't be needing this anymore," he stated matter-of-factly as he leaned it against my desk. "You can call the people at the museum and have them pick it up."

And with that he returned to his desk. I saw the new painting of the Rock River was proudly displayed on the wall behind him in the place of *Desert Below Julian*. He clearly was pleased with himself.

I, however, was in full panic mode.

The Rock River painting, while not awful, was not worthy of such prominent placement in his office. Positioned where it was, when heads of state and important visitors came, it would be the backdrop to every one of those photos. Also, the Rock River painting was much smaller than the Reiffel masterpiece. It looked ridiculous on the large wall behind his desk and under the lighting that was specially designed for its grand predecessor.

I dreaded placing the call to the museum curator to tell them the president had decided he no longer wanted their beautiful painting. If they asked what had replaced it, what would I say? The truth would sound preposterous. And I knew our own archivists would not be happy that the president had moved the masterpiece without wearing the special white cotton gloves meant for handling fine art and artifacts. And, how would I explain this to the rest of the office staff? I had to find a diplomatic way to undo what the president had just done, and do it quickly. I stared at the beautiful landscape leaning haphazardly against my desk and hatched my plan.

I walked into the president's office and stood at his desk. I looked at the Rock River painting and then at him, then back at the new painting, and then at him.

"Mr. President, that really is a lovely painting he gave you," I said. "I can see why you like it and why you want to keep it in your office."

His eyes sparkled with agreement and he smiled, thinking I was pleased with his handiwork. Then I started my sales pitch.

"I've been thinking, though, that with it hanging behind your desk, every time you want to look at it you have to stop what you're doing, turn your head and your chair for even just a quick glance," I said. "That seems like a lot of effort and wasted time for something you want to enjoy all day long."

I had his full attention.

"I had a thought that perhaps we could hang it over here," I said, walking to the wall opposite his desk and pointing to a vacant space there. "If you hang it here you could see it easily all day long."

He sat straight in his chair as if he were working and looked over to the spot I had indicated. Then he turned his neck and chair to look at the painting behind him, then straightened again and looked up at the proposed relocation area, and again craned his neck behind him to stare at the new painting. He then looked at me—the moment of truth.

"I think you're right."

Whew. Victory!

"If it's over there I can look at it any time I want all day long without having to strain my neck or stop what I'm reading or working on," he said.

I agreed with "his" idea.

"Yes, sir, I agree that would be much better. I'll go get a hammer and nail and get it hung up for you right away. But first, do you think the two of us can carefully return the painting you took down?"

He gave me a suspicious glance as if to ensure I was really going to hang the other one and wasn't just playing him.

"I promise to rehang this one right away," I offered, smiling and pulling it off the wall. "I just don't want either one of us to be in trouble for having removed the other one without permission."

"Oh. Well then, we better put it back. And quick!"

So with the president on one end and I on the other, looking all around us first as if we were on a top secret mission and didn't want anyone to see, we carried the massive painting back into his office, putting it back in its rightful spot.

I then dutifully went down the hall to borrow a hammer and nail from the Secret Service office, meeting a line of curious looks.

"Don't ask," I said with a smirk before the question came.

In no time at all, the new picture was hung, the old painting was replaced, and the crisis had been averted. I returned to my desk very pleased that a losing scenario had quickly been turned into a win-win proposition.

The placement of that Rock River painting was, in the end, better than what the president had first wanted, allowing him to regularly gaze at it whenever he desired. From my desk I could see the president at his desk, and periodically I would see him looking longingly and pleasantly across his office—and I knew exactly what he was looking at.

11

The Legacy of a Lifetime

One day, in a rush to find a particular document in the president's files, I came across something else unexpectedly that stopped me dead in my tracks. It was as if a neon light of patriotism was flashing boldly and brightly in my face, right there in the quiet of the office. I have no idea the purpose or the origin of this piece of paper, but since I knew his handwriting well, there was no doubt about its authorship. Written in the president's perfect, beautiful cursive were the words of a patriot—from his pen and from his soul: *"I Love this Blessed Land. Ronald Reagan."*

His patriotism was contagious. And genuine. Ronald Reagan believed God was sovereign and that the people of this great land had the right to make decisions that were best for them, their families, their communities, and the nation. He would often brag, with pride, that out of all the nations in all the world, ours was the only constitution that began with the three simple words "We the People." "Ours," he would say, "is the only constitution in which 'We the People' tell the government what to do, not the other way around." This wasn't just a nicely turned phrase to him; it was a core belief.

This love of country and love of its people was the foundation of his vision for his presidential library. President Reagan didn't want his library to be a stale reminder of the past, nor did he want it to be a glorified trophy case where the accomplishments and accolades of his presidency could be admired. Instead, he wanted the Ronald Reagan

Presidential Library and Museum to provide a snapshot of who we were as a nation during the 1980s.

He wanted it to celebrate all of us—and all that we had accomplished together—rather than a look at just one man and his role. His role, while vital, was not singular. Instead he had been the catalyst that gave Americans the courage, the confidence, and the opportunity to create and build, innovate and take risks, establish and expand during the Reagan years. He hoped his library would be a place of patriotism and pride, not partisan politics. He could not have known then what great success he would have in achieving those goals.

The scale model of the Reagan Library that stood on a table in the lobby of his offices in Century City often caught the eye of the visitors I greeted there. They liked to pause at the model and have me point out some of the features of the building, and it was always my pleasure to do so.

The Reagan Library is the largest presidential library ever constructed and will remain so since Congress has placed limits on the square footage that is allowed in these structures. The finished interior space has more than 265,000 square feet. Housed in that one facility are 63 million pages of presidential papers, a million photographs, and 60,000 gifts of state that were received during the Reagan era. The size, however, was not what struck visitors or me. We were all impressed by how its design perfectly reflected both the style and the values of the president.

The architecture was Spanish Mission style, with red tile roof, evoking California's casual elegance, while the grand proportions of the structure communicated importance and formality. Ronald Reagan was involved in the design of the building and its grounds, which expressed in tile and stucco the warm and welcoming environment that surrounded the president wherever he went. President Reagan didn't want his library to be merely four walls to house artifacts reflecting the achievements from his time in office. He wanted it to be a living, breathing center for civic events and important conversations about the issues of the day. He hoped this building would connect the history of the presidency to the people of the West Coast as it welcomed academics, thought leaders, and ordinary people of all walks of life and political philosophies.

I saw how this vision for a living library was manifest in its design the first time I visited, while the building was still under construction. One of the best exhibits there is not inside the library but rather behind it: a section of the Berlin Wall that came to Simi Valley after the wall fell in 1989. There was great interest in bringing a large piece of the Berlin Wall to the library grounds to mark President Reagan's role in the collapse of this barrier between East and West, between communism and capitalism. Germany was dismantling the wall quickly, and sections of it were available only for a short while. The section that was acquired for the library arrived before it was even open, meaning the ceremony for its dedication would take place in the middle of a construction site.

This section of the Berlin Wall was not one thick with graffiti, but rather it was graced with an artful symbol of freedom: a red butterfly painted over a mottled teal and blue background that looks like an open sky. Across the midsection someone had scrawled FREE. On the other side of the wall, the one that had faced East Germany, there were no markings, just plain concrete, offering a stark contrast between the freedom of the West and constraints of the East German government.

On the day the president dedicated this piece of the wall there still was heavy construction equipment on the grounds of the library, forcing the ceremony to be more casual than the usual pomp and polish of Reagan events. There was a German band in lederhosen playing traditional folk music, and individuals who had lived on both sides of the wall spoke about the impact this barrier had on their country and on their families. And although the ceremony was necessarily a bit informal, there was nothing casual about the significance of this symbol.

From that day on, every time prominent people, especially from the former Soviet Bloc, came to visit the president, they wanted to have their picture taken with him against the backdrop of this wall. I remember the big smiles on President Reagan's and President Gorbachev's faces as they stood before the wall posing for a picture. Even more amusing was the visit of President Lech Walesa, the founder of the Solidarity movement that helped free Poland from communist rule. Instead of merely standing in front of it, the two presidents placed their hands on this section of the wall and dug their feet into the ground, pretending to try to push it over, symbolic of what both of them had helped to do in reality. Truly this library invited people to interact with history and in some sense to claim its successes as their own.

The grand dedication ceremony for the Ronald Reagan Presidential Library was much more dignified, of course. I had been working at the president's office for two years when the Reagan Library was formally opened. I was proud to be part of the team that brought this event off without a hitch—or at least without a visible one. The weather was beautiful and clear, a classic Southern California day, one for which the preparations had been extensive.

The day prior we had done a dress rehearsal with staff members filling in for all the presidents, First Ladies, and dignitaries who would be featured in the program so that we could orchestrate the precise movements and finalize camera angles. After this sequence was calibrated just right, we all took a break. It was around this time when we discovered we had a major problem in the koi pond, which we had stocked with beautiful fish. All the fish were dead. As a groundskeeper cleared out the pond, one of the staff members determined brightly that this was no longer a koi pond—it was a "reflecting pool." And so it remains to this day.

On dedication day, November 4, 1991, I was overcome with the feeling that I was in the middle of a very realistic dream that, at any minute, I would wake from and in a blink it would all be over. Here I was, a girl who had grown up with her nose in books about presidents and First Ladies, and to have so many of them gathered in one place, to be face-to-face with all of these American symbols, was almost more than I could believe.

Presidents Nixon, Ford, Carter, Reagan, and Bush were there, along with their wives, and Lady Bird Johnson. Descendants of Presidents Roosevelt, Johnson, and Kennedy were also present. For the first time in history, five presidents of the United States and six First Ladies were gathered in one place.

Only the staff knew how hard it was to get all of these presidents to Simi Valley for the event. Whatever political differences presidents may have with one another, they all recognize they are members of a very exclusive club, and when that club is summoned to a special occasion such as this, they all put their ideologies aside to honor the office they had the privilege to hold. For the Reagan Library dedication, Jimmy Carter very nearly didn't make it.

President Carter was in Africa observing elections in Zambia, and due to the scheduling conflict, he declined the invitation to attend, although Mrs. Carter would be attending. Since he was the only Democrat in the group, we knew it would be written about as if it were a political play, though there was no evidence to support that. President Carter would be criticized for not attending, and it would be seen as an affront against something all the presidents did for one another, the breaking of an unspoken rule.

The staff decided it was unseemly to beg or cajole President Carter, though we very much wanted him to attend. We decided to make it as easy as possible for him to say yes—and difficult, if not impossible, to say no. We arranged for one of our donors who had a private jet to send it to the airport in Africa closest to where President Carter was working and to make him aware of it. No pressure (at least not any that was forcefully articulated, but was very much implied), just a fervent hope and offer of goodwill and convenience. And while we portrayed this as a casual and courteous action, the staff was anxious about whether or not this gamble would work. We all celebrated when we got a message from the pilot that he had taken off with President Carter onboard and would land in time to make it to the ceremony!

To see these five presidents talking casually and comfortably, as if gathered around the water cooler at work, was something I will always remember. As they waited for the ceremony to begin, I enjoyed watching them speak with one another: asking questions and telling stories, just like any other group of men would do as they awaited instructions for when to move toward the stage and take their places. Richard Nixon really did look like the caricatures of him and had a low, gruff voice that was distinctive and memorable. He clearly was the "elder statesman" of the group, even though he was born the same year as President Ford and, surprisingly, was two years younger than Ronald Reagan (though had served as president more than a decade earlier). President Carter and President Ford were understated both in appearance and in manner, overshadowed in the group by their predecessors and their successors, symbolic of their own presidencies. George H. W. Bush was the sitting president of the United States at the time, so he came with the biggest fanfare and entourage but was appropriately deferential to Ronald Reagan, as this was *his* big day and he wanted to honor his friend, mentor, and one-time boss. Regardless of current titles, there was an obvious respect and fondness toward Ronald Reagan, even though Bush was now the president and Reagan was now a private citizen.

From my vantage point in the offstage announcement area of the courtyard, I saw a sea of faces—guests, reporters, and photographers who were in attendance. More than six hundred media credentials had been handed out and 3,500 invited guests filled the outdoor hilltop venue, all eager to get a glimpse of this historic lineup of presidents and First Ladies. My role was to ensure that the program participants were appropriately lined up, knew their cue, knew where to sit, and were listening and ready to take the stage when their names were called. Now, seeing that we're dealing with grown adults, this sounds like it would be a fairly simple and straightforward task. Not necessarily.

I noticed a very prominent woman whose slip was showing below the hem of her dress. I knew if I was in her position that I would want to know, so I walked up to her and motioned her to lean toward me and whispered my observation. She was extremely appreciative and adjusted her dress accordingly. As her name was called she glanced back and gave me a wink and a smile.

As I returned to the next group who was about to be called to take the stage, I noticed that General Colin Powell, who was then the chairman of the Joint Chiefs of Staff, was not standing in the correct place in line. I approached this powerful and intimidating man to ask if he would please mind moving to the appropriate place in line before his name was called. He gave me a nodding smile of approval, joking that in the military, people are very used to being told what to do (though *he* is the one who tells everyone what to do and I'm sure not many people tell *him* what to do!).

I saw a big gap in the line for members of First Families and knew precisely who was missing: Caroline Kennedy and John F. Kennedy Jr. (and yes, he was as handsome and charming in person as you suspect, or maybe even more so—which is precisely why I knew immediately who was missing from the line). I heard their names announced and yet no one took the stage, much to the disappointment, I'm sure, of the women in the crowd that day. Everyone else was seated, the program was starting, and still no Kennedys. As I headed back into the building to look for them, they came walking out looking for me. Caroline had left something in the holding room and wanted to run back and get it. Her brother, ever the gentleman, had accompanied her. They wondered if they had missed their cue. Yes, unfortunately, I replied, but it was not a problem. I happily took them to the stage and got them to their seats belatedly, earning a smile and wave of thanks from JFK Jr.

The library was dedicated amid great symbolic fanfare and patriotism. President Reagan spoke about his vision for the future of this institution, saying, "Together we gather for a single purpose, to give to the American people and the world a presidential library. There is understandably a great temptation to look back, to remember, to share warm and fond memories, and to reflect on the events that have brought us here. And as we do, I hope we do not unduly focus on one man, one political party, or even one country. Instead our focus should be on the enduring fundamental principles of life that ennoble mankind."

He ended his remarks that day by saying, "My fondest hope is that Americans will travel the road extending forward from the arch of experience, never forgetting our heroic origins, never failing to seek divine guidance as we march boldly, bravely into a future limited only by our capacity to dream." The ceremony concluded with a military flyover, perfectly timed to punctuate the final line of Lee Greenwood singing "God Bless the USA." And with that, the library was now officially dedicated and opened. The public and the crowds came immediately and continued to come until it was quickly the most visited of all the presidential libraries.

Everyone who visits the Ronald Reagan Presidential Library and Museum finds something that has a special meaning. Some are struck by the majesty of the building itself. Others, especially kids, stand awed by the sight of *Air Force One* towering above them. For many, the replica of the Oval Office is the place they linger. For me, the place that always causes me to pause is something others may brush past with just a glance. It is a group of pictures of Ronald Reagan as a very young child.

There is an adorable picture of him only a few weeks old, dressed all in white, with his little hands clutched together and giving the world a sideways glance, as if he spots something the others in the room have missed. As a mother myself, the image I most treasure is that one of him as a newborn. I feel, as every new parent has felt, a sense of awe and wonder over the precious little life entrusted to us, one that already is independent with its own mind and thoughts and needs and desires— and time schedule! I think about Ronald Reagan's mother and what she saw in him and dreamed for him, even when he was still a baby. I'm sure she thought he was special, but I wonder, when did she know that he was exceptional and destined for greatness?

Just past that photograph in the library is a display of posters from the more than fifty movies Ronald Reagan made when he was under contract to Paramount and Warner Brothers. For many people, that would be the crowning achievement of their lives, but in this museum that is just one glass case. Then the visitor moves on to a beautiful room that honors his eight years as the governor of California during a time of social upheaval. It's one little room you stand in that, again, for most people would have been the pinnacle of an amazing life. And yet the museum is just beginning. Then, long past "retirement age," when life scales back for most people, Ronald Reagan still hadn't yet reached the pinnacle of his career. Artifacts from his presidency and reminders of actions he took and the changes he brought to the nation and to the world fill the remainder of this huge museum—starting primarily when he was in his seventies.

And all of that began in the eyes of the little baby with the adorable smile and the sideways glance.

One particular visitor who loved going up to the library time and time again was President Reagan himself.

Whether it was to showcase this beautiful, historic facility to a friend or a head of state or to open a new exhibit, there was nothing like walking through the museum exhibits with the president and seeing how people would respond to seeing him there. They had come to learn *about* him, never imagining they would ever *meet* him. It was a little like the movie *Night at the Museum* for some of the guests there—where history literally came to life!

People responded in two distinct ways when they saw him. The first group, as I had, took a step back, as if observing him from a distance was enough, or perhaps too much. The second group made a beeline for him (which drew a quick response from the Secret Service), putting out their hand to shake his. It was as if they had rehearsed this moment a thousand times and were fully prepared when their chance meeting occurred.

There wasn't much in between—an interesting, though unscientific, observation of mine. Kids, I noticed, usually fell into the second category, bold and unafraid to approach him. They loved him, and he loved nothing more than being surrounded by a giggling group of school-children at his library. I usually had to pull him along to keep him on schedule. The kids would boo me, but the president would just laugh and point to me saying, "She's telling me I need to go now. I better do what she says."

One time when we were getting ready to leave the library the sky was especially clear and the sun was beginning to set. We saw a distant glimmer of the ocean in the distance. It felt as if we were on top of the world and could see forever, atop a steep slope down to distant houses and fields. The president paused for a moment. As we stood silently, side by side, he looked over his left shoulder at his future memorial site, poorly disguised behind a few low hedges, the place where he and Mrs. Reagan would eventually be buried. He squared his body so that his angle perfectly matched that of the burial site, turned to me, and said, "I think I'll enjoy this view..."

He laughed to defuse an otherwise awkward moment. And in spite of making me smile on the outside, just the thought of the day when we would lay him to rest there pained me deeply. He, however, seemed unaffected by the joke, comfortable to the core in who he was and in the remarkable life he had been given. I savored this quiet, peaceful moment and lingered extra long that day to enjoy the incredible view— both the beautiful landscape in front of me and the iconic profile to my left, lit beautifully with the warm glow of the setting California sun.

Part Two

12

Balancing Act

As I learned from the first day I worked in the Office of Ronald Reagan as an intern, the office had a rhythm and a pace, like a metronome set at a very high speed, a pace that suited me and invigorated me. As part of a small staff with lots to do, I often had to step up and take charge of a project or a situation, even early on, when I wasn't sure I was completely up to it. Yet it was possible because I learned so much from the people I worked with.

Working for the chief of staff, Fred Ryan, taught me the mechanics of fundraising, the way the president's network of relationships operated, how he stayed connected to people, and the importance of follow-up. Joanne (Hildebrand) Drake, the president's scheduling director, ran the president's calendar. From her I learned to speak with authority and gained the confidence that comes from never missing a detail. No one was better at the minutia of a presidential event than she. And if Joanne could imagine it, then Sheri (Semon) Lietzow and Jon Hall could make it happen—the masters at advance work and detailed implementation. I also closely observed Lisa Cavelier, who was Mrs. Reagan's executive assistant, in action. She did her homework but didn't offer up everything she knew, which was her secret power. Lisa was a woman who knew a lot more than she was saying. She was equal parts elegant and formidable.

I was also trying to fulfill the much more complex and never-ending demands of being a young new mom. I welcomed my son, Taylor, who was born three weeks early, in September 1993. I was twenty-five. When

I think back on that time I can see clearly how the two skill sets—that of a working mom and that of a top-tier executive assistant—taught me so much about anticipating and avoiding problems, planning ahead with an optimistic offense, and remaining in control always, including staying calm in the middle of a crisis. Especially then.

While I was working for President Reagan, Greg and I got married and had three of our four children. Those were wonderfully blessed and busy years. Now that my children are older, I, like other working parents, wonder how we pulled it off, especially in those early years when babies and toddlers needed so much time and attention. On top of that, Greg was going to night school to finish his master's degree, an MBA in finance—one more element to juggle.

After Greg finished grad school, we moved into an old, tired house in need of some TLC, but big enough to hold our growing family. It was in a beautiful, peaceful suburb of Los Angeles with tree-lined streets, Blue Ribbon public schools, and a small-town feel. It was perfect for raising our family, but it was more than an hour's drive away from Fox Plaza. For nearly a year as we renovated, it felt like camping, with plywood on some of the windows, a toaster oven and a microwave to cook all of our meals, and a refrigerator in the backyard. I washed dishes and baby bottles in the bathtub and then would have to clean and sanitize it in order to bathe the kids! We didn't have grass yet in the backyard, nor were our washer and dryer installed yet. Once a week I would haul all the kids to the laundromat with more than a dozen loads of towels, sheets, and muddy clothes. We were quite the sight.

To keep this whole thing in motion, I used the skills I'd learned at the office: thinking through every step and every motion, planning what would happen, anticipating what might also happen or happen instead, corralling what I might need for any of those scenarios, and always making a contingency plan. I had packing lists for everything and tried to make the routine as predictable as possible and easy to replicate. Simplicity and efficiency were my friends, above and beyond aesthetics. After dinner and baths and books and bedtime prayers for the kids,

I would set out their clothes for the next day and pack three bags in the evenings. One was for the baby, making sure I had enough diapers, baby food, bottles, formula, pacifiers, blankets, juice, Cheerios, and a set of clothes and pajamas. For the older kids I would pack a bag of their spare clothes, jackets, favorite stuffed animals, books, toys, snacks, and drinks. A third bag for me had a change of clothes and shoes, lunch or snack, water bottle, and notecards or another project that I could work on if I ever had five minutes to breathe.

In the mornings I would get up around five thirty a.m., feed the baby from bed, and then get myself ready for work before starting the ritual of making breakfast and getting the kids dressed and out the door. And boy, was it a production: someone was always unhappy or crying or didn't feel good or didn't want to leave. Often it was heartbreaking, if I can be honest about it, because some days *I* was unhappy or felt like crying or didn't feel good and didn't want to leave, either. Inevitably at the very last moment before departure, someone would spill or spit up or worse, and the whole routine would start over for one or maybe two people. It's a miracle we ever left the house. And most mornings I had the help of my husband, who said when we went from two kids to three that we had to "switch from a man-to-man defense to a zone defense." I am so grateful we were a team. (Hats off to the single parents out there who do all of this alone. You're amazing, and I admire you.)

Then the bags and the kids and Mom would make their way to the car, where it was car seats and buckles and all the drama of settling in for the long commute. And even though it was a long drive for the kids, I preferred having them in a family daycare in a home close to my work. If there ever was a problem, I could be there in just a few minutes to get them. Besides, we had the drive time together, which I recall now with more fondness than I sometimes felt about it back then.

I always tried to leave the demands of home behind as best I could once I got to work, but sometimes they came with me—literally. One day I was in the Fox Plaza elevator and an older woman who was behind me tapped me on the shoulder and said, "I'm sorry to mention it, but as a mom myself I wanted you to know that you have just a tiny little bit of spit-up on your shoulder that you may want to clean up before you go about the rest of your day." I thanked her for letting me know as she exited the elevator on a lower floor. I went straight to the ladies' room once I got to the thirty-fourth floor and nearly screamed as I turned around in the mirror to discover that far from a "tiny little bit of spit-up" on my shoulder, I had an entire waterfall, which had started at my shoulder and went all the way down my dress and leg and onto my shoe. Thankfully, I kept a change of clothes in the office for just such an occasion. I laughed to myself as I changed my dress, grateful for the woman in the elevator and wondering how many people had noticed but not mentioned it as I made my way from the parking lot and through the lobby of the building.

On a typical day, after the frenzy that started my morning at home, when I got through the politics of the elevator, I felt like I was soaring up into the clouds and into an alternate universe. I craved the relative peace and quiet of the office. (It's ironic when work seems like the easy part of your day.) I finally arrived at the office to start my work day three hours after I woke up.

From my seat right outside the president's office, my job was both internal facing, focused on him and his work, as well as externally oriented, making sure that my words and actions were aligned with his and properly mirrored and reflected his thoughts, attitudes, tone, and personality. Not only was my role to reside in two very different and specific capacities figuratively, but my life literally existed in two completely separate worlds. One was that of dresses and heels, private planes, Secret Service–driven cars in motorcades, catered lunches, and beautiful, elegant surroundings that were quiet and secure. The other world consisted of shorts, tank tops, and flip-flops and involved driving a very old car that perpetually smelled like French fries and was too small for all the car seats crammed inside. In fact, by the time we added a third car seat to the back of my old Acura Integra hatchback, the doors couldn't shut without tightly squeezing the seats together. So before I could shut the door I would make sure the baby's hands were in her lap and would tell the others to put their hands up so I could slam the door, cramming the seats together and avoiding any pinched fingers. At home, far from the luxury of my work life, meals were often a derivative of mac and cheese on a paper plate, and our house with no air conditioning was hot and sweaty and always had someone in it who was crying or whining or both. And though it sounds like one world would be paradise and the other closer to hell, in actuality I loved both of those worlds and both of those lives and considered myself to be the luckiest person in the world to live in and appreciate the extremes of my life.

How? Because I never thought that the president's world was my world, and I always believed that I was fortunate to be even a small part of it. My reality was kids and noise and sometimes having to do without. It was appreciating the little things in life and striving for more and continuing to grow and work hard to build a future for our family. Two parallel lives, completely disconnected, yet overlapping every day for a few hours. In each world, part of me felt like an imposter, like I was pretending to be a mom when I was really a professional, and pretending to be a professional when I was really a mom. Life is incredible that way, and parents in particular are amazingly resilient to jump back and forth between two worlds and do so in the blink of an eye, like a chameleon, blending in seamlessly in both places. In both worlds they are called upon to perform feats of strength, patience, and endurance day after day.

As I juggled both, with varying degrees of success and ease, I realized that the feeling of never quite knowing everything you feel like you need to know is universal. Even my greatest role models at the office showed me that they were constantly challenging themselves to be better and do more. Together we enjoyed not only the exhilaration of the office but also the exciting milestones of life. Many of us got married while we were working together, shared the joy of being new parents together, and bought our first homes. We also experienced the heartaches of losing family members and the demands of caring for aging parents. We shared an environment of loyalty and respect that originated from the president himself. We were a family. We were in this together, for better or for worse. What a blessing to share life inside and outside the office with such remarkable friends.

In this way, I understand now how much I grew up while I was working for the president. I always hoped I would have the opportunity and the capacity to live an important and challenging life, but I did not know if that would ever be my reality. Successfully navigating the complex world of the president and pairing that with the equally complex demands of a growing family not only tested my ability to master logistics but also stretched the depth and range of my heart.

I realized I had tremendous capacity to love, learn, and accomplish if I would just give in to it and embrace the unknown, enjoy the moments when something was fresh and new and uncertain, and learn from both my failures and my accomplishments, taking note of what didn't work and what did, allowing myself to reflect with pride on those moments when I had found myself outside of my comfort zone and yet had successfully maneuvered through the situation. I had to do the job, do my best, and ultimately just get it done. Not only was I riding the elevator to the top floor every day, but there were days I felt like I was at the top of my game.

During the next few years in the office, I continued to pour myself into my job and into the president. I was determined to continue growing in my knowledge and understanding of him, learning to better anticipate his needs and how to read his body language and nonverbal cues. I continued to cultivate an understanding between us that was stronger than words. I became increasingly interconnected with the president, taking notice of the smaller intricacies of his life, appreciating him more personally, and learning to serve him with greater specificity and skill.

A great job keeps you learning, and at the midway point of my ten years with the president I found that this job would test me and make me grow in ways I had not anticipated. Just as I was finding my footing and becoming comfortable in his world and in this place, the world was about to change. And I would need to change with it.

13

Life at Full Throttle

Inaugurated just two weeks prior to his seventieth birthday, Ronald Reagan was at that time the oldest man in history to become president of the United States. Well past the age when most people retire, Ronald Reagan stepped into the most difficult job in the world. I met him when he had "retired" to Los Angeles, but even then there was still work he wanted to do. He had a strong work ethic and a zeal for life that continually propelled him forward.

He kept in amazing shape physically, as evidenced by his ability to still wear his clothes decades after he had purchased some of those pieces. He exercised regularly when he was at home in LA—swimming in his backyard pool, lifting weights in his home gym, working out with a trainer once a week, and enjoying long walks in Holmby Park near his home or along the coast near the Jonathan Beach Club in Santa Monica.

When the schedule would permit and the weather was beautiful, I would sometimes walk into the office and invite the president to lunch.

"Mr. President, it's going to be a beautiful day today, and your afternoon is clear. Do you have any interest in going to the Jonathan Beach Club for lunch?"

He never turned down my offer.

I would notify the office staff and Secret Service and call in a lunch reservation. After his last appointment of the morning, we would leave the office, and the Secret Service would drive us to the private Jonathan

Beach Club for lunch. I would tell my husband not to worry if he heard I was seen dining in public with a very handsome older man. He said if he ever had to play second fiddle to another man, he didn't mind that it was Ronald Reagan!

The president had a favorite table, outdoors on a patio balcony that had a stunning view of the sand and the water and pleasant ocean breezes. We would sit together at a table for two or sometimes three, if another staffer joined us. Secret Service would have the table adjacent to us. The president would typically order a sandwich with fruit or a half sandwich with a salad and always an iced tea to drink.

The other diners would try to be discreet but couldn't help but turn around to point or gawk, sometimes approaching the president for a handshake or an autograph—even in the middle of his meal. He was always gracious, though I would sometimes get annoyed and wish they would at least let the man eat first! (Being a bit of a germophobe, I always carried hand wipes or hand sanitizer with me, since those hands he shook with were also the same hands he was eating with!)

Those lunches were often followed by a short walk along the beach. A set of stairs led directly down to the boardwalk. And though we looked a bit out of place—the president in a coat and tie and me in dress and heels, trailed by Secret Service in suits—we enjoyed the gorgeous view and fresh sea air and worked off lunch. On the way back to the residence with the president, Secret Service would detour by Fox Plaza to drop me off to finish my day of work. These little day trips were a bit surreal—long coastal lunches with the president amid the busyness of the day. I enjoyed them immensely and always hoped that he did, too.

After golfing only eight times in eight years as president, Ronald Reagan played much more frequently in his post-presidency, a few times a month, typically, at Los Angeles Country Club. He often needed someone to fill out a foursome, as some of his elderly contemporaries had physical problems or were spending more time in the desert or at the beach on the weekends. Golf was not on my mind the Friday afternoon in early 1992 when Mrs. Reagan called the house and asked to speak with Greg. You can imagine the keen look on my face as I handed him the phone. As he listened to Mrs. Reagan, he had a mischievous grin.

"Yes, thank you, Mrs. Reagan, for asking. Of course I would be happy to."

As he hung up the phone he turned to me and said, "Peggy, I was really looking forward to mowing the lawn tomorrow and doing other chores around the house, but duty calls. I must serve my country. I have been summoned to play golf with the president," he said, putting his hand over his heart for dramatic effect.

Greg had grown up in a suburb of Los Angeles and had often dreamed of playing golf at Los Angeles Country Club, though he never could have dreamed it would be with Ronald Reagan. He wore his nicest golf attire that day (top brands, courtesy of my former Nordstrom discount) but self-consciously parked his well-worn Honda Accord out of sight in the corner of the parking lot farthest away from the club entrance, then trudged over, carrying his clubs, past the Benzes, BMWs, Ferraris, and Bentleys that the members drove. As he approached the entrance he was even more embarrassed when the caddies, men twenty or more years older than he was at age twenty-seven, rushed over to relieve him of his clubs. The staff pointed him to Ronald Reagan's table in the Grill Room, the one in the corner with a view. Greg was the first one to arrive and sat anxiously waiting for the president to arrive.

The routine was lunch at twelve thirty p.m. with a tee time of one fifteen p.m. When Ronald Reagan entered the room, the whole place got brighter. People looked up from their meals with smiles on their faces as the president came into the room beaming and waving and took his place next to Greg. Right behind him were the president's Secret Service agents, who brightened, too, when they saw Greg. They were excited to have someone they knew well enough to tease all day out on the course.

The president outlined for Greg his two simple rules for golf when the other members of the foursome, longtime friends of the president and definitely more his peers, joined them.

"Greg, let me tell you how I play golf these days…One: We don't keep score. And two: You can drop a ball anytime you want. Because at my age, I figure, what do I have to prove? We're out here to have fun. So let's go do that."

"Yes, of course, Mr. President," Greg agreed. When lunch was finished, they exited through the men's locker room directly onto the first hole of the South Course and inadvertently stepped into the middle of a wedding party.

The wedding guests, on their way to the gazebo to pose for pictures, suddenly found that Ronald Reagan had joined them. A few decided to pause for a minute to watch the president tee off. What started as a few curious bystanders quickly swelled into an audience of a hundred. Without hesitation, the president placed his ball on the tee and hit a strong drive straight down the center of the fairway about 175 yards, remarkable for a man in his eighties.

Greg was up next, self-conscious because he believed the audience assumed President Reagan would only be playing with a golf pro, which Greg certainly was not. The president was watching him, too. Greg decided to take no chance on muffing the shot or hitting one of the bystanders, so he went back to his bag to choose his five iron instead of a driver, a more reliable club. As he strode back to the tee, one of the agents mumbled Greg's worst fears.

"Careful, Greg," the agent said, mockingly. "Look at all the people around here."

"Yeah, careful," the other agent said. "Don't hit anybody," he added jokingly, "especially the president."

Greg popped the ball high up into the sky and it came to rest about 145 yards away. He was short of the president's ball, but at least he didn't hit him or anybody else.

The rotating members of President Reagan's golf foursome were men he had known since he first arrived in California, many from what he fondly referred to as his "kitchen cabinet." While they met regularly for golf, the game was no longer the point for most of them. They chose the South Course because it was the easier of the two courses at LA

Country Club, and while they intended to play nine holes, President Reagan was usually the only one who played all nine. Greg became a semi-regular in part because he also would play all nine holes.

The others in the foursome would often shoot the first few holes together but not walk to get to their balls. Instead they drove in the golf cart, laughing and telling stories. Greg remembers listening to their banter with interest, enjoying the close relationships forged through decades spent in one another's company. Most of them could finish each other's stories, and sometimes they did. By the fourth hole the other two men were done playing and were simply riding around in the cart watching the president and Greg play.

President Reagan didn't ride in the cart much, and when he and Greg were walking the course, the president set a quick pace. Like any other red-blooded American, when he hit a bad shot he would mutter under his breath and charge off toward the sand trap with quick fury, but his mood changed if he could get back onto the green with just a chip.

On one of those occasions when they found themselves looking for the president's ball in the rough, he turned and said, "You know, Greg, just last week I hit a ball that rolled right behind this very tree, and as I went to hit it I noticed right beside it was a frog. I didn't know whether I should move the frog or leave it, when all of a sudden the frog started talking to me." At this point, Greg was wondering whether this was a joke or if the president was imagining things, but he was soon to learn. The president continued, "The frog said to me, 'If you kiss me I will turn into a beautiful woman and will love you forever.'" Greg by now was fully intrigued. The president finished with, "So I picked up the frog, put it in my pocket, and hit my ball. Because at my age I think I'd rather have a talking frog!" Greg laughed heartily, relieved that it was clearly a joke!

On the fourth hole of that first game, the president paused on the fairway to point out the view. Just beyond the manicured greens and a group of tall trees stood the skyscrapers of Century City, including Fox Plaza—so close that Greg felt like they could touch them, although they were half a mile away.

"Ah, look at that, Greg," he said. "To me this is one of the most beautiful spots in the world."

Agreeing, Greg stopped to take it in and to see it through the eyes of the president.

"Let's see if we can break one of these windows," he said to Greg as he teed up his ball.

Greg was lucky enough to play golf with the president off and on for six years, and he always cherished that little pause on the fourth hole when he saw the president's worlds juxtaposed in that one view. And he never got tired of President Reagan's dare.

What helped the president stay so active was the disciplined way he ate, never to excess in either way. He didn't overeat, nor was he an extreme dieter. He was consistent in providing his body with the fuel it needed, never starving himself nor giving in to gluttony, while always saving room for dessert. He enjoyed fine food, of course, and loved chocolate, but didn't obsess over it or let it have control over him. He would have a drink socially, but never drank very much and preferred good Midwestern comfort food like macaroni and cheese and meatloaf served with an iced tea over a gourmet meal any day. In fact, that was exactly what we served him on his birthday each year, because we knew how much he loved it. That and a chocolate cake and he was content. (Though he never counted his birthdays—instead he called each one an "anniversary" of his thirty-ninth birthday.)

He stayed active socially with friends, many of whom he and Mrs. Reagan had been close with going back to the 1950s and 1960s. They would eat out together or meet in one of their homes for dinner. They would sometimes get away for a quick trip with one set of friends or the other, though their favorite getaway remained the ranch with just the two of them. The president also was thrilled to be able to attend church regularly again at Bel Air Presbyterian Church, starting the first week he and Mrs. Reagan were back in Los Angeles.

The president made sure to get plenty of sleep and turned in fairly early when he could. In fact, I remember one of the first times I had to make a delivery to his house. I had worked late, and it was around seven thirty p.m. when I arrived at the residence. I knocked on the front door and the president opened the door in his bathrobe! I apologized profusely for arriving so late, but he wasn't the least bit bothered by it and said he wasn't heading to bed quite yet, but had gone for a swim and thought he would just go ahead and shower before bed. His striped matching pajama set and white monogrammed RWR robe with leather slippers were quite a surprising sight for a young new staffer, but it didn't seem to faze him at all to stand there and conduct business with me, signing a few things and taking the items I needed to deliver to him. And though it was not what I expected to see on that particular evening, it was a sight that greeted me multiple times over the years, and it became a familiar and comforting one. It felt wonderful to be part of his life, in his home, and a regular part of his routine—monogrammed robe and all.

Looking around the office it was easy to see that the president enjoyed surrounding himself with young people. In fact, young people had voted overwhelmingly to return him to office for a second term in 1984, when he won support of people under the age of twenty-nine and first-time voters by twenty percent. Although I was the youngest staffer for a while, the median age in the office was probably twenty-eight. And the president was eighty. He enjoyed the energy, laughter, and enthusiasm young people bring. We had wonderful team camaraderie that made for a fun work environment. He never seemed to mind some of the antics, a natural byproduct of young people working together, often over very long hours, in a close-knit environment. These were people who loved their jobs, loved each other, loved life, and were committed to excellence and to a singular cause: the ease and comfort of the president's current life and perpetuating his positive legacy of influence.

Not only with his staff but also in his travels and at events, he always wanted to connect with young people: giving speeches on college campuses, visiting TKE houses (he was proud of his fraternity, Tau Kappa

Epsilon), and welcoming kids and students regularly into his office. Although he certainly could not control, slow down, or stop the aging process, he could rebel against becoming stale and grouchy, stagnant and irrelevant, and he did so by surrounding himself with those who were always looking forward and had their whole lives ahead of them. He kept a childlike curiosity, a wonder and desire to see and learn new things throughout his life. When life becomes known, life becomes small. Ronald Reagan was always reading, traveling, meeting new people, and committed to a full schedule. He never truly "retired." He felt there was always work to be done, people to encourage, and ways to use his voice for good. He never preached at me or told me to live life full throttle, but everything I witnessed him do day by day nudged me toward that commitment.

In his essay "The Station," Robert Hastings writes about a train journey on which a passenger looks out the window, enjoying the view and taking it all in, yet is constantly distracted by thoughts of the station, fixated on the arrival and dreaming about how wonderful it will be to arrive, to finally achieve everything we have dreamed of and live happily ever after. But, he says, "Sooner or later, however, we must realize there is no Station in this life, no one earthly place to arrive at once and for all. The journey is the joy...The station will come soon enough." Ronald Reagan had sustained enthusiasm for the journey. He was a happy warrior who brought joy and happiness to those around him, showing us all that it is possible to live life at full throttle, all the way to the final station.

14

On the Rooftops

On those days when the Santa Ana winds have blown through the San Gabriel Valley and out to the sea, the air in West Los Angeles is crisp and the sky becomes a deep, penetrating blue. The last place the president wanted to be then was stuck indoors. Although generally he was content in the office, when the clear sky beckoned him to breathe deeper, he got antsy to answer that call and yearned for some California sun.

I could sense his restlessness on those days. He would get up from his desk more often than usual and wander around the office, surprising staff. He was known to venture to the other side of the office when he wanted to ask someone a question personally, and I was usually close behind, notepad in hand in case an impromptu meeting hatched an idea or identified a question about an upcoming event. I always wanted to be in the loop so that I could follow up as needed, and ensure that he didn't lose track of time and wind up late for his next appointment.

But on these clear, blue, restless days there was no particular agenda for his walk to the other side of the office. He might just surprise the interns by approaching their desks, creating panic among them. Or the staff might find the president in the kitchen enjoying community snacks or standing in front of the open refrigerator door, staring at the offerings as we all do. He especially enjoyed walking into Mark Weinberg's office in Public Affairs because Mark and he had a close, jocular relationship.

I was right behind him one day when Mark stood up as the president entered his office and Mark handed him some papers.

"Oh, hello, sir! I'm so glad you're here," Mark said as the president took the papers from his hand. "I was wondering if you could go make some copies of these for me." Of course Mark was completely joking.

"Well, of course. I'd be happy to," said the president, always willing to play along.

As the men both laughed, I took the papers from the president's hands and gave them to Mark's intern so *he* could make the copies.

Eventually, the president's wanderings took him back to his office and to his window, where he would gaze outside longingly, like a bird in a cage, enjoying his view but eager for more and longing to fly. That would usually be the moment when the president would come out to talk to me at my desk, holding a pair of binoculars in his hand.

"Say, do you think those fellas with the building would let me go up to the roof and look around today?"

"I'm sure I can arrange that for you," I replied. "Can you give me a few minutes?"

As he turned to head back to his desk he grabbed one of the folders from my desk that held work for him to do and gave me an impish smile. I knew it was his way of saying, "I'll do this work for you if you do that favor for me." Quid pro quo!

Still, nothing involving the president was ever truly spontaneous or simple. Indulging his ordinary human wish to enjoy a beautiful sunny day involved the synchronized efforts of a dozen or more people. My job, along with the rest of the staff, was to make these tiny movements flow just as smoothly as the large-scale ceremonial visits we organized with international heads of state.

I called the head of building security, alerted the scheduling office, notified the chief of staff's office, and then called the Secret Service office down the hall to tell them we would be going to the roof at said time. All these calls for one little walk up to the roof—no wonder the president sometimes felt a bit trapped. After that, I'd walk into the president's office with the good news. He would start his mental count-down to freedom and fresh air, only half an hour away.

At the appointed time, two gentlemen from building security, dressed in matching suits and ties and armed with oversize walkie-talkies, gathered in the hallway with Secret Service and awaited my confirmation that we were ready to move. I would verify they were ready, then walk in to get the president, who didn't need to be asked twice if he was ready to go. I grabbed the office camera, he grabbed his binoculars, and with an extra skip in his step he would follow me out to the lobby, where we would enter the freight elevator.

The regular building elevators only went to the thirty-fourth floor, our floor, which was the top working floor in the building. The freight elevator, though, would allow key-coded access to the thirty-fifth floor, where many of the building's operating systems were housed. The access door was in our main lobby and looked like an oversized closet door. But once you opened it up you left the elegant office space and entered a loading dock that led to the freight elevator—stainless steel, beat-up walls from thousands of deliveries and moves, and always a bit of a stench as if a catering cart or two had spilled in there. The sights, smells, and slightly sticky floor were always part of the adventure as we loaded into the large elevator that easily accommodated us all: the president, his Secret Service detail, the building security team, and some staff members who paused their work to enjoy the view and to enjoy watching the president as he enjoyed the view.

The quick ride to thirty-five opened to a different world. Moments before, we were in the pristine sanctuary of the thirty-fourth floor, and then abruptly we entered a labyrinth of wiring and equipment and hot, blowing air that smelled like an auto repair shop. The pathway was narrow and noisy, flanked by humming machinery. We walked single file, following the man with the keys, who led us toward one small flight of stairs that provided access to the roof and fresh air. With a gust of air as the door was opened, we stepped out of the working floor of Fox Plaza and onto the roof, where the heliport was located. The president didn't notice or care about this grubby journey. His eyes were set on blue sky, a warm breeze, and endless views. And on days like this, he had all three in abundance.

While it seemed like you could get too close to the edge and step off, in reality when we were on the roof there was no fear of falling. It was surprisingly much larger up there than you'd think it would be. Every time we went to the roof, the president would pause first to take in the entire view. He would select a spot, plant his feet, and turn from the ocean to the mountains, to downtown, and then toward LAX and the South Bay. He knew every block of this city, and I saw this full revolution ritual as his way of assessing it all before picking a direction and putting his binoculars up to his eyes.

These were not ordinary binoculars; they were military-grade, special-issue binoculars given to him by the armed forces when he was commander in chief. They made you feel as if you could see forever, because you practically could. I was used to the standard binoculars that from row twenty of a sporting event make you feel as if you were in row five, but these filtered out glare and made distant objects so clear and seemingly close that you could see leaves on the trees, details on the homes, and practically read license plates on the passing cars—even from five hundred feet up. Everyone in the office, myself included, would periodically go into the president's office, usually after he had gone home for the day, and pick up these binoculars and look out his window. They made us feel like top-secret spies.

On the roof, the president would turn away from the view toward the boats of Marina Del Rey and the planes of Santa Monica he saw every day from his west-facing window to look south toward the Hillcrest Country Club, a hidden gem of a private golf course and social club, nestled in the middle of a wealthy neighborhood. Although President Reagan was now a member of Los Angeles Country Club, in his earlier years in LA he had been a member at Hillcrest. He would pause and look with fondness at the expansive tree-lined course. I could see him mentally walking down the fairways, approaching the greens, and imagining sinking a perfect putt. He told me why he had joined Hillcrest when he first came to Los Angeles: because it was one of the few clubs that accepted members of all races and religions. He hadn't wanted to be a member of a club that discriminated.

If he decided to stand at the other side of the building's rooftop, facing north, he'd look among the trees for his home in Bel Air, pretending to wave at Mrs. Reagan. I loved seeing his childlike grin when he waved to her as if he was delighted to be swooping in to say a brief hello and give her a quick kiss. To the east was downtown Los Angeles, whose skyline had changed drastically since he first moved to LA, back when the twenty-eight-story City Hall building was the tallest in downtown.

He would pass the binoculars around, wanting to ensure that everyone else got a chance to look, too, pointing out something of particular interest he had noticed or enjoyed. I always appreciated that he included his Secret Service agents. He showed the agents the park where they had taken him to walk after work the week prior, or looked down at the hotel that sent over his lunch every day. The joy he had in these moments, not only for himself but for sharing this enthusiasm with others, was contagious. I especially appreciated and needed to be reminded to take advantage of beautiful days when they came and not look back on a cloudy day with regret that I missed an opportunity to see LA from the rooftops with a man who loved this town and who made me love it even more.

And maybe these rooftop visits were symbolic of something much deeper and more significant about him. Ronald Reagan was a man who, as an actor, had not only honed his craft but mastered the art of timing, which made all the difference in the world in how his work as an actor was received. And this was a man who didn't ever miss his cue or let the opportunity to make a point or a positive impact bypass him in life. We saw this time and time again when he was president: in swift and decisive action like taking on PATCO when the air traffic controllers went on strike, to his bold challenge of Gorbachev at the Berlin Wall when the Soviet Union was on the cusp of collapse. His words and actions, deliberate and timely, were delivered in the right way at the right time and changed everything.

Now, while I know that these rooftop visits weren't on par with historical aspects of his presidency, the impact they had on me was life changing nonetheless. Prior to this time I always thought that someone this important and powerful and accomplished must work longer and harder than anyone else on earth to achieve all that they had. Instead in Ronald Reagan I saw a man who worked extremely hard, efficiently, and effectively, and yet he knew that in order to get your work done on a beautiful LA day you sometimes had to stop wandering around the office, ignoring your work, and dismissing the call of the outdoors and go ahead and answer the call of the sunshine and find your way to the rooftop. There you could admire and appreciate the beauty, remember to reflect, and breathe deeply, leaving feeling refreshed, renewed, ready to tackle the day, and, most of all, content that you had seized and embraced this opportunity of the moment.

When we finally left the rooftop together and returned to our respective corners of work and routine, I am sure I wasn't the only one who would forever gaze out the window on a beautiful clear LA day and see things differently, watching the world bustling and busy all around us, deeply breathing in the beauty, the fresh restorative air, and the opportunity of the moment. How glad I am that I did. The work was still there when I returned to my desk, but I had a brightened spirit and a fresh perspective that only a visit to the rooftop with the president could bring.

15

Visiting the Residence

The Reagans loved children, and Mrs. Reagan especially always seemed a little disappointed if I showed up at the residence without mine. Visiting with the kids was such a production, however, that I didn't always have time to take them. Inevitably, if I showed up alone, as I was leaving she would say, "Peggy, it's always nice to see you, but... I haven't seen the children in a while..."

Her not-so-subtle hint was well taken!

President and Mrs. Reagan were an important part not only of my life but that of my family as well. They had warmly welcomed my first child, my son, Taylor, in 1993. My second, my daughter Courtney, arrived in 1996. My third, my daughter Paige, entered our world in 1999. And when I told Mrs. Reagan I was expecting my fourth child, she looked at me and said, "You know how this is happening, right?!" Embarrassed, I promised her, "Four and no more!" Nonetheless she and the president joyfully greeted my fourth child, my daughter Jocelyn, in 2001. Taking young kids into a beautiful home filled with priceless items was a nerve-racking endeavor that required a full day of preparation. Getting four little ones dressed up was an adventure in and of itself, including ruffled socks, hair bows, pressed shirts and dresses, and of course packing up an appropriate stash of bribes for the diaper bag, like special snacks, candy, or juice boxes.

Before each visit to the Reagan home, we made two stops. First, we stopped to buy an orchid for Mrs. Reagan (she loved them), a tradition that started the day my son, Taylor, was old enough to stand on his own and give it to her. Our second stop was at Holmby Park, about a mile away from the Reagans' house, so the kids could use the public restrooms. I'm serious. I didn't want them to have to go during the visit. I'd end up wasting our visiting time there shuttling kids back and forth to the powder room, leaving the others unsupervised. With so many priceless objects tempting their busy little hands, I just couldn't risk it.

I would then assess the state of their clothes and fix their hair as we loaded back into the car at the park and buckled back into car seats. As we climbed the hill to the residence the kids would get "the speech." If Ronald Reagan had his famous speech from 1964, this was mine—and I gave it on a regular basis. "You are very fortunate to visit these special people. Most people never get a single chance to meet them, and you are blessed to not only visit with them but to be guests in their home, and to get to do so often. Please use your best manners, be polite, answer questions, and enjoy the conversation, but don't offer up too much information or talk too much, and please don't do anything embarrassing. And *do not touch anything*!"

They got this talk every time we visited, and they can still recite it by heart. I am not sure "the speech" ever really worked, but thankfully they never did embarrass themselves or me—and, in fact, on one particular occasion in 1997 Taylor made me especially proud.

Taylor was about four years old and standing nose-high to a side table in the impeccable living room of the Reagans' home in Bel Air. On this particular visit he was eyeing an enticing collection of decorative elephants. They were trunk to tail, trunk to tail, in a line around the perimeter of the round table, each elephant different. One was crystal, one jade, one silver, and one stone, none like the others, all priceless. As Taylor intently studied this pachyderm parade, I nervously watched him, ready to block his hand if he reached for one. I was always on high alert when I brought my children to visit the Reagans.

Mrs. Reagan was watching him closely, too. Not to scold him, though. She wanted to ask him a question: "Taylor, do you know why I would have so many elephants in my house?"

Without pause he replied, matter-of-factly, "Because the elephant is the symbol of the Republican Party and you and the president are Republicans."

I was shocked he knew that—and was so proud. I couldn't have scripted it better myself if I tried. His response got a big grin from the First Lady, as the children usually did—and got ice cream from Mom on the way home as a reward.

My children were very comfortable with the Reagans—hugging them, holding their hands, and even climbing up on the president's desk to get up high enough to give him a real hug, not just a leg hug. That's the great thing about kids—they don't get bogged down with titles or status like adults do. When they were young, my kids didn't necessarily know or care that he had been president of the United States. They loved him and enjoyed him because they knew that he loved and enjoyed them. And for them, this was just part of their daily lives.

The Reagans enjoyed the energy, laughter, and enthusiasm that children brought and, in that phase of their lives, they craved the company of youth. Fortunately for them, there were a lot of children around. Many of the office staff were starting their families, with all the joy and chaos that entailed. Each of us from time to time had childcare gaps or mixed-up plans that resulted in one member of the staff or another bringing a young child to the office.

Although it wasn't conducive to work, the president loved it.

It's not as if the Office of Ronald Reagan was a daycare center, but I will admit that the kids played together so often in the hallways, colored in the conference room, and had snacks together in the kitchen that they have remained friends and still get together at least once a year. Every year the Reagans were alive, the children of their staffs would take a picture of these annual gatherings to send to the residence for President and Mrs. Reagan to enjoy.

I can still picture Taylor, napping on the floor of the conference room on his little farm animal blanket, surrounded by glossy jumbo pictures of world leaders and priceless art. I remember watching the president "sneak" past my desk, thinking I hadn't seen him, so he could peek in on Taylor. He didn't have much on his calendar that afternoon, so his thoughts had drifted back to that little boy asleep in the adjacent room. After a few tiptoe trips back and forth to the conference room, exasperated, he stopped at my desk and said, "When is that boy of yours going to wake up and play with me?!"

Taylor was always excited to go to the office because he wanted to see "his friend" the president. They were eighty-two years apart in age, but they both enjoyed tossing the football around in the office. When the staff surprised the president on his birthday with the notorious fish tank, I think the president appreciated the present even more when he saw what a draw it was for the children.

Taylor remembers how when he would visit, the president and he would always spend a bit of time assessing the fish and inventing creative story lines about their relationships to one another, something they both enjoyed. The president also would pick up Taylor, holding him in the windowsill to look out toward the ocean. Taylor enjoyed listening to his voice and always felt like he was telling him things of importance, so he listened intently, even when he didn't necessarily understand. When Taylor thinks about the president, it's as if he was another grandparent. "He always made me feel loved, welcomed, and most importantly for a kid, he always remembered my birthday!"

In many ways, the Reagans treated the office kids like additional grandkids, inviting them into the office in costumes on Halloween and handing out candy. Whether the little ones dressed as farmers, bumblebees, Robin Hood, ballerinas, or construction workers, the president loved the kids' costumes and would take pictures with them to commemorate the day. He would have the office kids in on their birthdays and on his birthday as well to help him open his gifts and blow out his candles. He was not only tolerant of the noise, sticky fingers, and occasional crying baby (and God forbid a smelly diaper!), but seemed to truly enjoy the new life, the energy, the laughter, and the joy that accompanied kids wherever they went.

It was fun and memorable to get together away from the office, too. The president would invite my kids to come up and swim in his pool with him at the residence and would ask them to join him at the polo grounds to watch polo matches at Will Rogers State Park on Sundays. Although he tried to maintain a low profile, people couldn't help but notice Ronald Reagan sitting in a plastic lawn chair with a cute baby beside him. And there was nothing more surreal than being at the Los Angeles Zoo for the dedication of one of their new exhibits and looking over to see Ronald Reagan pushing Taylor's stroller, surrounded by Secret Service agents! The president thought it would be much more fun to go with a little one who would enjoy the zoo along with him— and we all agreed.

I don't think any of my children enjoyed the big fuss I made before I took them up to the residence or the office or on an adventure with the president, but that preparation was designed to instill in them respect for these important individuals and a reverence for the occasion. But the truth was that my children, like all children, just wanted to have fun. Courtney had a special connection since she and Mrs. Reagan were both dancers. Courtney felt very grown-up when Mrs. Reagan talked to her seriously about dance, as if she was speaking one professional dancer to another.

Mrs. Reagan would ask what Courtney was working on in her classes. Courtney would describe the routines they were practicing, and then Mrs. Reagan would ask her to show one to her. Courtney didn't have to be asked twice. I remember one visit in the summer when Courtney described the eight-count combinations the class was working on and leapt up to demonstrate. Soon Mrs. Reagan was up, too, holding Courtney's hand and asking her to teach her the steps. What a great memory of these two dancers, with big grins on their faces, holding hands and sharing choreography on the back patio of the Reagan residence.

Mrs. Reagan enjoyed watching with amusement the joy and the chaos that so many young children created in my life and the ways in which they forced me to learn and grow. I recall a Saturday when I had driven up to the residence to take photos for a meeting with a visiting head of state. I left Greg in charge of the kids, including the dance class schedule for Courtney, who was about three at the time. Just as I rang the driveway buzzer to the Secret Service command post at the residence, identified myself, was being given access to the property and pulling up the driveway, my cell phone rang. It was Greg, and he was trying to figure out how to get Courtney dressed for her ballet class.

By then I was out of my car and standing on the Reagans' front porch, but hadn't yet rung the doorbell because I wanted to finish the call. Secret Service had notified Mrs. Reagan that I was on property, though, so she opened the front door to let me in. I apologized to her that I would be just one more minute because Greg was in the midst of asking me, "Does the thing that looks like a bathing suit go on first? Or the long, skinny leg-looking thing?"

Mrs. Reagan watched with a smile as I explained that the tights (the long, skinny leg-looking things) go on first and then the leotard (which looks like a bathing suit) goes on next. Greg said, "That's what Courtney was trying to tell me. I guess she was right."

Counsel from a three-year-old!

By this time Mrs. Reagan was fully engrossed in our conversation.

"Tell Greg hello—and good luck with ballet today," she said. "And thanks for the laugh this morning!"

On a few occasions, however, the kids weren't exactly an asset to a conversation. Mrs. Reagan would often call in the evenings with a question, and those of you who have kids know what dinnertime looks like and sounds like in a household of toddlers. It's not quiet, nor is there a lot of patience for Mommy being on the phone. I couldn't exactly tell Mrs. Reagan to call back at a more convenient time, so it became almost a game of hide-and-seek, or more like a game of chase.

Our house at the time made a huge circle between the living room, the bedroom hallway, and the kitchen. I would be talking on the phone with Mrs. Reagan and seeing how far opposite the kids I could be while they were "chasing" me in a circle. It was probably not a very good mommy moment, but it had been a lot of years since Mrs. Reagan had little ones of her own, so I wasn't sure she would understand my being unavailable.

Other times, if it was still too loud to talk to her, I would make sure the door was unlocked and step out into the backyard and hold the door closed and make silly faces as I would duck and hide and play peek-a-boo with the kids while simultaneously having a serious conversation with the former First Lady. Good thing video calling wasn't yet available!

For my children it was completely normal to visit the president, or come to the office, or talk about the president—and they did so nearly every day. When I would be dressed up in the evenings, Taylor would look at me and ask, "Mommy, are you having dinner tonight with Daddy or the president?" And when the kids in the office would get together and play, Taylor would take charge and give everyone their roles to play, saying, "You be the First Lady and I'll be Secret Service, okay?!" Then he would put on his sunglasses, talk into his sleeve, and spy around the corners, moving protectively around the "First Lady." Standard kids' play, right?

While this was their norm growing up, the children eventually developed a new appreciation for how extraordinary this everyday experience was to other people. Each of my kids has numerous photographs in their scrapbooks and pinned to the corkboards of their rooms of moments with the president: the birthday parties or snapshots of them playing ball or enjoying his beautiful backyard. When their friends see these casual images of the children embraced by the Reagans they are amazed that they don't brag about it or think of it as the biggest thing that ever happened to them. As little ones, they only knew of the warmth, the fondness, and the fun. Now that they are older they understand the significance and the importance of these gracious people, yet the history book recitations of what they accomplished or what they meant to the world will never supersede their own personal thoughts, warm feelings, and fond memories, which they cherish dearly.

Ronald Reagan was known for so many grand accomplishments on the world stage, but for me personally, he embodied kindness and graciousness, especially when I would watch him interact with my kids. There was nothing sweeter. When I thought I couldn't admire or appreciate this man any more than I already did, he would warm my heart further with these endearing grandfatherly-type interactions. I treasured those moments and know my children do as well.

16

Tru Luv Marriage

S tretching out behind the Reagans' Santa Barbara ranch home is a tranquil pond called Lake Lucky. At the end of the dock there floats a canoe named *Tru Luv*. Nancy Reagan once remarked to her husband that she thought the perfect marriage proposal would be one made in a canoe while the woman sat back, trailing her fingers in the water. Ronald Reagan always remembered that description. In 1977, when he was between his governorship and his presidency, he took Nancy out for a row in the *Tru Luv*, a gift to her on their twenty-fifth wedding anniversary. On that trip around Lake Lucky he repeated his original proposal of marriage while she trailed her fingers in the lake.

When we were up at the ranch, if I could get away for a moment, I'd walk out to the edge of that dock and breathe in the sweet Southern California mountain air: the aroma of earth and grasses with a hint of the sea that was just below this hilltop retreat. I'd think about the Reagans when they first bought this place, 688 acres of heaven. I could imagine them out on the water. I pictured the president sitting tall, his back straight and arms strong, as he paddled his beloved across the water. He is looking at her as she relaxes in her seat at the front. She admires the beauty around them there and her magnificent husband. This is a romantic image, but, to me, it is more than that: it is a metaphor for their marriage and for the best in all marriages, and it is what I as a young woman learned by watching the Reagans.

When a couple marries they find themselves figuratively in the same

147

boat. Whatever floods the boat floods both of them. They have to work together, each alert and aware, to stay afloat. Rough waters may come, but it can also be calm and steady. In those calm times, it is important to sit back, relax, and take the time to appreciate each other and the beauty of the world, remembering what a blessing it is to share that boat with someone you love and trust, someone who sees the best in you, wants the best for you, and enjoys your company above all others.

I had a strong model of marriage in my parents, Terry and Susan Giboney, as did Greg with his, John and Virginia Grande, though we knew our marriage would never look the same as our parents'. I hoped that, like my mother, I could be a loving and supportive wife, create a happy home for my family, and be active in my church and community. I wanted all of those things, and I wanted more, but I wasn't sure it would all be possible.

Both Greg's parents and mine showed us what true partnerships look like, making a huge impression on us and helping shape our own marriage. In the Reagans, too, we saw firsthand the importance of little gestures that strengthen a loving and lasting bond.

So much has been written about the Reagans and their love for each other, including a book of love letters from the president that Mrs. Reagan published entitled *I Love You, Ronnie*. The president said that his life "truly began when I met Nancy" and that he would miss her every time she left the room. I can attest to the truth of that statement, as I saw what happened when she returned. The Reagans couldn't stand being apart.

Mrs. Reagan used to love dropping by the office unannounced. She would call me to find out if the president had an opening in his schedule and, if he did, she would make me promise not to tell him that she was stopping by. When she arrived, I would tell the president we had an unexpected visitor and ask if he had time for a quick hello. When *she* walked into his office, he would practically leap out of his chair to greet her.

The Reagans were truly best friends. They were so comfortable in each other's company that often no words were exchanged, just a touch or a glance. They were like magnets drawn together with a force no one else could see and only they could feel. It didn't matter where they were or how many other people were around as long as the two of them could see each other across the room. They would always somehow find their way back together, back to each other's space, back to where they completed each other.

His delight in her was not just when she surprised him. Mrs. Reagan had an office down the hall from the president that she used from time to time. Sometimes they would meet in the hallway between the two offices, and if you happened to walk around the corner, you might catch them in full embrace and kissing. Really kissing. The posted Secret Service agent would smile laughingly, roll his eyes, and turn his back to give them some privacy. It was pretty funny, actually, and amazingly sweet, especially considering their ages and how long they had been married.

They were constantly holding hands, and he was always putting his arm around her or his hand in the small of her back as they were standing. People talk about the gaze that Nancy Reagan gave her husband as he spoke at events. But that loving gaze wasn't just reserved for public moments; that is how she always looked at him. But then there was the way that *he* looked at *her*. He had a gaze of his own, one that said without words that he was looking at the most beautiful woman in the world, someone whom he was exceptionally proud of, loved being beside, and adored in every way. She completed him—a real-life love story.

I saw how the two of them faced challenges together as a united front. Nothing came between them. They aligned themselves against the intruding problem. I loved watching that in action, the way that trust allowed them to shine independently because they appreciated and relied upon the qualities each uniquely brought to the relationship. They say opposites attract, which was very true with the Reagans. The president approached life in a way that was open and friendly, easygoing and optimistic, while she was more selective with her friendships and practical and realistic in her outlook on life. He was warm and affable with everyone, even strangers, while she was more proper and formal. He assumed the best in people and immediately treated everyone with trust and respect, as if they were old friends, while Mrs. Reagan was a bit more shrewd and intuitive in sizing people up and warmed slowly to new relationships, more hesitant to attach herself to people immediately.

This "other half of the whole" played itself out in many aspects of their lives. What I took from watching the Reagans was that a good marriage needs to achieve balance, a give and take, for the little boat to remain stable. I saw how the president ceded the territory of style to Mrs. Reagan, who helped him always look his best (sometimes with his knowledge and sometimes without). He never minded either way, because he, too, wanted to look his best and wanted to stay fit and be handsome and polished for her—and for himself. And while he certainly had opinions, he would often defer to her, but she knew how to give ground, too. At the ranch, she allowed the president to have his own style in his cowboy's paradise. I know she would not have chosen all the items and décor he selected to fill their little adobe home, but she was happy to be supportive and play along (maybe as part of a deal that their Bel Air home would be decorated the way she wanted).

I sometimes think about the irony in the Reagans' powerful partnership. Mrs. Reagan wasn't the one who was interested in politics, and she certainly didn't push her husband into it, and yet I'm convinced that he wouldn't have achieved all he did and had all the success in the political arena he had without her. Her personal support, her intuitive insights, her ongoing encouragement, and her graciousness as a political spouse were essential to his accomplishments. So she made possible something that she wasn't necessarily advocating for personally because she knew he was made for this. He was called to this. And she helped him thrive and succeed and become a powerful figure on the world stage, in spite of her own preferences, not because of them. She truly devoted her life to him and his pursuits, regardless of what she would have preferred or

With my parents, Terry and Susan Giboney, at my December 1989 graduation from Pepperdine University. I was named "Outstanding Woman of the Year" and was excited to see what life would hold.

Not long after I started my internship in 1989, President Reagan gave me a Snoopy birthday card on my birthday—November 6. I was ecstatic since I didn't even think he knew who I was yet.

Private air travel with the president spoiled me at an early age. I look back on it longingly every time I now take a commercial flight.

Office life could be hectic and demanding, but I loved the challenges of each day and cherished my role.

All five living presidents gathered for the opening of the Reagan Library. It was a thrilling day for me, someone who had been obsessed with studying the presidency since childhood.

President Reagan was so proud of his Presidential Medal of Freedom that he wore it all the way home from the White House in January 1993. He always modeled discipline and gratitude—even writing his own thank-you notes on the flight back. *Photo by the author.*

People loved President Reagan and wanted to be near him, or just shake his hand, as seen here as he was leaving a large political rally in summer 1992.
Photo by the author.

President Reagan and President Lech Walesa of Poland, symbolically and humorously trying to push over a section of the Berlin Wall at the Reagan Library in March 1991.
Photo by the author.

A special visit to the Century City office from Mother Teresa, now a saint, in December 1991. One of the many "pinch me" moments I had while working for the president. *Photo by the author.*

Mrs. Reagan and Margaret Thatcher in the Oval Office replica at the Reagan Library, shoes kicked off and deep in conversation following an event in February 1993. The president looked eager to head home! *Photo by the author.*

The former commander in chief welcomed and honored American hero Captain Scott O'Grady, who had been shot down behind enemy lines in Bosnia. Here they are in July 1995, saluting each other out of deep mutual respect. *Photo by the author.*

The Reagans embrace in the White House East Room following the presentation of the Presidential Medal of Freedom by President George H. W. Bush to Ronald Reagan in January 1993. It is the highest honor that can be bestowed on a civilian in peacetime. *Photo by the author.*

The adobe home at Rancho del Cielo was built in 1871. Modest by most standards, it was a beloved retreat for President and Mrs. Reagan where they enjoyed hosting world leaders as well as cherished private time together. *Photo by the author.*

Former Soviet leader Mikhail Gorbachev in the Stetson cowboy hat that took me on a worldwide quest to find his size.

The president was like an excited kid behind the wheel of his Jeep at the ranch, since he hadn't driven much in his eight years in office. And, yes, that's Gorbachev riding shotgun in the passenger's seat.

The Reagans enjoyed the ranch visit of Prime Minister Brian Mulroney of Canada and his wife, Mila, in April 1993. The president and the prime minister both had Irish heritage, which made them great storytellers. No one laughed harder at their jokes than they did. *Photo by the author.*

I loved working with the president in his beautiful Century City office. It was warm, welcoming, and elegant, filled with historic artifacts as well as Western art and cowboy bronzes.

Happy birthday, Mr. President! Although the cake I was holding on February 6, 1993, said 82, the president preferred to celebrate by saying it was the forty-third anniversary of his thirty-ninth birthday.

The president golfing at the Los Angeles Country Club with my husband, Greg, and dear friends Erik Felten and Bill Drake.

Five hundred feet above the streets of LA, the president could see forever with his binoculars. I treasured visits with him to that rooftop oasis.

President Reagan loved having the kids come visit him at the office, especially on holidays. My son, Taylor, dressed as a farmer on Halloween, enjoyed candy, pumpkins, and the president. *Photo by the author.*

The president was never too busy to play a quick game of catch when the kids dropped by the office, and he always had a football on hand! *Photo by the author.*

No "trick," just a "treat" for my daughter Courtney on Halloween to be dressed as a ballerina and gazed at so lovingly by the fortieth president of the United States. *Photo by the author.*

Sunday polo matches at the Will Rogers Polo Club were always more fun when the kids came along. Courtney got almost as much attention as the president when they were seated together at this match in summer 1997.

Nine months pregnant with my third child in April 1999. This was my last day at work before my daughter Paige was born just four days later.

Introducing Paige to President Reagan. My kids grew up knowing this iconic man as an important part of their lives.

Paige meeting Mrs. Reagan for the first time. My kids enjoyed the Reagans' warm hospitality and loving attention over the years.

When I told Mrs. Reagan I was expecting my fourth child, she quipped, "You know how this is happening, right?!" Nonetheless, she warmly welcomed my daughter Jocelyn into our family and into her home in 2001.
Photo by the author.

On my kids' last visit with the president in summer 2000, they took turns sitting with him. Here, Taylor holds the president's hand in the Reagans' beautiful backyard and says his final goodbye. *Photo by the author.*

Taking four children into the Reagans' beautiful home, which was full of priceless artifacts, was always nerve-racking. Fortunately, the kids were respectful, well-behaved, and enjoyed and treasured their visits—like this one in summer 2009. *Photo by the author.*

Dutchess, a purebred Chinese shar-pei, was given to Mrs. Reagan as a puppy after the president died, but she grew too strong and lively for Mrs. Reagan and came to live with my family instead. We loved her for ten years and said goodbye to her a few months after Mrs. Reagan's passing. Dutchess was buried up at the Reagan Ranch with all the other beloved Reagan pets. *Photo by the author.*

My family, up at Rancho del Cielo in September 2016, on the patio outside the Reagans' little adobe home. The kids, left to right: Taylor, Paige, Jocelyn, and Courtney.

pursued on her own. And though neither one could have ever predicted back in 1952 that they would wind up in the White House together, I know they would have been happy together even if life took a different path and they wound up sharing only that little adobe house at the ranch.

During the first year I was serving as the president's personal assistant, I was in his office one day and talking about some upcoming events when I flipped the calendar to March, which was labeled on the fourth as the Reagans' anniversary.

"There it is—your special day!" I said.

"Yes, it is—a very special day!" he replied with his eyes sparkling.

"I'm not sure if you need me to do anything for you before then, but of course please let me know," I offered.

"Well, I usually get her two cards, so if you could pick some out for me to choose from, that would be great."

"Of course. Anything in particular?"

"I always give her Snoopy cards—she loves those. I give her one that is cute or funny and another one that is more...you know...more appropriate for an anniversary," he said with a little wink and a big smile.

I suddenly felt myself blushing, as if I was embarrassed to be the one to choose the cards to express his feelings to his wife on their anniversary, but replied, "I'll have some options for you tomorrow."

As I walked out of his office I wondered if there was such a thing as a wink-and-a-smile type make-you-blush Snoopy card. I guessed I would have to go find out.

That day after work I stopped at a Hallmark store near my house and went straight to the anniversary card section, laughing to myself as I realized what a simple stop this was for me—and what a huge logistical production it would have been if the president had gone card shopping himself. Surprisingly, there was a large selection of Snoopy cards and, as hoped, a wide variety—from entertaining and funny to sweet and even romantic, in an old-fashioned type of way. I purchased a few options for the president to choose from. And though I wouldn't say that Snoopy was racy, there certainly were some surprisingly sentimental and loving Snoopy cards I thought would be perfect for him to give Mrs. Reagan.

The following day he chose two from the several I had brought for him and seemed very pleased.

I saw him pull a pen from his desk and get busy, eagerly writing in the two anniversary cards to his wife. I saw him concentrating, then smiling, spending a few minutes thinking about and then writing in each one. Ultimately satisfied with what he had composed, he put the two cards in their envelopes, sealed them, and brought them to me at my desk, asking me to give them back to him again when he was heading out the door the day before their anniversary. He seemed so happy after writing to her, knowing that his words meant the world to her. He wanted to do anything he could to please her, honor her, and make her feel cherished and treasured, because she was. It was as if the very thought of her was an oasis of comfort and delight for him in the midst of an otherwise busy day. He loved putting his thoughts in writing to her, nearly as much as she enjoyed receiving them. She inspired him and energized him. He had the glow of a newlywed at the mention of her name—even though he was well into his eighties and they had been married more than forty years!

While Snoopy isn't exactly known or revered for being a great philosopher, I think there is something much deeper and more powerful than first appears in the president's two-card routine to honor his wife on their anniversary (and for her birthday, too). Ronald and Nancy Reagan had a love story that on the outside may have looked very storybook and too-good-to-be-true. In reality, their love and relationship was far more deep and layered—a dynamic too complex to ever be captured in a single anniversary card. The two cards in many ways symbolized the essence of their marriage and the way in which he wanted to honor both aspects: a solid foundation of love, support, stability, and true romance, partnered with a side of their life together that was playful and cute and funny and didn't allow either of them to take themselves or their life together too seriously. What a wonderful balance of complementary traits to possess, especially for a couple in the political spotlight!

Over the years, several times on my birthday I also received a Snoopy card from the president, which meant the world to me—especially knowing that Snoopy cards were so near and dear to his heart. My favorite one had Snoopy on the front, waving a little pendant that said "Happy Birthday" on it. Inside the card was a treasured inscription: "Dear Peggy, From One of Your Biggest Fans—Ronald Reagan." Though I'm not sure who bought cards for him to give to me, I always was extremely grateful and cherished seeing his name signed on those cards (but just *one* Snoopy card on my birthday, though—of course).

The long, happy life the Reagans had together was truly a gift, yet even the greatest love stories don't always wind up having fairy-tale endings, as Mrs. Reagan knew—as does my mom. My mom and my dad had known each other since elementary school and started dating when my mom was finishing high school and my dad had just started college. They married very young and enjoyed having and raising a family together. Life was wonderful and loving. Yet cancer had its eyes set on my father and relentlessly pursued him until he succumbed to it at the young age of fifty-seven. He died only a few days short of my parents' thirty-sixth wedding anniversary, but, ever the romantic, my dad had planned ahead and left my mom a letter that he had written to her when he was still able to, with instructions for her to pull a package out of the safe-deposit box he had left there for her. He had taken a family heirloom diamond and designed a ring for her, calling it her "forever" ring, saying it sparkled like their marriage. With it, he wanted to declare that his love for her would endure forever, and that their separation, though painful now, would be brief in eternity's time.

Though there's never enough time with someone you love, I learned from watching my father pass away at such a young age that we need to live each day as if there's no guarantee of tomorrow—because there's not. Even if you wish and plan and save and look forward to those "golden years" of retirement, even when you do everything "right," life doesn't always cooperate or turn out as planned. Cherish and celebrate now—don't wait. Live and love with an intensity, a passion, and a pace that is worthy of the treasure of love. That's what the Reagans did. And even though they were blessed with many years together, they never would have said it was enough. When you lose something you truly have loved, you know what it's like to lose half of yourself.

17

Seasons of Change

I don't remember the exact day, but I will never forget the exact moment. I had been working for the president for about five years. I had taken the initial pictures of his greeting with a visitor and snapped a few of the president speaking with his guest. I could tell he was having a good time because he had started down the on ramp to one of his favorite stories, the one where he was announcing the baseball game based only on the wire feed and his imagination, and then the wire stopped and he had to imagine what was happening on the field. I was already finishing the story in my mind while simultaneously daydreamingly looking out his beautiful windows at the expansive view. I always enjoyed experiencing how his visitors would be enraptured by his ability to masterfully tell a tall tale. And then it happened.

He was about to describe the fight he imagined taking place between two boys beyond the outfield and the peanut vendor making his way through the stands. Just as he was building to the crescendo of the story, the punch line, there was an awkward pause. It was just a moment. But it was there. And I couldn't help but notice. He seemed surprised as well that he had lost his place. But the president, ever the professional actor and showman, just backed up a few sentences, emphasizing the previous lines, and made it appear as if it had been on purpose, for dramatic effect. He did it masterfully, completing the story this time without missing a beat, even convincing me that maybe he was just trying out a new way to tell an old story. The guest laughed and had a wonderful visit, and the day resumed as normal. I didn't give the moment another thought—until later.

A few weeks later I was in another meeting with him and a similar scenario occurred. A friendly greeting with his guests, photos, warm welcoming conversation, a look around the office, and the telling of one of his favorite stories—the one about two brothers, one an eternal optimist and the other an eternal pessimist. Their father put the pessimist into a room piled high with toys, thinking surely this would make him happy, yet he still lamented that they might break, or need batteries, or not work. The story was flowing off his tongue effortlessly. This was one of his greatest hits, one of his oldies-but-goodies favorite stories. He continued by saying that the eternal optimist was put into a room piled high with horse manure, sure to elicit a complaint, "but rather than complaining, the boy said..." And there he stopped. And he looked at me with a look I would eventually get to know very well but didn't understand yet. I knew what he was supposed to say and knew that he did, too. But it didn't come out. So I jumped in quickly and awkwardly.

"Mr. President, aren't you so nice to let me say the punch line?! The optimistic boy said, 'With all that manure—there has to be a pony in there somewhere!'" The guests laughed and the president managed a smile as well.

I quickly ended the appointment, walked the president's guests out to the lobby, and thanked them for coming. Instead of returning to my desk, I walked back into President Reagan's office.

"Are you all right, Mr. President?" I asked.

"Oh, yes, I'm fine," he said. "I just got distracted and lost my place in that story."

He did seem perfectly fine, but he had been right in the middle of a familiar story and had stopped. Again. Even though I brushed off the earlier incident, subconsciously it hadn't sat well with me. I had been trying to confirm or deny the fact that it had even happened at all or had meant anything at all. And yet there it was again: an uncharacteristic pause in an otherwise unremarkable moment. I definitely hadn't imagined it this time.

I returned to my desk. My mind was spinning. I wanted to assure myself that it didn't mean anything, that it was just a momentary brain freeze and was to be expected. It happens to us all. I also knew, of course, that I worked for an elderly gentleman, and older people do funny things and get confused all the time, so maybe he was just showing his age. Yes, that had to be it. He was well into his eighties—of course even he, a consummate storyteller, would periodically have a misstep in telling a story. I tried to return to my work but was distracted. I couldn't shake the unsettling feeling there was something wrong. As soon as I thought that, my own defenses rose up in protest. No, there was nothing wrong. He said he was fine. I should believe him.

No matter my internal argument, I knew now I would be more aware of any lapses in his speech or action, even the smallest ones. As the weeks unfolded, I noticed more and more little things. He seemed quieter, a little more lost in thought than his usual engaging self, and a bit distracted. He was less attentive to detail, and not as focused on time as he had always been. When I started working for the president he was seventy-eight years old but still energetic and fully engaged. I saw periodic reminders of his advanced age, such as technology he didn't understand or terminology he used that was very old-fashioned, as being part of his charm. As with other older people I knew, I saw these aspects of their personalities as hints about the era they lived through, their experiences, and their life's adventures. These never gave me concern. And even after his lapse in telling a favorite story or two, I was not frightened because I didn't yet realize that I had noticed the very tip of an enormous iceberg, and I was currently unaware of its depth or its potential for future devastation.

But in the ensuing months the episodes became more frequent. Something was changing, but, as a staff person, I did not know if it was appropriate for me to comment on his behavior, as it seemed to be a personal issue, one that surely wasn't my place to discuss. Also,

I didn't know whom I could discuss it with without feeling as though I was breeching a boundary or betraying his privacy. Even though Mrs. Reagan and I had a comfortable working relationship, it was a professional one, and I certainly didn't want to rush to her with something that wasn't my business or exaggerate a behavior that would be considered typical for a man his age.

I was conflicted, so I did nothing for a while except continue to take notice. And worry. And pray. Finally, I could ignore it no longer. I decided that perhaps I was the only one who worked with him this closely, and since no one else had mentioned anything around the office, maybe I was the only one who was in a position to notice. I felt I must share my observations, without knowing what the consequences might be. I summoned up the courage to confide my concern with one of the other women in the office, who was a dear friend and part of the senior staff.

I waited until the president had left for the day, walked down to her office, and shut the door. The senior staff office doors typically were left open, so when a door was shut we all knew it was serious. And this was. It started as one of those conversations where each side knows something they are not sure whether the other person knows, so they each dance around the truth and drop hints to indicate that they know, hoping the other person will also indicate they know so that both people can then share freely. After a few minutes of not talking about the elephant in the middle of the room and dancing around it instead, we finally got to the place where I stated that I was concerned about some lapses and behaviors I had noticed, and I was relieved when she admitted the same. She had noticed little things here and there as well and had mentioned them to Mrs. Reagan, who recently expressed her awareness and her concern as well. Their annual visit to the Mayo Clinic in Rochester, Minnesota, was scheduled for the summer, as usual, so they would discuss it with his doctors there at that time.

I was relieved I wasn't alone in my observations and in my concern and glad that they were going to look into it. I would proceed as if it was business as usual, remain aware and supportive, and keep a positive, optimistic attitude as always.

The summer trip to the Mayo Clinic came and went. The president came back to the office and nothing was said to me about the visit. No information was offered, and I didn't feel it was my place or appropriate for me to specifically inquire, especially into personal issues like the status of his health. And despite my close proximity to the president, I was not part of the senior staff. I imagine they might have been discussing the president's state of mind for a while, but I was not privy to those conversations.

The fact that they did not instantly call me in to tell me anything was wrong was oddly comforting. I decided there must not be anything worth sharing. Besides, I wanted to be respectful of the president's right to privacy. So it was business as usual. Mostly. The schedule was normal, visitors came regularly, guest visits were polite, events were attended, and speeches continued to be given and were uneventful for the most part, with glitches that were now becoming the norm. Yet there was this underlying sense that something had changed. There were more closed-door meetings, a new sense of secrecy and concern, and the feeling that a little black cloud was hovering above an office that had previously known only sunshine. On Friday, November 4, 1994, less than a year after I had first noticed, that little black cloud burst into a full storm.

After the president left the office for the day, I was called into the chief of staff's office, where the senior staff was already gathered. It was one of those moments when you walk in and everyone is suddenly perfectly still, as if you're interrupting something important. And I was. I was asked to take a seat and shut the door behind me. I was nervous and worried. They looked very serious and grim. I was understandably alarmed, but not in the way you feel when you have been called into the boss's office and think you're in trouble or have done something horribly wrong. This was different. I could tell from their faces. I knew it wasn't about me. I feared it was about the president. And unfortunately, I was right.

We had been through challenges in the past as a team and as an office family, and we had always done so with a unified front and a grace that disguised the heavy lifting that was often taking place behind the scenes. Yet even in the midst of crisis we managed to portray a lightness, a Reaganesque optimism, a confidence that this, too, would pass and we would once again get back on course. But this felt heavy and fearful. I had so many questions. And they were about to be answered. The chief of staff handed me two pages of beautiful cream-colored paper with a gold presidential seal at the top and the gold engraved name of Ronald Reagan underneath. He asked me to read it. The stationery and the handwriting both belonged to the president and were very familiar, but this letter was not. I held in my hands and read for the first time the heartfelt letter from President Reagan himself, which the rest of the world would read the following day:

November 5, 1994
My fellow Americans,

I have recently been told that I am one of the millions of Americans who will be afflicted with Alzheimer's disease.

Upon learning this news, Nancy and I had to decide whether as private citizens we would keep this a private matter or whether we would make this news known in a public way.

In the past, Nancy suffered from breast cancer and I had cancer surgeries. We found through our open disclosures we were able to raise public awareness. We were happy that as a result many more people underwent testing. They were treated in early stages and able to return to normal, healthy lives.

So now we feel it is important to share it with you. In opening our hearts, we hope this might promote greater awareness of this condition. Perhaps it will encourage a clear understanding of the individuals and families who are affected by it.

At the moment, I feel just fine. I intend to live the remainder of the years God gives me on this earth doing the things I have always done. I will continue to share life's journey with my beloved Nancy and my family. I plan to enjoy the great outdoors and stay in touch with my friends and supporters.

Unfortunately, as Alzheimer's disease progresses, the family often bears a heavy burden. I only wish there was some way I could spare Nancy from this painful experience. When the time comes, I am confident that with your help she will face it with faith and courage.

In closing, let me thank you, the American people, for giving me the great honor of allowing me to serve as your president. When the Lord calls me home, whenever that may be, I will leave the greatest love for this country of ours and eternal optimism for its future.

I now begin the journey that will lead me into the sunset of my life. I know that for America there will always be a bright dawn ahead.

Thank you, my friends. May God always bless you.

Sincerely,
Ronald Reagan

I wanted to cry. But couldn't. Not yet. Not here. As tears began to well up in my eyes I was overwhelmed by the goodness, the graciousness, and the faith of a man who was being tested and in his time of trial was not crumbling, but rather was rising up with strength and courage and even optimism in the depths of life's darkest place. I would have expected nothing less. Yet to expect anyone, even him, to endure this and to do so with transparency and hope was extraordinary. He and Mrs. Reagan had privately come to terms with this news as best as they could, and now, he, like always, was going to find a way to shoulder the burdens of his wife and his nation, pointing the way to acceptance. And to peace.

When I finished reading, we agreed that I would be part of the small team that would come into the office the next day, Saturday, November 5, 1994, to let the world know President Ronald Reagan had been diagnosed with Alzheimer's disease. Of course I would do anything that was needed. Professionally I remained strong. Personally my heart sank and my stomach was in my throat. I felt overcome with conflicting emotions and thoughts and feelings and questions. Inside I was angry. *Why him?* And scared. *What does this mean?* And worried. *How does he feel?* And intimidated. *How can I help?* And sad. *How can I face him? And how can I ever face losing him?*

After the Mayo Clinic diagnosed his illness, the Reagans decided this news could—and should—be used to help others who also shared their struggle. They always believed that awareness saved lives and brought lifesaving funding to causes that needed support, answers, and cures. As they had done with Mrs. Reagan's breast cancer and President Reagan's own cancer scares, they believed that in sharing their lives with others, the lives of others could be bettered. And maybe even saved. The easier path would have been to just fade from public view. Move full-time to the ranch or stick close to home. Perhaps the world would never know, and they could live out their days together in peace and with privacy. Yet that is not the Reagans the world knew and loved. They had no idea then how much they would positively impact the Alzheimer's community of families, physicians, and patients in the years to come.

The meeting ended and a few of us stayed behind and started working on preparing the fax cover sheets for the various news agencies, determining the order of release and making the appropriate copies. There was so much to say, and yet words failed us all. Lost in our own internal conversations, we finished efficiently and quietly and locked everything away until the next morning. We headed out together—a wordless elevator ride down, a silent walk to the parking garage, each dreading tomorrow. The pain and grief we were experiencing now privately was about to be unleashed publicly. We were going to be the bearers of heartbreaking and devastating news for the world the next day. And they would look to us for answers we didn't have, for strength we were still trying to summon ourselves, and for optimism and hope, which was uncharacteristically absent from the Office of Ronald Reagan at the moment. As we would do several times in difficult situations yet to come, we would soldier on, band together, and put on a strong and brave face in the midst of our own fears and doubts and grief and deep sadness. The president would have it no other way.

I got in my car and headed for home. I expected to be sobbing but was too shell-shocked and distraught to even find tears. I was about to become an expert on something I knew nothing about and wanted to know nothing about.

18

My Fellow Americans

We've all had a day we have anticipated with dread. Yet regardless of how hard we fight against it or want to ignore or avoid it, the clock ticks forward, the calendar page turns, and the day arrives. Thankfully we tell ourselves that however hard and painful the day is, it will ultimately pass and become a memory.

Such was my feeling on Saturday, November 5, 1994, as I was facing a day of dread, but more than that, I was turning the page into a new chapter, one I didn't want to write. I got up early and enjoyed an easy morning of getting out the door alone and a significantly lighter commute. My birthday was the following day, November 6. I would not be celebrating much this year. I was turning twenty-seven, but on this particular day I felt much older, painfully aware of the gravity and burdens of life that were far beyond my own years.

On my radio-less drive to the office, my thoughts went to all the individuals and families and friends and admirers of the Reagans who were going about their day—at soccer games, at birthday parties, running errands, visiting relatives, or cleaning their homes—likely in the midst of a carefree and productive typical Saturday, not yet burdened by the news we were going to share about the president's Alzheimer's diagnosis. It was news I knew they would take hard and personally. I saw in my mind the faces and heard the voices of all those people who in the past had taken time from their busy lives to write to the president to wish him a happy birthday, or called to express their admiration for him personally or their appreciation for the leadership of his presidency.

I thought of all those who had sent in pictures of their adorable chubby babies they had enthusiastically named Reagan, both boys and girls, or their sons in baseball uniforms at that cute age where they are missing more teeth than they have left. There were Golden Retrievers and white fluffy poodles and mutts of unknown origin who were perhaps adorable to their owner yet a bit peculiar-looking to me, all named Reagan. All named out of love and affection. All named as a reminder of him. He meant something to them. They had brought him into their homes and into their lives.

These were the people I thought of who would hear the news and be devastated. They were ordinary Americans who just wanted to share in his life, be part of his life, and have him be part of theirs. They felt connected to him and valued by him. They had looked to him in their time of need, when America had lost its way and its sense of self. When we were floundering as a people in the 1970s he had been the rudder, steering the ship in a better direction in the 1980s. When we didn't believe in ourselves or in our future, he was a bright beacon of hope who got us moving in a direction that led us to growth, pride, and prosperity. When we were suffering economically he established a revised framework of regulations and taxes that allowed people to once again be innovative and explore and take a risk.

For much of America he had been a rock, an unmovable object of stability we could trust to stand firm in principles and be unflinching in conflicts, never wavering. For all those, myself included, who had pictured him as a gigantic superhero, riding his white stallion with his sword of freedom held high, traveling around the world liberating oppressed people everywhere and bringing life and liberty wherever he went, he was about to be seen as a mere mortal, not superhuman, but human, with a chink in his steel armor, just like the rest of us. The image of the mythological superhero Ronald Reagan was about to be shattered. And I, still his biggest fan and admirer, was going to be part of the shattering of that image. I dreaded it. By nature I was a protector, but I hadn't been able to protect him from this hideous disease, nor would I be able to protect the world from sharing in his pain.

When I walked in the door the night before, Greg knew by my face that something was terribly wrong. I hadn't called him on the way home, not wanting to risk talking about something so secret and sensitive over an insecure cell phone line. I told him the news in person, and we sat in silence. In saying the words it made it seem real. I could no longer pretend I just imagined it and was in the middle of a horrible nightmare from which I would wake up. We didn't talk about it any further. I just sat in shock and stared off into the distracted distance of my own racing and anxious thoughts.

I didn't know much about Alzheimer's then, and I would guess most people didn't, unless they had a family member personally affected by it. In fact, through the president's diagnosis I finally had a name for the illness that had afflicted my great-aunt Opal. As a young child I just thought she was odd and silly, yet after the president's announcement, all those years later, the realization hit me that she, too, had been a victim of Alzheimer's. I was sure that as I learned more about it, the symptoms of the disease would give explanation to some of the behaviors I had noticed in the office and had been concerned about. But maybe it was better I didn't know too much. It would have been too frightening, too intimidating, and too terrifying. Yet as everyone who is in a professional or personal relationship with someone affected by a similar diagnosis knows, you commit to the person, to the relationship, and to doing everything you can to walk the journey with them, regardless of what that entails. And as much as I feared doing so, I wanted so desperately to be there with him and for him in this uncharted, unknown, and unthinkable future ahead.

The morning of the announcement, a small group of my co-workers and I met in the very quiet office. The thirty-fourth floor was empty, except for us. There was work to be done, and we were committed to doing it, knowing it was what the president wanted. Yet we were burdened by the ominous feeling that an enormous genie was about to be let out of the bottle and could never be put back in. We had sent lots of press releases out in the past, but this one would rock the world as it had already privately rocked each of our worlds.

A cover sheet, a press statement, and the president's handwritten letter were being faxed to every news agency on our list, starting with the Associated Press. We had a favorite AP reporter we had known for years and had worked with often. He had been alerted that morning to stand by for a statement. He would receive it, then route it to the wires, and the news would be out there within moments. He would take it hard personally as well, since he had met the president on many occasions and was very fond of him. Although the other news agencies would inevitably hear through the wire, we also sent the release as a courtesy to other reporters with whom we had regularly corresponded. We pushed Send on the first one, holding our collective breaths, knowing we couldn't undo what had just been done and knowing that things in our office and in our lives would never be the same. My thoughts went to the president, enjoying the solitude of the ranch that day with Mrs. Reagan, safely away from the press storm that was about to erupt. That poor beloved man. I wondered what he and Mrs. Reagan were thinking about on this day, knowing their private suffering was about to become public.

As anticipated, the office phones began to ring within minutes. My greeting was the same—"Office of Ronald Reagan"—yet the tone and feel were entirely different. We knew the only people calling the office number in the middle of a Saturday were people who were calling with questions for which we had no answers. Their questions were similar to ours. We stayed in the office for an hour or two, verifying receipt of the faxes, validating that yes, it was true and that the release had come from our office on the president's behalf. Everything else was referred to the director of public affairs, who fielded as many questions as possible initially and had us take specific messages or direct the caller to submit their questions in writing to be answered at a later time. These were the typical things we had anticipated. However, the unanticipated deluge was yet ahead.

Monday came, and I headed into the office a bit earlier than usual. I arrived to the sound of phones ringing. And ringing. And ringing. By then everyone on the staff had heard the news. Even the interns had been briefed and given talking points so they could help handle the tsunami of calls flooding the office. That was a huge help to triage the influx, but anyone who had my name was routed my way for me to talk to. The volume alone was overwhelming, but even more so was the nature of these calls. People were calling me to share their outpouring of emotion and grief and feelings of loss. In many ways this was the beginning of goodbye for all of us. Realizing that he was not invincible and that, like all of us, he would eventually pass on into the history books was a painful reality that affected people greatly.

They would call with a favorite memory, a story, a thought or emotion that they wanted to share as if he were already gone. There was a gentleman who had served in the military, calling through his tears, telling me how he had almost left the armed services in 1979 but was so glad he had stayed because Ronald Reagan as commander in chief had made him proud again—of his service, of his country, and, most importantly, of himself. There was a woman who called, sobbing, saying that she had been working in the kitchen at an event and he had met her and shook her hand and looked at her, really looked at her, connecting to her with his eyes in a way that she felt seen and acknowledged and valued for the very first time. She would never forget it, or him. People were calling with beautiful tributes, sending well wishes to him and surrounding Mrs. Reagan with love and prayers of support. They were calling with tears and sadness and heartbreak that they weren't sure how to handle.

I guess by calling the office it made them feel connected to him, supportive of him, and close to him for as long as they could be. Yet in doing so, they were dumping their emotions and their grief on me, who was already overwhelmed and weighted down by my own mountain of grief and emotion I hadn't yet processed. I wasn't even sure how to begin. I knew I wasn't alone in my pain and in my feelings of loss and sadness, which was helpful, but I felt ill-equipped to carry the tears of the world on my young shoulders. I was just trying to get through my own day and prepare for the president's return the next week.

I'm known as a person of action, not emotion, especially with people I love. Problem? I have a solution. What do you need? I'll do my best to provide it. How can I help? I roll up my sleeves and do it, not just talk about it. Where does it hurt? I have a fix for that. What is hard for you to do? I will tell you how to do it better or more efficiently. I'm a fixer. A do-er. Yet this scenario was different. There was no easy or good solution and no positive resolution, which made this extraordinarily challenging and tough to face—and I was having to walk others through it as I was walking through it myself. They wanted him to be strong and secure and bear their burdens and live up to their expectations as he always had. Yet he no longer could. And the devastation of that reality often landed in my ear on the phone or on my desk in the form of heart-wrenching, beautifully written mail.

Since my first day in the office I knew I had been blessed with the opportunity to answer the calling of a lifetime. I often wondered, why me? How was this possible? What am I supposed to do with the blessing—and burden—of stewardship with which I have been entrusted? Would I be worthy and up to the tasks asked of me? How could I show my gratitude for the opportunity and give back the lessons and truths to which I was exposed every day? I couldn't help but think that maybe I had had it all wrong. Maybe the past five years had not been about answering that initial call of a lifetime, but perhaps they had just been a training ground, a proving ground, a boot camp of instruction and practice in order to stretch me, grow me, challenge me, and prepare me to answer my true calling, which was this very moment. Was I ready? Could I handle it? Would I be able to face it and help shoulder his burden? Help those who were suffering under the weight of their own grief? I knew the president would expect nothing less and would believe me to be capable of nothing less. Yes, this was my calling. I needed to confidently and courageously step into it. And it would start with facing him again when he returned.

The president would be back in the office the following Monday. I couldn't wait to see him, to see if he was okay, to give him a comforting hug of love and support, and to remind him of my commitment to him regardless of what was ahead for him. I would be honored to walk this journey with him as long or as short as needed. Yet part of me dreaded seeing him as well. What would I say? What should I say? What should I not say? Or do? Would it be awkward and uncomfortable? Would he appear upset or seem like it was business as usual? Again, there were more questions than answers. Again, there was the emotion of wanting to be nowhere near this devastating illness, yet also not wanting to be anywhere else in the world except by his side.

Although I would typically meet him at his car in the morning, knowing there was such a firestorm of press interest and being concerned that there may be media staked out in the lobby, his director of public affairs walked down to meet him at his car that day. I waited at my desk for the sounds of the outer doors opening. Secret Service strode in a few steps ahead of him, per usual. And there he was. Instinctively I gave him my usual greeting: "Good morning, Mr. President. It's so nice to see you back in the office."

The page had been turned and the next chapter had begun.

Part Three

19

The Journey into Sunset

Since I was a little girl I had longed for more. I always wanted what was bigger and better, more important, faster-paced, and more challenging. With the president's diagnosis, the world that up until then had continually expanded for me suddenly began to contract. As a result, I needed to become bigger, stronger, more patient and resilient, finding a way to become a larger part of the life of the man who had previously expanded my world.

I was still very young, only twenty-seven, with most of my professional life ahead of me, and was faced with a monumental choice: Would I step away from this role and continue pursuing a world that was "bigger, better, and more"? Or would I stay? My job had the same title, but it was changing. It was contracting while simultaneously forcing me to stretch in untold and uncomfortable ways and to grow up—quickly.

In some ways it would have been easier to walk away. The office was beginning to downsize anyway, and other people were moving on. I considered doing the same—but only briefly. My job had become this man, not my desk or my duties. As Alzheimer's took more of him away from me and from all who loved him, I began to recognize that my attachment to him had deeper roots than I first thought when I was hired. I committed to serve him and would do so as long as he would need me.

Ronald Reagan was someone I somehow felt close to long before I met him. There was something familiar about him, and I couldn't understand why until I got to know him. When I did, the reasons for this feeling of connection were obvious—the president was a lot like my dad.

They shared the same small-town values, the by-product of their Midwestern childhoods. Both grew up poor yet were emotionally wealthy. They each had mothers with unshakable faith who kept their sons on the right path of life in spite of their fathers being alcoholics. Considering their tough early lives, you might have expected them to be bitter or hardened, suspicious of the future. Instead, my father and Ronald Reagan were eternal optimists, big dreamers, enthusiastic and tireless workers, and they were loved and respected by people everywhere they went.

For the Reagans and the Giboneys to survive, the children had to learn how to do things for themselves. As a result, both men liked to stay active tinkering and fixing things. Just like the president wanted to get up to the ranch and dig some fence posts or clear some brush, my father, Terry Giboney, went straight to the garage after he got home from work each day, always staying busy with one project or another. They wanted to make things better. Since both were professionals who wore suits and ties to their desk jobs, working with their hands was an escape into the tactile and the practical. They could see progress and complete tasks, which was satisfying to them. I must have sensed these similarities when I was just a kid admiring Ronald Reagan from a distance. Among the many things I loved about him was that he made me feel comfortable and safe, just like my dad.

My father's early years were spent in Belle, Missouri, a wide spot in the road thirty-five miles southeast of Missouri's capital, Jefferson City, which is where my father was born. When he was four years old his father headed off alone to California in search of work and a better life for his family. Several months later his mother took her five small children and followed him west by hopping aboard a troop train. Each of the children was only allowed to take what they could carry. Little Terry Boy (which his mother called him throughout his life, even when he grew to be six feet tall and she was barely five feet tall) brought with him a small knapsack of clothes and a teddy bear he clung to throughout that long journey.

The life they found when they got to Monrovia, California, was still difficult. The family expanded to eight children, five boys and three girls, with my father landing in the middle, the fourth of the eight. My father described going to church without shoes and the lean lunches he and his siblings took to school, grateful some days to have any lunch at all.

His native intelligence, charisma, street smarts, and lots of persistence not only earned his acceptance into George Pepperdine College but also got him elected as student body president. Before coming to Pepperdine, he served in the National Guard while earning his AA degree in engineering. He later graduated Pepperdine with a BA in religion while also earning his teaching credentials. He worked for a few years as a draftsman and a youth minister, then went back to school to get his master's degree in school administration, and later his doctorate degree in education. He worked first as a teacher and rose quickly to serve as a principal, eventually being promoted to a district administrator. By the time I was in high school, he had become superintendent of schools. With every step of his improbable rise to the top of his field, just like Ronald Reagan, he thanked God and this great country for the opportunities to work hard doing something he loved, which was leaving a positive and lasting impact on those around him and being a good steward of all he had been given.

Despite these similarities, there was one big difference: the way they looked. I was very conscious of style even as a young girl, but my father was decidedly not interested. He was six feet tall—lean, with big feet and long fingers. Unlike the president's striking profile and lush head of hair, my dad wore glasses and had a bit of a comb-over. Nonetheless, I thought he was the most handsome man in the world. He drove an older model car because he saw no reason to get rid of something that was running just fine. Besides, he enjoyed working on cars, so if it broke down, it gave him a project to work on. He used things until they wore out, a value system he extended even into his wardrobe. He wore clothes until they literally fell apart.

I'll never forget my teenage humiliation the day I accompanied him to the hardware store in his normal after-work attire of frayed Bermuda shorts, black dress socks, white tennis shoes, and a well-worn V-neck undershirt. He dropped something in the middle of the store, and when he bent over to pick it up, he completely split open the back of his shorts. I wanted to run to another aisle and hide or just disappear, but he offered up a quick solution, saying, "I needed some duct tape anyway." He had a big smile on his face, thoroughly amused with himself. Believe it or not, I still had to convince him when we got home to throw those shorts away!

I loved being with him so much that I would tag along with him anytime I could, even at the risk of embarrassment. There was something that drew me to him and drew others to him as well. Everywhere we went, people who knew him were delighted to see him, and he made new friends easily and quickly. The people who worked for him adored him, regardless of whether they were high or low in the hierarchy of the school district. He treated everyone with equal respect and in turn was widely respected.

People loved my dad's corny sense of humor, another quality he shared with the president. They both liked to tell jokes that often made their audiences simultaneously laugh and groan. Neither of them was afraid to use self-deprecating humor, which put everyone around them at ease. While I don't share in that same sense of humor, I certainly got my optimism and drive from my father, and I grew up believing that anything was possible and that hard work, persistence, and dedication were essential components to success. My dad was my staunchest ally and my greatest supporter. He taught me things most dads don't teach their girls—how to ride a motorcycle, tow a trailer, change a tire and the oil in my car, shoot a gun, swing a hammer, run a table saw, use a soldering gun, paint a house, strip wallpaper, mow the yard, and drive like I was headed to NASCAR, even testing me with a backward slalom course, orange cones and all! I was always "Daddy's girl" and lived to make him proud.

When I was twenty-six and had been working for Ronald Reagan for five years, my father was diagnosed with colon cancer. Our family went into shock. He was a vigorous fifty-four years old then, and all of us, especially him, believed he would beat this. And he did, for a while. Yet shortly after the president announced he had Alzheimer's, my father's cancer returned and spread rapidly. He was given three to six months to live. His illness advanced much faster than the president's, and unfortunately gave me experience in finding a way to be dignified and respectful in saying goodbye. In many ways, it was through my father's illness that I learned how to respond to the president as his disease progressed.

My father declined quickly, appearing to age several decades in just a few months. It was hard to start treating my father as an elderly treasure instead of a young and vital man. He had taught me so much but very quickly was unable to do many things for himself, though he would still try.

Before his relapse, he had retired from the school district and moved to Malibu to serve on the board of regents and work in the development office at Pepperdine. He loved his professional role there, but his favorite title was that of grandpa. His grandchildren brought the kid out of the executive. He saw leftover boxes and packing material as excellent opportunities to play with my kids, creating tunnels from boxes for them to explore and creating a "California snowstorm" out of packing peanuts. Even when he became very ill, he lovingly took a large board and affixed model train tracks on it for his boyhood vintage toy trains. He wanted to ensure that the kids had a gift from Grandpa on Christmas Day, even if he didn't live until Christmas. It was a beautiful gift that the kids enjoyed for years.

When his cancer returned a second time, it became more and more difficult for him to do all the things he loved. It was frustrating for this previously active man to be idle and rely on others to help him do basic tasks. Some days he would have bursts of energy and would write or do other things that had been on his mind. Other days he was listless and slept a lot. Though the calendar said he was still young, his body was tired and failing. Helping care for him showed me that when you love someone dearly there is no limit to what you will do for them. You will go to any lengths for their comfort and peace, in spite of your own inexperience or fear. Through my father's example I saw how it was possible to face death with unshakeable faith and unwavering confidence in God's love, even amid pain and suffering. And I experienced how a life can end in a beautiful way when you have lived with goodness, have left a meaningful legacy, and are surrounded by love. And I realized that life can finish the same way it begins: strong and optimistic and faithful, regardless of how young or old you are.

We had him with us for less than six months after the cancer came back. We said our final goodbyes to him on December 6, 1996. Taylor was three and Courtney was just six months old. Though I only had him as my father for twenty-nine years, I was grateful that I had been his daughter, albeit too briefly. I learned the hard way that life goes on and that the pain of those first days without him would eventually develop into appreciation for his life, rather than a perpetual mourning of his death. Those last six months with my father were a daily exercise in letting go and letting him go, accepting that I would soon be facing the rest of my life without my first hero. It was only after the thickest part of my grief started to diminish that I recognized how what I went through in losing my dad would help me navigate a similar future very soon with my other hero, the president.

Much of the nation and the world started saying goodbye to Ronald Reagan in their hearts and minds once he announced his illness. Yet I was still saying hello to him every morning. They assumed it meant his death was imminent, and they prepared their hearts to let him go. Yet that was far too premature for reality. Of course we didn't know it at the time, but the president would continue to come into his office for another five years following his announcement, and he would live almost ten years after he wrote his letter to the American people. As most people were letting him go and writing long, depressing goodbye letters, he was very much still alive and living a life of meaning and purpose. I continued to greet him in the mornings, welcoming him to the office every day, five days a week, for another half decade.

During that time, the pendulum of Alzheimer's continued to swing. Anyone familiar with the effects of this dreadful disease knows at first the days are mostly good, with a moment or two here and there of confusion, a sense of loss, or unfamiliarity—but that passes. As time goes on, there slowly become fewer good days and fewer good times during those days, replaced by more difficult moments, challenging hours, and days that are completely "off." In moments of self-doubt, I felt ill-prepared to deal with the realities of working closely with a person with Alzheimer's, and yet at the same time I felt prepared to work with him, a man I knew well, cared for deeply, and with whom I had a well-established routine that worked.

I also knew, from the passing of my father, that no one ever feels equipped to lose someone they are fond of, whether it's slowly or quickly. No one ever feels confident in meeting the changing needs of someone in the process of decline, so I guess that made me as qualified as anyone else to fulfill the duties of the next five years.

Far beyond just me, the president had incredible support from his entire office staff. A little extra time was built into his schedule in the mornings in case it took him longer to get out the door that day. The afternoons were also scheduled more lightly approaching his typical departure time so if there was the need to leave early it wouldn't create any complications. Yet we wanted him to still have a reason to come to the office, to feel needed and important and valued professionally— which he was. We wanted the schedule we sent home with him each evening to have appointments and visitors on it that gave him something to look forward to, so he would feel the need to get up and come to the office, keeping his routine and staying mentally active. And we welcomed him joyfully and with open arms every day he was there.

I never thought of myself as a caregiver to the president—that was

Mrs. Reagan's role, and one that she did amazingly well. He also had household staff who assisted and supported him. We all worked together to ensure the president's comfort and to coordinate everything as seamlessly as possible. Yet in a much smaller way, I'm sure I shared many of the feelings and emotions that caregivers everywhere feel daily. *Am I doing this right? Am I being loving enough? And patient enough? Am I giving him the freedom he needs, along with the support he needs? Am I doing too much for him, and in doing so, am I insulting him? Am I not doing enough for him so that he's feeling inadequate or frustrated? Do I have what it takes to not only get through this myself but be a champion for him as well? What will he ask of me? What will he not ask of me that I need to do for him anyway? Do I have the physical stamina and the emotional fortitude to withstand the heartbreak I will endure a little bit more every single day?*

Whether or not you have the title of caregiver, if you care about someone and are giving of yourself on their behalf, then you have likely shared these emotions and these doubts. It's a constant reckoning with yourself, being stretched beyond what you thought possible. In many ways you need to double your capacity to do and to love, providing enough of both for both of you. Can you find a way to forgive yourself for not being enough or not living up to what you think you need to be? Can you give yourself the grace to be enough just as you are, flawed but willing, available, and present, regardless of qualifications or lack thereof? Showing up is noble, courageous, and fearless in and of itself. In the midst of it all it's hard to see the value you add, but in hindsight you will hopefully realize that you gave all that you had. And that was enough.

I was so young when these responsibilities fell on my shoulders, yet having already endured a similar crisis and loss, I had learned that you can regret the circumstances and endure the sadness, while still embracing the opportunities for growth. You can find within yourself heroic strength and poise and patience and goodness you never knew was there. I learned to seek and find a sense of balance amid a life of imbalance.

20

Surrounded with Love

After the president announced his Alzheimer's diagnosis to the public, he and Mrs. Reagan spent a week at the ranch, taking time for personal reflection far away from the media circus. We staffers were still trying to absorb the information, but as we fielded hundreds of calls each, we were forced to talk about it and answer questions about it from the many people who called wanting to know more. Working to help the public understand what this would mean for the president, we slowly embraced what his diagnosis meant to each of us and to our individual roles in the office. We already knew it, but when we saw the outpouring of concern and affection from people all across the nation and around the world, it reinforced how blessed and honored we were to be part of surrounding this man with love and support at a time when he needed it most.

Anyone familiar with Alzheimer's knows that the illness expresses itself differently in each individual. I had no idea how long the president would continue coming to the office, nor could I anticipate how engaged he would be on any particular day. I did know, though, that there was no cure. I also knew that, following his example, I was resolved to soldier on. If he could do it, I most certainly could, too. In every crisis, in every dark place, there is a danger of being entirely overcome by the darkness. Yet there is always some light and hope, too. I vowed to look for those glimmers, regardless of how hard they might be to find in the future. He deserved nothing less.

When the president returned from the ranch he smiled and waved at me as he walked into his office, as he always did. He looked refreshed and rested. I'm sure that I did not look the same! It had been quite a week, to say the least, and though he had seen the newspaper and television coverage, overall he had been insulated from the response that had drowned our office the week prior. We were still reeling. The surface of my desk was clean, but the piles underneath it were tall. I was still trying to stay afloat. Nonetheless I was excited to see him and was delighted that he appeared to be his usual cheerful self.

Once he entered his office, though, I felt my heart breaking. This was going to be harder than I thought. Although his positive demeanor would make our new situation more pleasant, it only further showed his tremendous resolve and strength, despite the deep pain and fear that he, too, had to be experiencing.

We staffers were determined, as a team and individually, not to hang our heads in sorrow. We wanted to ensure that the president's office remained a comforting and welcoming place for him to proceed with business as usual as long as that was possible. It was clear that was exactly what he intended to do. That would require us to remain professional as always but also to become more personally connected to the president, to watch for and be aware of the nuances of his behavior, not just his actions and words, and to take greater initiative when we sensed he needed more from us.

When he arrived at the office each morning, I usually would let him settle in for a few minutes before I interrupted him. On this day, however, I didn't want another moment to pass before acknowledging how much things had changed since I last saw him and also reassure him that nothing would change with us in the office.

He was seated at his desk and looked up, surprised to see me standing next to him.

"Mr. President, I am so very sorry to hear about your diagnosis and want you to know how much I admire you for sharing something very private with the world. There are so many people who will be helped and encouraged by what you have done, and I want to thank you for that. Also, I hope you know that I am here for you, as I always have been. I care very much and will keep you and Mrs. Reagan in my prayers. I love working for you. That will never change." I managed a smile of encouragement.

His blue eyes didn't quite sparkle as usual, and understandably so.

"I hope you know how much I appreciate that. And you," he said.

Before I turned to walk away I hesitated, doubting if I should proceed.

"Mr. President, do you mind if I give you a hug?"

He smiled broadly and got up from his chair.

"That would be just fine," he said as he received my hug.

All these years I had worked for the president, I had never given him a real hug before. Our relationship was warm and close, but also appropriately formal. The diagnosis would change that, and I wanted to indicate this to him in a way that did not require words. This hug was my way to comfort him and to demonstrate that I was willing to make myself vulnerable, as he had done, and to show that I would remain at his side in this next phase of his life, fully invested personally, not just professionally obligated. I wanted to ensure he knew that whatever he needed, he could count on me.

With this, a new chapter in our working relationship began. Yet on that day, nothing else in particular would change.

"Thank you, Mr. President," I said. "You have the funnies that need reading and I have work at my desk that needs doing, so let's get this day started."

He smiled and nodded, grabbing the comics from his desk and starting right in.

I sat down at my desk and exhaled deeply. Wow, that had been hard. We did not yet know what his limitations would be or how soon the changes of Alzheimer's would alter his routine. I realized my skills as his assistant needed to expand beyond thoroughness and attention to detail. Now the president would need me to lead with my heart, acting out of care and fondness first. I would need to retrain myself not to worry about doing things "right." Instead, I should make my decisions based on my own estimation of what was most loving. That was all I could do.

I can't fathom how helpless he must have felt, unable to control or defeat the invasion of this unwelcome enemy. I felt weak and ineffective, too, as this intruder was taking control of someone who was so dear to me. Part of me was angry. I wanted him to resist it with every ounce of his being, but instead I sensed he was quietly accepting it. He trusted that God, who had directed and appointed every step of his life this far, was present—even in this. God would orchestrate the rest of his tomorrows according to His perfect plan and will. The president's faith was unwavering, his commitment to God unshaken. It both challenged and confirmed my own faith to observe his.

Before the diagnosis, my life with the president had been black and white, right or wrong, approved or not. Now we were entering a gray space where everything suddenly seemed unknown and uncertain. For a "fixer" and a "do-er," this is much worse than being given even the most monumental task to complete. I prefer to have a list of tangible tasks I can accomplish to make things better. In this case, there wasn't much I could do. I certainly couldn't fix it. But the things I could do, I would do with increased purpose and intention.

He and I had a system and an order to the day that didn't change, unless the day became too taxing for him, in which case it was adjusted. Periodically there were moments when it appeared he felt lost or was unsure about something. Without him saying anything, I could tell by just his quick glance my way, his eyes pleading for reassurance or certainty, that he wanted me to jump in, offer up the answer to his unspoken question, or provide the assurance for his uncertainty. When I did, he would give me a look of relief, his eyes immediately changing from concern to gratitude. If I saw him becoming overwhelmed like that, I made changes discreetly and gently so as not to disturb the other elements of comfort and familiarity. I never wanted him to feel as if he was messing up the system or disappointing me in any way, so I was careful about the adjustments I made and then watched closely to observe that the change indeed was helpful and positive for him.

My goal was to make the days as predictable and manageable for him as possible. Routine became extremely important, as did simplicity. I became acutely aware of how and when I did things, the placement of items in the office, and the time and way in which I asked the president to do his work. Instead of having all of his work files out on my desk as I had always done previously, I would give him one thing at a time. This let him set the pace for his day, without feeling rushed or hurried.

And his eyes always revealed it all. When they were a clear blue and dancing and sparkling, it was wonderful to see. He was fully there, engaged and eager to press through his work. Under my desk I kept a secret stash of things that needed his attention. I was ready to take full advantage of those times when he was at his best. It was wonderful when those times came, as I felt close to him and connected to him again. The real him, the person who was still there, though now sometimes veiled behind this hideous disease.

In the months following the announcement, his diagnosis continued to generate a huge reaction. People all around the world responded to the simple beauty and authenticity of his letter. That plain and heartfelt way he had of communicating with every citizen was clear in the way he revealed his new reality. He had spoken directly to them, authentically from his heart, not through a spokesperson. That resonated with people and was deeply appreciated. Every day when the mail was sorted, my inbox was stacked high with letters for my attention or the president's, probably ten times the normal volume. And the plastic crates of mail that were delivered every day to the correspondence office took twice the amount of staff to deliver. It was almost too much to handle, both the sheer volume as well as the emotion behind these messages. They were personal, tragic, sweet, nostalgic, prayerful, mournful, full of the entire spectrum of feelings and life experiences. Reading them every day took me on my own emotional roller-coaster ride, with highs and lows and laughter and sadness. I continued responding to all of these letters on behalf of the president but believed it would be better if we had a specific response that acknowledged the writer in a more personal way, communicating how much this outpouring of love meant to the president himself. I went to him with my idea.

"Mr. President, I have been showing you a small percentage of the incredibly kind and heartfelt mail you have been receiving recently, and there are crates and crates of mail in the correspondence office which arrive every day from people expressing their admiration and appreciation—you're extremely loved! Everyone who writes in is being sent a nice reply from the office, but I thought it might be nice to send out something more personal to people who write in. Something directly from you they will keep and treasure and appreciate. What do you think?"

"Well, I think that sounds just fine. What do you have in mind?"

"I think a nice notecard in your writing on your stationery would be a lovely and very personal gesture. I'll write up a draft, and you can see what you think. If you write it out once, I will have it duplicated."

"I am happy to do that."

"Terrific. Thank you. I'll be back shortly with a draft."

I sat at my desk happy he had agreed with me about this. I knew him well, this Great Communicator. I had written letters in his voice and worked on his remarks for so many years that I knew his voice and tone better than I knew my own. It had to be short and succinct, as it had to fit on one small notecard. I also wanted those few words to be heartfelt and mirror the tone of his letter to the nation.

Later that day I walked back into his office and read him the draft. He liked it and approved it on the spot. He seemed eager to get these printed so those who were writing in to him could start receiving them right away. Without hesitation he pulled out one of his special signing pens and started writing on his cream-colored, gold embossed cards, using my draft of the text as his guide. Just below his name in block letters at the top, he began. I had brought in an extra notecard in case he needed it, but as I watched him carefully, he handwrote it from start to finish flawlessly. I looked at each letter and each word, lovingly written, and I intuitively knew how much it would mean to its future recipients. I also wondered how many more opportunities I would have to write for him, to have him add his name to my words. A well-established routine and relationship now felt fleeting.

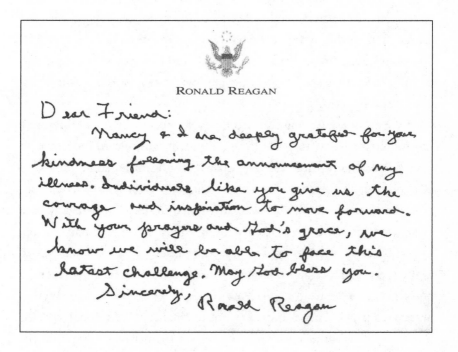

RONALD REAGAN

Dear Friend:

Nancy & I are deeply grateful for your kindness following the announcement of my illness. Individuals like you give us the courage and inspiration to move forward. With your prayers and God's grace, we know we will be able to face this latest challenge. May God bless you.

Sincerely, Ronald Reagan

I prepared a FedEx envelope to overnight it to the engraver in Maryland who was the only one allowed to print the presidential seal. His was not the exact seal used by the sitting president, but was a variation of it, one that removed the outer ring of words that said "President of the United States of America" and featured just the stars and eagle inside the seal. It made a striking impression when anything was received on this elegant paper that bore his name, especially when it was in his own handwriting. Yes, I was holding a very special card that would connect and resonate with people the world over. At that point, though, I had no idea how much so.

A few days later we received several large boxes back from the engraver and began to send the cards out—not just to anyone and everyone who sent in a generic signed "thinking of you" card, but to those who had written a particularly beautiful and heartfelt letter articulating what President Reagan meant to them, sharing a story of their own family's experience with Alzheimer's, or thanking the president for something in particular that had changed their life, or to anyone who had a personal connection to the president or had worked in the White House. The mail was abundant and this was a quick and easy yet very special and personal way to respond. And people loved these cards—really loved them. Too much!

We soon began getting calls from people specifically requesting these cards. They were writing not to the president now, but to inquire as to how to get one of these cards. Oops! In trying to do something very nice on behalf of the president, we had actually created additional work for ourselves, not at all what we had wanted to do. Unfortunately, as a result, not long after we started sending the cards out, we had to stop. It had become a frenzy, a collector's item rather than a personal way to show the president's appreciation. Instead, people would now receive a more generic note from me or from the correspondence office, one that was made particularly bland so as not to create any additional interest. I felt awful that others were missing out on the personal note from the president, but unfortunately, a few people wound up ruining something special for the rest.

We all took our cues from the president. As I reflect back and think about the first day he walked into the office after his announcement, if he had come in with an attitude of "it's over" or "I might as well say my goodbyes now," my response and my actions would have been very different toward him. But as it was, would I have done anything differently had I known we would still have our routine and work together for five more years? No, not really. His positive attitude gave me no reason to say goodbye to him yet, although the reality of his diagnosis did give me every reason to treasure and savor each day. And I did. I look back with no regret on our working relationship and how it evolved and developed and changed in those next five years. Although the changes were not always noticeable from one day to the next, it did change dramatically from 1994 to 1999. It had to.

President Reagan kept on his desk a sign that had four simple words on it: "It CAN Be Done." He kept it as a reminder that even when things seemed impossible there was always a way to get things done. In the later years of his life, I don't know if it carried the same meaning for him, but for me it became a symbol of strength, a sign I took personally and took strength from every time I walked into his office. Regardless of the circumstances, the day, the challenge, or even the crisis of the moment, his words of comfort, his words of courage, reminded me that in spite of my own shortcomings and doubts that indeed it *can* be done. And it would be done. Anything for you, Mr. President.

21

One Last Project

While the president was at the ranch the week after announcing his diagnosis, the staff assembled to reassess the president's funeral plans. From the time they take office, presidents (and First Ladies, too) have funeral plans on file that are updated regularly until they pass away. The logistics and security for a state funeral are staggering and cannot possibly be generated instantly upon the person's death. Such measures need to be well planned and agreed upon long before they are ever implemented. The occasion of the president's diagnosis made all of us aware that we should make sure his plan—and our plans—were up to date.

We walked in somberly, each of us carrying our own binder of the funeral plans. Normally we held our informal meetings in the chief of staff's office, but since this one involved the entire staff we met in the conference room, spreading out across the long, broad table of dark polished wood. The powerful response from the nation and the world to the announcement of the president's illness reminded us of this great responsibility and of the urgency to ensure we were ready when the time came. Surrounded by the president's artifacts and Western sculptures and facing the view he loved, I felt the warmth of his presence. Everyone was dealing with their own emotions individually, but this was not a therapy session; it was time to confirm the plans that were already in place and advance them a bit further than before.

As we opened our binders, our hearts were heavier than last time we reviewed them, knowing now that we might need these plans sometime soon. The chief of staff ran through the timeline, recapped the high-lights, and pointed out things that had been adjusted or changed since our last meeting. Additional assignments were handed out to each member of the staff. One of my tasks was to finalize the design of the president's funeral program. I had an earlier draft of the program already on file, but I wanted to work with the president to make sure it still reflected his wishes.

This was a conversation I dreaded having with the president so soon after his diagnosis was made public. I worried it might seem as if I was anticipating his passing instead of appreciating his presence. I realized I would have to figure out exactly when and how to bring up this sensitive subject with him. I envisioned a very awkward conversation in my near future: "Mr. President, I wanted to discuss your funeral program with you…" I would need to give thought to a better opening line before then, but in the meantime I could work on a revised draft to propose to him.

I spent several weeks on the initial draft of the program the year prior, wanting to ensure it was a powerful reflection of his magnificent life. It wound up being more like a lavish magazine retrospective, slick and glossy and colorful. I included pictures of him as a small child back in Dixon, glamorous headshots from his Hollywood days, patriotic images of him as president of the United States, and accompanying text in a story line format that tied the images together. While it was beautiful, I now considered it with the fresh perspective that time offers. After the recent outpouring of affection from the public, and considering all the ways we were simplifying life around the president, this glossy display now felt wrong for the occasion. The big national magazines were sure to put out special issues once President Reagan died. They were better equipped and had more experienced staff to make a memorable keepsake. As I looked again through the photos, I also felt that the formal, polished presentation did not accurately reflect his approachable warmth, nor did it capture the elegant simplicity of this humble man.

Much of the order of a president's funeral service is determined by

protocol, so there were only a few ways in which the president's personality would come through on the program, things like the type of paper
it was printed on, the typeface, and the color of the ink. He would select
which quotes he wanted on the inside pages, a big choice, as they would
have to sum up some aspect of his character and his legacy in just a few
words. He also would choose the music to be played and the Scriptures
to be read. I decided we did not have to rush these things. I would wait
until I thought he was having a good day and in the mood to review his
previous decisions.

We had worked together previously on the original program, but mainly
he trusted me to do what I thought was best. Looking back now, I realized he might have been uncomfortable with something that could have
seemed to him to be too self-promoting. I was determined with this draft
to make a program that was a clearer expression of his values, believing
that less would be more in this case. I instinctively knew he would agree.

I recognized that the right moment to bring this up with him would
take some intuition. He had moments when he seemed distant and
distracted, lost in faded thoughts that were faraway. I had come to grips
with the realization that this was the last chapter of his life. When I
originally consulted with him on this program, he was fully of sound
mind and body, and I needed to conclude these discussions as well
while he still was. Though the senior staff and Mrs. Reagan would all
weigh in, it was important to me that I receive *his* approval. Having his
blessing on the final version only seemed fitting, no matter how long it
took or how uncomfortable bringing it up made me feel.

Prior to the diagnosis, I would set the signature file on my desk, and
he would pick it up at some point during the day and plow through the
stack of photos and letters quickly, bringing it back to me at my desk
with great pride as if he was presenting me with a special gift, which he
was. As the disease progressed, I did more to set the pace and the order
of the day, pulling back and slowing things down as needed to make
sure he never felt rushed or pressured. I wanted him to feel useful and
needed. It was easy to see when he was engaged and eager.

I could identify how he was feeling and his state of mind by working with him on something fairly straightforward first, seeing how he responded and how interested he seemed in discussing the business at hand. I would start by asking him to sign a few things that only required an autograph, not an extensive inscription. Then if that went well, I would move through the increasingly demanding and difficult work I had for him. I kept everything tucked away in a folder so that if he wasn't engaged or eager, I would thank him for signing one or two things and return to my desk, waiting for another time to approach him. On the days when he was focused and feeling good, I would keep giving him things to sign and other work to attend to until it was clear he had reached his limit.

A few weeks later the right moment arrived for our conversation. I had my mental list of the items on which I wanted his agreement and approval. He had signed several items in a row and his handwriting was strong and clear. He was having a good day and was fully engaged, so I asked, "Mr. President do you have time to discuss something else with me?"

"Of course," he said.

I hurried to my desk, trading the signature folder for the funeral program folder that contained the new proposed layouts and paper samples. I walked around his desk so that I was standing behind him while he sat in his chair.

"The last time we talked about this program you and I agreed we should make it simpler," I said. "I want to get your opinion on the scaled-back version I have put together."

I laid out the two side by side for comparison.

"Are you okay with moving away from the red, white, and blue color scheme?" I asked first. "I know those colors are fitting, but do you think they seem a bit too celebratory for such an occasion?"

"I prefer this one," he said, pointing to the sample of the new program I had put together.

Instead of an extensive glossy layout, I wanted a presentation that reflected more than just the time he served as president. It was only eight years of his life, albeit monumental ones. Yet when many people think about Ronald Reagan, they also picture him in his cowboy hat that he wore on his iconic campaign poster "Reagan Country." They recall his love for the ranch and horses and working on the land, and especially his love of the West. I wanted something warmer to embody that aspect of him as well.

Far from formal, slick, and glossy, the new sample was earthy—with a warm ecru paper that was soft to the touch and soothing to the eyes, with a hint of yellow like you see in California's dry summer grass when it's lit by the sun. The ink I proposed was not a traditional jet black, but rather a rich, deep brown that was bold and warm, reminiscent of the color of his favorite brown suit. I added small star embellishments across the bottom of the pages, also in brown, that seemed both formal and familiar. While I loved this combination, the president had the ultimate say.

I stood behind him watching closely. The president picked up the sample, rubbing the paper between his fingers and gazing intently at the text. As he studied the sample, I studied him. He was taking his time, as if he was picturing when it would be printed, pondering the reality and the gravity of that day in the future. After a lengthy silence, he finally replied, "I like this. I really like this."

We moved on to talk about other elements of the program. He had previously selected Psalm 23, a very common Scripture verse to be included in memorial services. I could only imagine the new meaning verse 4 had taken on for him recently: "Even though I walk through the valley of the shadow of death, I fear no evil, for You are with me; Your rod and Your staff, they comfort me." He was definitely in the midst of his own very real "valley of the shadow of death." He confirmed he still wanted that verse included. I'm sure that God's promise to provide comfort and to remove the fear of evil were of great solace to him then.

As we moved down the proposed order of service and talked about the music, it was no surprise to me his first choice was still "The Battle

Hymn of the Republic," which had always been one of his favorites. I remembered back to a day in 1994 when a beautiful, bubbly, red-headed young woman performed a chill-inducing rendition of this song when we arranged for her to sing at one of the president's birthday parties. He loved it and was so moved by her performance that he started tapping his toes in time to the music and singing along to every verse.

President Reagan's voice was easily distinguishable, even amid a chorus of voices in the room, because he was not merely mouthing well-known lyrics from a song; he knew how to express a depth of feeling with his voice. The emotion that moved him to sing was one of genuine pride and heartfelt love for our country.

He also confirmed "America the Beautiful," which I knew was particularly special to him. I remember watching him at that same birthday party be so deeply moved by the singing of it that as the second verse began—"O beautiful for pilgrim feet..."—without a glance around or giving it a second thought, he instinctively rose to his feet, put his hand over his heart, and started singing along, louder now. We all rose to join him in this beautiful heartfelt expression.

When the song went into the fourth and final verse, I looked over at the president, and his eyes were misting over with tears. Thinking back on that day, I knew indeed that yes, this song would be a definitive choice for the program. He also confirmed "My Country 'Tis of Thee" along with "Amazing Grace," two more of his longtime personal favorites, which now also symbolized his faith that "grace will lead me home."

The final part of our collaboration was choosing the final quote for inside the front cover. I selected and printed out several options to recommend to him. Each one would have been an appropriate statement, reflective of his beliefs and worthy of his life's legacy. Many in the office had favorite quotes of his they were pushing for, and the president, always eager to please, seemed to be content with whichever quote others would convince him was the best one.

I didn't want him just to be content, though. I wanted him to be in control and to choose one that expressed how he desired to be remembered.

Once again, I studied him as he studied the list. Ultimately he pointed decisively to one particular quote, the one I liked and had hoped he would select. I could picture the mourners on that sad day in the future being inspired by it, as I was now and as the audience at the 1992 Republican National Convention in Houston had been years ago when he first uttered these words:

> Whatever else history may say about me when I'm gone, I hope it will record that I appealed to your best hopes, not your worst fears; to your confidence rather than your doubts. My dream is that you will travel the road ahead with liberty's lamp guiding your steps and opportunity's arm steadying your way.

To me, in its beautiful simplicity, it cut to the heart of his legacy and was the essence of this great man.

"Thank you, Mr. President," I said. "I appreciate your graciousness in making a task which could have been very uncomfortable something I am happy we did together."

"Thank you for working so hard to get this right. I appreciate it," he said. "I really like it now. It's just the way I want it."

"That was the goal, Mr. President. I'm glad we accomplished it."

I returned to my desk and made the necessary changes to the document. As I put the folder away, I dreaded the day the printer would be called to place this order. Yet I believed when the day came that I could approach it with confidence and hope, not fear and doubt, knowing this truly was *his* program.

22

A Faithful Life

I'm not a crier, but I remember back to one night a few months before my father died, I was walking through the grocery store filling my cart with essentials. The kids were in bed at home, sound asleep, as was Greg. It was quiet and my thoughts were elsewhere, completely preoccupied with my father's rapidly declining health. When I turned into the freezer section and saw shelf after shelf of ice cream, I immediately burst into tears.

The sight of the ice cream reminded me of just one more cruel insult that cancer was inflicting on my dad before it would ultimately steal him from me. It was mid-1996 and he recently had started having problems with his blood sugar, another by-product of the illness's advancement. As a result he was no longer able to eat ice cream, a treat he had enjoyed nearly every night of his life. My father was tall and thin. He maintained an active lifestyle and never gained a pound. A bowl of ice cream was his one indulgence in life—the perfect reward for him at the end of a long, hard day. To take away his one and only remaining pleasure in a life that was terminal anyway seemed cruel and unnecessary and just wrong.

The notoriety that followed the announcement of President Reagan's Alzheimer's diagnosis stirred similar feelings of outrage and deep sadness in me. The place he most wanted and needed to be during this challenging time—his church—was being taken away from him. When President Reagan returned to California from Washington, he was happy to be able to attend church again and could be found most

Sunday mornings with Mrs. Reagan sitting in a pew at Bel Air Presbyterian Church, close to his home. It had been difficult for him to attend church regularly as president, so being back in church as a private citizen was a great joy for him. He enjoyed going every week, feeling connected once again not only to God but to a church community as well.

But once he told the world of his illness, people showed up at church just to get a glimpse or a photo of him. Even worse, the paparazzi would pretend to attend the services, attempting to get a poor picture of the president inside the church. Or they'd try to catch him on camera, coming or going from the service, hoping to get a statement. The published stories and photos only increased the interest in this despicable behavior. Sundays were taking on a circus atmosphere, and it wasn't fair to the church or the other members, so the president made the difficult decision, once again, that he could no longer attend. Mrs. Reagan reluctantly agreed. This broke my heart.

There are times in life during which we are called upon to pour ourselves completely out in service to others. We give to the point that we feel there is nothing left. Yet such periods are usually short and we tell ourselves that if we can just endure and just keep going, eventually we will catch a break and catch our breath. And sometimes, in the midst of that intense focus on others, just when you need it most, unexpected support surprises you.

While I was working for the president, both of my grandmothers passed away, along with my remaining grandfather and my father. Grief stretched my emotions and shattered my heart in many ways. Thankfully, having young children ensured that life went on and that every day was filled with love and laughter on the outside even when my heart was heavy on the inside. In these difficult times, I still managed to find joy. I especially appreciated the way the president became a surrogate father figure to me and a grandfatherly figure to my kids. Yet I was also coming to grips with the fact that I was losing him as well.

Ronald Reagan talked about his faith openly and unashamedly, even as president. In fact, it was President Reagan who designated the first Thursday in May as the National Day of Prayer and also declared 1983 to be the Year of the Bible. Yet whether or not you were a person of faith, the president would never have imposed his faith or beliefs upon you. He believed that in America the right to worship as you choose— or to choose not to worship—was sovereign. He was tolerant and supportive of others' faith while remaining completely committed to his own true north—Almighty God. His faith provided order, meaning, and stability to everything he did.

Over the years he stayed connected to others in the community of faith, including friends like Billy Graham, who liked to drop by the office to visit with the president now and then. Seeing these two men together seated in the president's office was endearing and inspiring. Both were advanced in years yet young at heart. They had seen so much of life with undying faith in God's plan and in His providence for their lives. After Reverend Graham's visits the president always seemed peaceful, content, and full of the blessing that fellowship with another Christian brings. These visits, along with his church attendance, up until then, had sustained the president's spiritual needs. I wasn't sure what to do, but I knew there had to be a way to continue to support him in this regard and nurture and encourage his faith in God to the very end.

As a Christian myself, I knew how important it was to find a way to meet the president's spiritual needs on a regular basis. We arranged for the president's pastor at Bel Air Presbyterian Church, Reverend Michael Wenning, to come in to the office to pray and read the Bible with the president. This tall, white-haired, South African–born man had developed a close relationship with both President and Mrs. Reagan and was pleased and honored to be asked to make these personal visits. He spoke in a thick, deep-toned accent and carried himself with an air of distinction, coupled with the warmth and easy smile of a dear friend. He was someone you desired to know and were blessed to be known by. He interacted in a natural, effortless way with the president, treating him with the respect that was due him, coupled with the transparency of someone who could be vulnerable and stand before God as a sinner in need of a Savior, just like all of us.

It was beautiful to observe these two faithful men of God together in the president's office. Reverend Wenning would bring in the weekly program from the church, read the Scriptures that were shared the previous Sunday, and give the president a little vignette of the sermon. He would finish their visit bowed in prayer, reaching out to place a hand on the president and praying a blessing over him. After a benediction, he said goodbye to the president, leaving him still seated in his favorite corner chair, looking through the Sunday bulletin as if he was in a church pew. The president would often remain there for several minutes in silent reflection and prayer. In those moments he seemed most at peace, serene and satisfied. He had been filled with God's love and provision and lingered there, savoring that feeling.

I would escort Reverend Wenning to the elevators. He always asked how I was doing with the president's illness. He encouraged me to be strong, convinced that serving the president at this time in his life was part of my calling and part of God's higher purpose. He believed it was no accident I had been placed right outside the president's office, especially now. He also would ask about what was happening in my own life personally, which he knew was stretching me nearly to my breaking point. Though we only had a few minutes together, in those brief moments he would grab my hands and bow his head and pray for me and with me—right there in the office. It was in those very moments that, in actuality, God was showing He hadn't forgotten about me in my own time of need, but was standing alongside me, offering the very comfort I craved. That comfort was in the form of this man whom I had brought in to the office for an entirely different reason. I was humbled by the notion that God would remember me, care for me, and send a comforter to me at the time I most desperately needed it.

Faith is very personal and at the core of an individual. It is not something we directly inherit like a birthright, but it is certainly influenced by those around us. Ronald Reagan "inherited" his faith from his mother, Nelle Reagan, a faithful woman of God. Nelle taught her son the value of prayer and how to have big dreams and believe they could come true. A small woman with auburn hair, she had a deep faith and belief in God's sovereign will. She regularly said, "God has a plan for everyone, and seemingly random twists of fate are all part of His plan... and in the end, everything will work out for the best." Ronald Reagan grew up hearing this, believing this, and embracing this, not only from a place of optimism but from a place of deep personal faith.

He faithfully attended Sunday services in Dixon, Illinois, with his mother, and when he was eleven, the future president decided to become a member of her church, the First Christian Church of Dixon. He was baptized into Christ there on June 21, 1922. He was passionate about his faith and involved himself in church activities with his mother. She was always thinking of those in need and found ways to help them, setting a powerful example of charity and service for her sons. She had a natural and intuitive intelligence that went far beyond her limited formal schooling and had a drive within her to help her sons make something of themselves. Nelle's belief in the good in everyone and her eternal optimism helped Ronald Reagan look beyond the confines of his small town and dream the seemingly impossible. Even when setbacks would come, Nelle's encouragement helped Ronald Reagan see the opportunities that were still there.

Nelle Reagan volunteered her time in the care and service of others her entire life. Even after she moved to California to join her son, she worked in the jails with prisoners and volunteered regularly at a tuberculosis sanitarium. Later in her life, Nelle suffered from the effects of dementia or senility. Although it wasn't called it back then, she likely was a victim of what we now know as Alzheimer's disease and likely also gave her son the genetic propensity toward it.

Although Alzheimer's is typically a genetic condition, trauma to the brain can spur its progression, which is what many speculate happened to Ronald Reagan, possibly accelerated by his fall off a horse in Mexico a few years earlier. That injury on July 4, 1989, was followed by surgery to remove fluid on his brain in September of that same year. He appeared to make a full recovery, and medically he did. But perhaps there were hidden consequences at the time that wouldn't be fully revealed until later. There is no way to prove the cause or the timeline of the disease's progression, but this has always made the most sense to me and aligns with what I saw.

I certainly am no doctor and don't know all the science and the research behind the disease and its effects, but I can tell you what I observed. The effects of Alzheimer's seem to me like the peeling back of layers of a person, losing a bit more of themselves each time. But when each new layer is peeled back, a deeper truth is exposed, showing that person's true heart. For the president it was as if his ability to be anyone other than who he was at his true core was gone. Although he had always been consistently the same behind the scenes as he was in the public eye, Alzheimer's stripped away the capacity to put on a more formal manner, to act in a way that was expected or required, and what was left was the true Ronald Reagan—and what a pure heart was revealed. Although he was quieter, he continued to exhibit his gentlemanly manners, waiting for me to pass through doorways first and walk ahead of him, never behind him. He continued to be warm and smiling to people who talked to him, waved at him, or shouted well wishes from afar. He made every effort to stay engaged, communicating with the public and being a gracious host to his guests as long as he could. When the façade was stripped away and any ability to create or sustain a public persona was gone, what was left was genuine and beautifully consistent. True goodness. It was bittersweet and heartbreaking to see.

My talks with Mrs. Reagan became more important and more frequent. In the early years we may have spoken once a week. As the illness progressed, we spoke daily, often multiple times. We wanted greater consistency between home and the office, so we collaborated about what seemed to be working really well in either location and what wasn't. I tried not to call her while the president was at the office, since I didn't want him to hear us discussing him. Besides, I knew that when he was at work it was usually her time to get away from the house to see friends and attend to any pressing business. I would always check her schedule before calling so that she could get away undisturbed. I wanted her to take breaks from his care whenever she could. It was a long and difficult time for her. We spoke freely and openly, but only to a point. She always put on a brave face, even for me, as if she didn't want to further burden me with her concerns, and as if some of it was too personal and too painful to even articulate. I, too, never wanted to add any of my worries and fears onto hers, so I constantly tried to find the perfect balance with her between sharing and oversharing. It was always a bit of a conversational dance between us, sticking to facts and to things that we could control or change, while being sensitive to the emotions that saturated each of those hard-to-face facts. I always knew there was much more that could have been discussed, but wasn't.

I can't imagine how devastatingly difficult it must have been for Mrs. Reagan from day to day as she bore the brunt of the president's care and continued to be the center of his world. I would encourage her on the phone about the heroic job she was doing in caring for the president. I tried to support her with my words and also in my actions toward her husband. Periodically I would drop a little note to her in the canvas White House bag that was headed home, telling her of my appreciation for her and how remarkable I thought she was in faithfully caring for her husband. It was sometimes easier to express what I truly wanted to say to her in writing.

She was always good about acknowledging my notes, sometimes popping a quick little note jotted on her Nancy Reagan Post-it pad back in the bag to me the next day, saying something brief but sincere like "Thank you for the note. It was timely and appreciated." Other times when we would next be on the phone she would acknowledge it, saying, "Thank you for your note, Peggy. You're very thoughtful." She didn't ever need to thank me, but she always did. She was a true lady, even in the midst of great heartache.

I admired the grit and determination it required to be a faithful, supportive, and staunch defender of her husband's legacy and of his privacy to the very end. And she was. It would have been easy to become the center of attention, to make it all about her—her grief, her struggle, her heartache, and her ongoing painful loss. Yet it never had been about her, and it wouldn't be, even now. I noticed behind the scenes the changes and sacrifices she made in order to be there for the president and care for him fully and lovingly. She greatly contracted her social circle and cut back her schedule drastically. Her previously frequent lunches with friends became sporadic and now were always close to home. Her periodic trips to New York, which she always enjoyed, became nearly extinct. The only travel she did was to represent the president, champion his legacy, or speak out in support of the Alzheimer's community. She would have it no other way. There was no place she would have rather been than with him.

In many ways Nancy Reagan rewrote what comes to mind when we think of First Ladies. While they are typically an extension of their husband's legacy, in her case, despite her initial reluctance, in the later years she became his primary voice, a champion for causes that were important to him. Though he was still alive, she had to press forward as his advocate and spokesperson. She took on this new role bravely, going where she was needed most, even though her heart was always with him at home.

The days became increasingly difficult for her as the president's demands for care increased, yet she always kept up a brave and strong face. I admired her for putting on her game face and finding Herculean strength within that petite frame of hers. We all were watching her and followed her lead and her example—me especially. She was teaching me with her actions and words without even realizing that they were guiding me on the path forward. I was following her lead in how to think, what to say, and how to navigate the deep potholes on this rough and rocky road of Alzheimer's.

In every previous crisis, she and the president had faced it together, yet she had to face much of this one alone. It was evident in the deep and lingering sadness I saw in her eyes, despite her brave exterior. This woman who had taken comfort in standing behind her husband and had enjoyed watching him with that gaze of pride now was forced to center stage. She much preferred to be a support to her husband, behind the scenes and in his very public shadow as she had always been. Yet now she knew the best way to support her husband was to step out of his shadow and assume a more visible presence. As his own abilities to do so were fading, she stepped up to be the embodiment of his life and his legacy. I sensed that her determination to honor him far outweighed her personal comfort, and she would see to it that she served our beloved president to the very end with dignity. And she did.

I took strength from her strength and tried to mirror her poise. Yet inside sometimes I was enraged. I was angry at an illness that was affecting this man who had a lifetime of priceless memories that now were slowly but surely being erased from his mind. Angry at the thought of this couple, who had shared so much and loved so much, having their love story end with such tragedy and sadness. Angry that distance and separation would grow between them even as they continued to coexist. Angry that some of the very people who were closest to them and should have bolstered them up during this darkest hour instead betrayed them, often publicly revealing intimate details that should have been implicitly private forever. Angry that some who had walked so much of life's journey with the Reagans for decades prior were now abandoning them because it was too hard for them to see the president or face him in decline. Angry that others made it all about them and lost sight of who the true victim was in the process. It was not them, and I didn't feel sorry for them. I was disappointed in them. And I was angry that the storybook ending that I would have written for his life was taking a plot twist that no one saw foreshadowed and no one wanted to accept.

Yet my outward face and voice remained in line with hers—and his— and I continued to represent them both with poise and professionalism. I focused on those who still loved him and were thinking of him. I was grateful for the letters and calls offering up prayers from people of faith all around the world. They would call with beautiful well wishes, write to him with incredible sentiments, and send in Scriptures and prayers. In doing so, their words ministered to me as well, bringing comfort and peace even though I was just the messenger passing them along to the president. Even though they weren't directed toward me, these messages still soothed me. Yet in spite of the multitude of people beseeching God on behalf of the president, there was no healing. And no respite. And no sparing him from the effects or from the ultimate end.

Ronald Reagan believed the ways of God were not always revealed here on earth but trusted that everything in life was part of a higher purpose and was within God's perfect plan for his life. I would, likewise, have to trust, in faith, that even this was not outside of God's will but squarely in the midst of it, not just for the president's life, but for mine as well.

President Reagan spoke publicly of his faith often, as well as the values and character that faith produces. In a 1993 speech he said:

> Character that takes command in moments of crucial choices has already been determined... It has been determined by a thousand other choices made earlier in seemingly unimportant moments... It has been determined by all the day-to-day decisions made when life seemed easy and crises seemed far away...
>
> Because when life does get tough, and the crisis is undeniably at hand—when we must, in an instant, look inward for strength of character to see us through—we will find nothing inside ourselves that we have not already put there.

For Ronald Reagan, the diagnosis of Alzheimer's was a crucial moment that would test his faith, his fortitude, and his ability to embrace and live out all the values he had spoken of his entire life. The opportunity to invest more into his life, his character, and his future was gone. He would be left to ride out the remainder of his days using what he had already put in there and would rely on God for the rest. And it would prove to be more than enough.

Several times in those later years I would find the president's Bible opened on his back shelf as if it had just been pulled down for a quick glance or reminder of a verse. Many times it was open to the Psalms, a beautiful book of poetry filled with praise and encouragement. Perhaps he was reading Psalm 121:1–2—"I will lift up my eyes to the mountains; From where shall my help come? My help *comes* from the LORD, Who made heaven and earth"—which was a favorite verse of his and reminded him fondly of his ranch. And though my typical reaction in the past would have been to pick up his Bible and put it back on the shelf as I was straightening his office, on those days I would leave it just where it was, just as it was. The open book was a reminder not only to the president but to me as well that God and His word were always available, always there and always sufficient, even in our greatest time of need. Especially then.

23

Farewell to the Fairway

As the president's world got smaller, my job changed from being an assistant who watched him move smoothly through the world to becoming a guardian of a much tighter circle. I saw my role, in part, as smoothing out his day and ensuring that his life was as routine and orderly as possible and that he was surrounded by familiar faces who would greet him with love.

Many longtime friends asked to see him after the letter about his diagnosis was made public, and I was, at first, happy to welcome these people who had been so important to him at different stages of his life, from Hollywood all the way through his presidency. This living memory bank I hoped would fill him with joy and warm reflection. Yet as I escorted them from the lobby to visit with the president, I watched how they girded themselves, as if they were putting on their game faces before they entered his office.

Often when they met with him, I could see the surprise on their faces and their attempts to control their reactions to how much he had changed since they had last seen him. A warm handshake or sometimes even a hug would close off these meetings, but as I walked some of these friends out the door, they felt free to express their feelings to me. Sadly, their feelings were usually about *them*, how difficult it was for them to see him in decline, how hard it was for them to accept, and on and on about them. My thoughts would be screaming internally, "*You?!* What about the president?! This is not about *you*!" Some of them even breached the privacy and dignity we tried so hard to maintain by writing sorrowful, revealing essays about the president's condition and how it had so adversely affected them to see him that way. Again, it was all about them, not about what was best for the president. It was discouraging and disappointing to say the least.

Those who have cared for someone with Alzheimer's know that while those who suffer from the disease may not be able to communicate their feelings as easily as before, they still have a very strong sense of when they feel safe. I hoped that visits like that did not disturb the president as much as they agitated me, but it was difficult to know. Over time we unfortunately had to become much more selective about who was invited in for a visit.

One day in late 1997, a friend of mine, Dan Quiggle, who had worked for the president several years prior, called to ask if I could schedule an appointment for him to see the president and introduce his newborn daughter.

"You know how much the president loves babies, so I hope you will give my request some extra consideration," he said. "I would love to bring my daughter in to meet the president and take a picture of them together. Do you think it would be possible?"

"I'm sure the president would love to meet her, but I'll have to check and get back to you. But I promise to ask."

"And one more thing," he continued before I could hang up. "Don't be mad at me for pushing my luck, but I have three friends who would also love to meet the president. Will you at least consider it?"

"I will, but only if you know these friends very well and can answer one question truthfully for me. I have to know: Do they love the president as much as you do?"

"Yes, they do," he replied confidently.

"Give me some time. I'll call you back."

As I hung up the phone I realized this instinct was now my new criterion for who I would recommend to be approved for a visit. Did this person love the president as much as I did and as much as we in the office did? They needed to come to see him with their hearts open and embrace him just as he was: a great man still, a beautiful soul, and a treasure who needed to be treated with unconditional love and support.

Dan's request was approved, and the big group had a wonderful visit that the president enjoyed as much as they did, maybe even more. He was having a good day, and it was made even better by seeing a beautiful baby and being surrounded by loving friends who adored him. What could possibly make for a better appointment?

Or perhaps loving the president as much as I did was not the only consideration. Love had to drive the decision, but I also was wary of people who, despite their love, might expect him to be different than he was or were unable to adjust from the man in their mind to the man that he had become. Some people found it difficult to face him, because in essence, it forced them to face their own mortality. I understood the pain they felt in seeing the president, as it was difficult for everyone. We all were handling our feelings about this great man in our own way and within our own limitations.

In maintaining the president's routine, we continued to arrange for his weekly golf games at Los Angeles Country Club. More and more, the members of his foursome were the husbands of the women at the office, the women the president affectionately called "my gals." These men had formed a bond based on being married to hard-charging, highly focused women. We always had our husbands at our sides at big events for the president, and frequently, before the event started, we would commandeer them to help us handle some last-minute crisis like relocating the podium or rearranging the seating. As there became fewer and fewer events, our husbands enjoyed staying connected to the president and loved seeing him whenever they were asked to fill out his foursome at Los Angeles Country Club.

Years earlier, Greg had been the last-minute add-on to a group of the president's contemporaries. As the circle of friends aged, they were less and less inclined to golf and more inclined to chat. Greg saw how uncomfortable these foursomes became when the president's longtime friends still wanted to discuss politics or international affairs rather than play golf. For their whole lives they could count on the president to say something they never had thought of before or state an old opinion in a new and fresh way. As his disease advanced, he paid less attention to those aspects of life and the world, and some of his friends were unable, or maybe unwilling, to adjust their conversation to accommodate him, so the president became more and more interested in playing golf with the husbands of "his gals."

Every time Greg came back from golf with the president, I was full of questions for him. In the early days I wanted to hear what jokes the president had told and hear about the way he would banter when it was just the "fellas." Even with all the time I spent with the president, I was always curious about how he interacted outside of the office setting when it was just he and the "fellas" out on the golf course. In the later years I wondered more about how well he was managing to still do things he enjoyed, like golfing. Because I sincerely wanted him to be happy and be well, I appreciated getting another point of view. I am an eternal optimist, which I feared might sometimes cloud my ability to see evidence of decline. Greg played golf with the president four or five times a year. With those long gaps between rounds, he was in a good position to assess changes in the president's health more objectively than I could in seeing him every day. I wanted whatever information he could provide.

One day he came home shaken after a golf game with the president. They had played nine holes and the president had barely spoken a word.

His speech was retreating, but he still communicated so much with his body language and his eyes. His gift of expression had not left him, and Greg saw that vigor and joy when he entered the Grill Room for lunch before they hit the links. He wasn't walking as quickly, but he was confident in leading the way, definitely knowing where he was going. He was happy to see Greg in his customary seat at the president's corner table. President Reagan didn't ask very many questions, but Greg knew from experience that he wanted to hear about the kids, about sports, and maybe a few jokes, which Greg was glad to provide.

The president knew his schedule instinctively. Exactly at one fifteen p.m. he stood up and started for the men's locker room, which had a door leading directly to the first hole. Ronald Reagan still drove the ball strong and true down the fairway but didn't charge off after it as usual. Instead he sat in the passenger seat as Greg drove him to his ball. Over the years Greg had become so attuned to the president that he could sense him focus or fade as they motored down the fairway. He'd feel the president relax and look at the trees, breathe deeply, and appreciate the vivid colors of the beautiful course. He looked over at Greg and smiled, but sometimes his smile pulled back for a few seconds as if he was not exactly sure of himself, but then he would recover quickly, grinning his lopsided smile and grabbing Greg's arm like they were dear old friends.

When they got to the fourth hole, the one with the stunning view of the Century City skyline, they paused, as usual, to admire the beautiful solitude of the golf course contrasted with the bustling enterprise of the city. Greg always looked forward to this moment in the round and was happy to stand with President Reagan on the green as long as he wanted to be there, honored to be the person alongside the president in this special place.

That afternoon when they paused on the green, Greg did not look at the view but instead looked at the president. His profile was still strong in the afternoon light filtered by the trees. Greg knew he should save this snapshot in his memory because he was not certain when it would happen again, if ever. He extended his arm toward the skyline, as the president had done every other time they stood there, and said what he knew the president was thinking: "What do you say we break a few of those windows?" The grin the president gave him then is one he still carries in his heart.

When they did play golf again a few months later, I was surprised Greg was home at three p.m. instead of closer to five p.m. With him was our good friend and Reagan staffer Erik Felten, who had rounded out the foursome that day. When I greeted them in our kitchen I saw they both seemed concerned.

"Peggy, I think we played our last round of golf with the president today," Greg said, looking down at the floor in resignation.

"Yes," said Erik. "I don't think we will be going back."

They said that as the president approached his table at the country club it was as if he did not recognize Greg and Erik. As they sat together over lunch, he looked often to his Secret Service agents, who were just a few feet away, for reassurance. His gaze was faraway, and he didn't seem to be following the conversation. He still knew when it was time to go, though, so they all rose on his cue and exited to the golf carts.

After they teed off, Greg joined him in the cart but could sense the president was very anxious until they started to drive to his ball. Then it seemed the president was enjoying himself again. Greg decided to align his thoughts with the president's and just savor the moment, realizing how privileged he was to share this special time with a man he admired greatly. Though he had been offered his first tee time invitation because he was my husband, he quickly earned his own place of respect and enjoyment with the president, which resulted in many additional invitations. He had so many cherished memories, yet today's would be especially treasured since they were likely to be among the last.

The president, he could tell, was just not himself. Perhaps he wasn't feeling well, Greg thought, or was especially tired. He had been unsure getting into the golf cart with him at the first hole and that had not improved. Greg drove him to get to his ball on the third hole, and when the president got out of the cart he froze, seemingly distraught. He turned to Greg, but still seemed anxious and concerned. His lead Secret Service agent came alongside him, reassuring him kindly and nodding and pointing toward the ball that was waiting to be hit. He seemed calmer and finished the hole. Everyone was very quiet. There was none of the previous banter and typical teasing between the agents and Greg that was a feature of every other time he'd played with the president. When the president sunk his putt, one of the agents walked up to him.

"I'm right here with you," he said. "Everything is okay. Would you like to go home now, Mr. President?"

The president headed decisively toward the cart.

"Gentlemen, I think we're done for the day," the agent said.

As the cart turned toward the clubhouse, now driven by the lead agent, Erik and Greg took off their hats and approached it. The cart stopped so the president could shake their hands one last time, and then it was gone.

Erik and Greg just stood in silence on the green after he departed. They would not continue play. They, too, were done for the day, and done playing golf with the president forever. This was the end of an era, and it needed to be acknowledged. It was yet another milestone, another evidence of decline and of having to let go, another heartbreaking reminder of the reality that the president was slowly losing everything he loved and being lost by those who loved him.

I felt it through them and saw it day by day myself in different ways. Like Greg and Erik, I tried to savor those moments when it all seemed to be going along well and was enjoyable, and I also had to know when to be done for the day and not play on. I wanted to continue to pour life into the president and cherish every memorable minute that we had, maneuvering through the rough spots, just as Greg had on the golf course, not focusing exclusively on the sadness of heading toward the clubhouse early, but rather of holding on to the memorable images of that recognizable profile bathed in the golden light of the fading afternoon sun.

24

End of an Era

The pendulum of my life was swinging, and I could feel the previously gentle tug toward home getting stronger and stronger. My last day in the office before my daughter Paige was born was bittersweet. I was due in just a few weeks and excited about expanding our family from four to five, but I also was torn. What would this mean to the president? To his daily routine and his schedule? To his comfort and well-being? While there were certainly other very capable people in the office who would fill in while I was away, those people might not have the same intuitions, regardless of their best intentions. Even if I could articulate the motions of the day, it was the moment-by-moment assessments and adjustments—reading his eyes, behaviors, and words and aligning my responses with his—that could not be precisely communicated to whoever filled in for me while I was on leave.

I had done my best to prepare the president, the office, and my replacement, but I was worried about him. It was April 1999, four and a half years after his announcement. He was still coming into the office most days and was well into the middle stages of Alzheimer's. And I was well into my pregnancy. I wanted to work until the very last minute, and did, but my other two children had been born several weeks early (typical for me, life at hyperspeed; my husband always said I was a microwave, not a Crock-Pot, when it came to pregnancy!), so my doctor was concerned that I might deliver my third child on the 405 freeway during my hour-long commute if I didn't stick closer to home.

(Thankfully, I listened, because Paige was born just a day or two later—two weeks early!) That final day before the president left the office, I took a picture with him, unsure if I would see him in the office again once I returned after a brief maternity leave. I was hopeful he would still be coming into the office every day by the time I got back, but at his age and at this stage of his life, the only thing that was predictable was unpredictability.

I called Mrs. Reagan the evening Paige was born to share with her our happy news. She, of course, had already heard through the office about Paige's arrival (she always knew everything). She thanked me for the call and asked me to please bring Paige by the house once I was able, as she couldn't wait to meet her. I asked her to give the president my love but, since Alzheimer's only advances, never retreats, I didn't ask her how he was doing. There was no need to. I already knew.

Though I loved being at home with my three small children, my thoughts were often with the president and with the office, and I felt an urgency to get back to him. I knew his condition would continue to deteriorate and I wanted to be there to support and help him. Though I was still on my maternity leave, I took newborn Paige and the other kids, who were now three and five, up to the office to see the president a few weeks after she was born. I was thrilled to get to introduce this new little one to him, and I treasure the pictures we have of that day. But mostly it was great to see him. I felt complete again. It warmed my heart and helped at least momentarily to assuage my guilt over having left him for a few weeks.

Six weeks after Paige's birth, I was ready to return to work, though I felt torn, especially with a new baby at home. But I knew this was the right thing for me to do. I had to do it. I had come this far with the president, and I had to finish strong and go all the way to the end, whenever that would be and whatever form it would take.

That first day back after my maternity leave I enjoyed walking around his office, inspecting every shelf and corner, adjusting this, moving that, rearranging a few things, and tidying everything just the way

I liked it and had always hoped the president did, too. The president's schedule was clear that day, which meant he may or may not come into the office. I had plenty to do, so I dove into the pile waiting for me on my desk, hoping and praying my phone would ring to tell me that the president was on his way. But the call never came that day.

I volunteered to take the canvas White House bag up to the residence that night. When the president wasn't able to serve as the messenger himself, one of the staff would be his understudy, filling in by delivering Mrs. Reagan's work to her. I asked her assistant not to tell Mrs. Reagan that I was the one who would be bringing the bag, so, as hoped, when she opened the door she was surprised and happy to see me. She greeted me with a hug and invited me in to say hello to the president. Before we could walk back toward his den, he walked into the entryway and I gave him a hug. He looked good, still dressed as impeccably as ever, though he was wearing his glasses instead of his contact lenses, which he typically had worn to the office. It made him look a bit older and grayer, and he seemed to shuffle his feet more than I remembered, taking his time now, with nowhere to go in a hurry anymore. I told him I had missed him in the office and that my corner was much too quiet without him there. He nodded and smiled in acknowledgment and seemed happy to see me, but not nearly as happy as I was to see him. As I drove away, I reflected on the day. It had felt good to be back at work, back in a routine, and back in their lives, and I was hopeful that tomorrow the president would be back in the office.

The next day I was back at my desk and went through my usual routine, preparing the president's office for his arrival. But he didn't come. Nor did he make it in to the office the next day. Or the next. I finally acknowledged, reluctantly, that I would never see him in his office again. And I was right. Sometime between the birth of Paige and our subsequent visit to the office to introduce her to the president, and now, unknowingly he had gone to the office for the very last time. Each scheduled day in the office had always been followed by the next scheduled day in the office. Yet somewhere that chain had been broken, and it had happened quietly, without fanfare. The expectation of his return was now overshadowed by the reality of his absence. We hoped every day he would miraculously wake up one morning and be eager to get back to work, but that proved to be folly. He wouldn't return.

After Paige was born, I had needed to come back to the office, to feel like I had done everything I could to try to continue the president's routine, to be there for him, to will him well, to coax him back to health and vitality and full ability. Yet no desire or longing on my part could make that happen. It was over. I was no longer serving him personally; I was now working in an office that proudly bore his name still, but didn't have *him* anymore. To me, he had been everything. The office still served an important purpose, but it had lost its very soul. The heart of my job had been working directly with the president. But there would be no more visits from old friends or photo ops with starry-eyed admirers. He was done giving speeches and signing photographs. I couldn't bear the thought of pushing papers in an office without the presence of the man at the center of the work. I knew it was time for me to listen to that voice inside my head that continued to get louder, telling me it was time to go home. For good.

I believe that everything in life has a season, a purpose, a lifespan, and a predetermined end. I actually never thought I would be a working mom at all. I was raised by a combination of June Cleaver and Betty Crocker—and I mean that in the best of ways. My mother had been a home economics teacher and ran our household with the precision of a top executive coupled with the love of a woman who had always wanted to be a mother and was living out her calling and purpose in life in that regard. And though she was highly educated and went on eventually to become a college professor, my mother's favorite title was always Mom and her deepest passion was her family. I respected, admired, and appreciated her for that. I always thought I would follow in her footsteps and once I had kids I would be home with them full-time, leaving behind, at least temporarily, any professional pursuits.

Yet my job, this job, wasn't just a job—it was my destiny. I felt called to it and felt like everything in life had ensured I was perfectly positioned for a role that was so unlikely yet so perfect for me, it had to be God's plan, not mine. There was no other logical explanation for it. I could never have planned for or earned it; it was a gift I was prepared to receive, and I had done everything I could to be a good steward of it. God had called me to this and made it all possible. I look back on the chaotic days with all the little kids and the travel and the illness and the moves and wonder how it all worked out as well as it did. Yet it did work out. And it was wonderful, for the most part, and I am convinced it's because it was part of God's plan. When He is in charge things work out in ways that otherwise would not be humanly possible. On paper there's no way that it should have ever worked. And I knew it.

In the summer of 1999, shortly after I returned to work from my third maternity leave, I started feeling a bit like the wheels were coming off, that things were unraveling at home and that perhaps God's hand of blessing was no longer over my being there in the office. It was nothing in particular but everything in general. My kids didn't seem as happy, and I wasn't as happy. My husband was always supportive, but I also felt he was trying to hold something together that was dissolving quicker than he could fix it. I spent ninety minutes in traffic one day getting home. Once I finally arrived, I said goodbye to the nanny, scooped all the kids up on my lap at once, and looked at Greg.

"I don't think I can do this anymore. I don't feel like I'm supposed to be there anymore. I feel like I'm supposed to be here."

He walked over and embraced his entire family with his large strong arms that had carried so much these past ten years.

"I think it's time, too. We all need you. And need more of you."

With that it was decided. After ten years of working in the Office of Ronald Reagan, I would be "retiring."

Taylor was starting kindergarten soon and his first day of school was also his birthday, September 7, 1999. He would be turning six, Courtney was three, and Paige was five months old. We decided there would be no better way to start this next chapter than to have that be my first official day as a full-time mom. So I submitted my resignation letter, set a date, and prepared my exit. I had left on three previous occasions, all for maternity leave, always with the intention of returning. This one, though, felt different. And it was. It seemed surreal to be leaving for good. And yet looking back on the past ten years it *all* had been surreal, so maybe this was just the ending of a very vivid, very realistic, and extended dream.

I thought back to my first glimpse of the president as a Pepperdine student and how exhilarating that was. Never could I have imagined how every detail of that man's face and his hands, voice, and mannerisms would forever be engrained in my mind, and now in my memory. I recalled the emotions of excitement when I was invited in for my interview and drove up Avenue of the Stars for the very first time, riding the elevator that rocketed to the penthouse. I thought of my surprise at how comfortable the office was from the outset and how uncomfortable, yet special, my first moment of meeting the president was. It seemed like yesterday when I answered the phone for the first time, "Office of Ronald Reagan." And now, ten years later, I had to consciously override that habit and remember to answer my own home phone with a simple "Hello."

I pictured how carefree and simple my life was back then—going to the gym, dressing for work, commuting, traveling, socializing, and pouring my whole self into my career. By contrast, now, I sometimes felt like I was barely staying afloat, let alone swimming along through life with the relative ease and grace of a few years ago. I was thirty-one years old and felt like I had lived ten lives in the last ten years. I had seen more, done more, met more people, and experienced more of life than most people would in a hundred years. I had gone from feeling young and green and out of place to feeling comfortable, accomplished, and confident in my work. I had known what it felt like to be at a place in my life where the pace and the people and the productivity thrilled me, brought out the best in me, and allowed me to offer my best to my boss and my workplace.

I knew what it felt like to be jolted out of bed in the middle of the night by the 1994 Northridge earthquake, unsure if the house around me would stand, and similarly jolted out of my comfort zone with the realities of cancer and Alzheimer's invading my life and trying to steal the joy from some of my greatest, most memorable and celebrated years of youth. Yet the experiences of all of that had also taught me that life doesn't happen by accident—you need to prepare and plan and dream and be ready to grab an opportunity when it comes your way, regardless of how inadequate you feel for the task at hand. Keep trying, keep growing, keep absorbing the best in your surroundings, and eventually you, too, can become accomplished and become a valued contributor in an environment that previously seemed foreign. I learned we all have a greater capacity to work and multitask and achieve and celebrate and even mourn simultaneously, and we can do so with a genuine sense of joy and purpose and contentment, even at times in the midst of sorrow. Sometimes especially then.

I learned that life truly is a circle, and just as I was welcoming new life, I was also reluctantly letting go of a life that meant so much to me and had taught me so much. I realized that gifts we are given that seem to be unearned and undeserved are sometimes recalled later in life with the demand that they be returned in the form of blessing on others, service to others, and unconditionally loving others, even when their capacity to reciprocate is gone. I learned that nothing is forever and had to accept that this amazing chapter of my life was now ending. I mourned its loss yet was filled with gratitude that it ever happened at all.

On my last day in the office, September 3, 1999, there was a typical office party—a giant decorated chocolate chip cookie, a card signed by all, a thoughtful big collage of pictures from the office in a nice frame, kind words, and tearful goodbyes. Yet unlike so many office parties of the past few years, there was no grand entrance of the president from the side door, no cheers from the staff and guests to welcome him, no entertainment or kids or candy or noise. It was just grown-ups. And it was very sweet. But also very quiet and sad.

Nothing was the same without him, and nothing would ever be. But how grateful I was for all those parties that had happened beforehand, for holding his birthday cake and watching him blow out his candles, for watching the kids "help" him open his presents, his enjoyment as great as or greater than theirs. All the memories in the office that included him, all the times I had interacted with him, flooded my mind. Even now he was still very present, but only in all of our thoughts. It was hard to say goodbye, and yet I had already said goodbye to the best part, to the reason for being there, to the reason for the office's very existence. Since I knew the relationships I was leaving behind would endure far beyond the walls of the office, I straightened the phone on my now bare desk, grabbed my bags, and said goodbye to my co-workers. I turned in my keycard, and rode the elevator down alone. No politics of the elevator on this day. Or ever again.

That weekend was busy, preparing my son for his first day of school and planning for his birthday party that next week. Life would go on. And it was very much going on. When we were walking around the mall over the weekend doing some last-minute back-to-school shopping, I had this overwhelming feeling that I was supposed to be somewhere else, that my phone would ring at any moment, requiring me to drop everything and go do something for the president or answer a call from Mrs. Reagan or be asked a question about the office or the schedule or an upcoming event. But the phone didn't ring. And I had to adjust to a new reality. It was completely fulfilling in some ways, yet in other ways left me missing my former life, not because I necessarily missed all that was involved in being a working mom, but because I missed him. I missed my boss. I would have to find a way to see him. And stay connected. And ensure that he knew of my love and support to the very end. I knew what I had to do.

I picked up the phone and called Mrs. Reagan at the residence.

25

Saying Goodbye

At the other end of the call, the phone was ringing at the residence, just as I had heard many times before. I could picture where each of the phones was and wondered which one Mrs. Reagan would pick up or if, perhaps, one of the household staff would answer instead. Though I had called the residence often in the past, I was a little anxious about this call, wondering if I should even be making it. Now that I wasn't on staff anymore, should I call through on the Office of Nancy Reagan line and go through her assistant? Was I supposed to use her private, direct line for personal purposes, not office purposes now, which this clearly was? My departure from the office was planned, and yet my exit seemed very abrupt, as if there was unfinished business, which there was, at least in my mind. The unfinished business was him. The president. I had always been there for him, and yet when I left, he was not there. It was like an open wound that I knew would never heal until I made it my business to finish strong and right and well. I had to see him.

The phone picked up on the other end. It was Mrs. Reagan.

"Hi, Mrs. Reagan. It's Peggy."

"Hello, Peggy. It's nice to hear from you. How are you? And how is the baby?"

"Thank you for asking. We are all doing well. Things are a bit crazy around here with three little ones, but it's a lot of fun and I'm certainly putting all my office skills to work still. In fact, I don't know how someone can do this job without having run the life of a president! And

I'm not sure yet which one is more challenging, but probably being a full-time mom!"

"Are you calling to see if you can bring the baby by to meet me? I hope so."

She was always direct and to the point. No hint dropping—just state it.

"She and Ronnie have met, but she and I still haven't, you know," she said.

"Yes, Mrs. Reagan, that's exactly why I was calling. We hope we can both come see you soon. I'll call your office and get on your calendar," I said.

On the scheduled day in the fall of 1999, I asked Greg's parents to watch the two older kids so just Paige and I could visit with Mrs. Reagan. It was a very cold day, too cold for a cute little dress, so I chose a bright red one-piece romper—Mrs. Reagan's signature color, which I knew she would like seeing on Paige. Yet I also knew the heat in the house would be on full blast since Mrs. Reagan was always cold, so I had no fear of it being too cold for the baby once we got there. As I drove toward the residence, I was little bit worried. Paige was about six months old and a darling baby—beautiful olive skin and the most enormous, deep-brown eyes you have ever seen. We were surprised since the other kids all had big blue eyes, but these were definitely deep chocolate brown and the most beautifully sparkling shade.

Paige also was born with very definite opinions about life and about people. How telling that would be of her strong and confident personality, which would develop later in life! She was passionate on both ends of the spectrum: she liked something with full delight or hated something with a vengeance. There was no in between, and she made her position very clear. It was the same with people: she either loved you dearly or she didn't. There was no in between. And some very important people in her life had sometimes been the recipients of strong negative opinions. It was embarrassing, but you can't exactly ascribe logic to a baby. I was worried. What if Paige didn't like Mrs. Reagan? What if she gave her "the scowl"? We jokingly called her Winston after Winston Churchill, since she would get this intense stare where she jutted out her lower chin, the jowls of the baby fat around her face sitting directly on her shoulders, looking just like the iconic black-and-white image of a scowling Winston Churchill from early in World War II.

The farther I drove, the more anxious I felt. This was my first visit to the residence since I "retired." Would it be the same? I had been looking forward to this visit, but now I was terrified. I should have thought more about this earlier, but I didn't, and here we were. As the gate opened, one of those celebrity tour vans was driving by, windows down, with tourists taking pictures out the window, the tour guide on his microphone telling the occupants of the van about the occupants of the residence. Although I could only hear a bit of what he was saying, he was definitely talking about the Reagans. They stopped in the middle of the road, watching as the gate opened and they looked up the long driveway toward the house. I prayed not to stall out my old stick-shift car as I started heading up the steep driveway.

One of the household staff invited me into the study and said Mrs. Reagan would be right with me. I pulled out a little toy for Paige to amuse her. All my anxiety was for naught. The moment Mrs. Reagan came around the corner, Paige lit up as if she was seeing a favorite, familiar face. I was relieved. Paige was perfectly behaved, and Mrs. Reagan was thoroughly enchanted. That quiet house on St. Cloud Road was suddenly full of life and joy that had been absent there just moments earlier.

We took a few quick pictures while Paige was still content and then Mrs. Reagan turned and started walking toward the president's den, motioning for us to follow. He was seated at his desk, looking through a book.

"Honey, look who's here," Mrs. Reagan said.

The president saw us and immediately jumped up from his chair and walked over to say hello—not to me, but to Paige. I loved seeing the president interact with her, especially since she had grown so much since he last saw her as a newborn. I finally interrupted their little mutual admiration society meeting for two.

"Hello, Mr. President. It's so nice to see you again," I said, and reached around to give him a one-armed hug and a kiss on the cheek, still holding the baby in our tight little circle.

He looked really good, dressed in slacks and a sweater with nice color in his cheeks, though he looked thinner than before, especially in the face. His hair had recently been cut, his nails were well manicured, and he smelled as good as ever. He was well cared for in all ways. It made me so happy to see that. His appearance had always been important to him—and to her.

Our visit was fairly brief, as a baby is often like a ticking time bomb, and you never know when it will blow—especially this baby. I promised to return again soon, believing it is better to leave when people want you to stay, rather than staying too long and having them want you to leave. We said our goodbyes with hugs and kisses. There was laughter and love and joy—and life.

Mrs. Reagan walked us back to the front door, telling me how good it was to see us and how much they had enjoyed our visit, and she implored us to please hurry back and bring the other kids, too. I gave her a little plate of cookies to share with the president later. I could picture the president lighting up when he was given his dessert as he had so many times in the office. It made me smile inside to know there were certain things you could still count on about him. As we pulled away from the house I was relieved it had gone so well. It felt great to be up at the residence and to see Mrs. Reagan again—and of course to see the president, too. He looked so good on the outside, which was comforting, though the changes inside were becoming more and more obvious outside now, too. He spoke less, moved slower, and seemed less engaged, which was sad and hard to see.

Over the next five years I continued to visit the residence many times, sometimes by myself and sometimes with Greg and the kids, experiencing the full range of the Reagans' hospitality. I remember the bittersweet moment when I first went to the residence to visit President and Mrs. Reagan by myself for the first time after I was no longer an employee of the Office of Ronald Reagan. Mrs. Reagan greeted me with a hug and invited me to sit in the den to wait for the president to come out and say hello. She also offered me some iced tea. In my mind I was still a staffer, but in her mind I was now a guest. The hug, the invitation to be seated, and the offer of iced tea were not the typical work visit protocol when there was business to conduct and the pace was hurried. It felt so strange and yet wonderful. I experienced another side of her then and appreciated her subtle, yet gracious acknowledgment of our new relationship. Although it was unspoken, it was clear to me that she saw me differently.

Perhaps it also was that after I left the office and my life had changed dramatically, things were continuing to change in her life as well. The residence was quieter and lonelier. Even though the president was still around physically, his world was shrinking and her role in it was continuing to expand. Maybe she saw me as a connection to the past, someone who brought back memories of happier times for her and her husband. We talked about the president, the kids, politics, people she knew I had seen or kept up with, the usual girl talk. And though we were friendly, I would never have presumed to see myself as her friend. She was forever in my mind the exalted First Lady of the United States. And I just happened to be the luckiest woman in the world to have my life intersect hers and the president's.

On one very special visit in late 2001 I got to introduce my youngest, Jocelyn, to President and Mrs. Reagan. I wasn't nearly as nervous this time since Jocelyn was a smiling, happy baby with a very even temperament—a perfect fourth child! I was pleased to be able to introduce her to the president, though his ability to respond and react was significantly different than when he met Paige two years earlier. He wasn't able to jump up and greet her; we took Jocelyn to him. He wasn't able to talk with her and interact playfully; instead, he quietly touched her soft skin and gazed at her with curiosity and wonder. While that saddened me deeply, I took comfort in the fact that I was able to introduce her to the president at all—an introduction I would have loved to have made to my own father, but couldn't. If my father couldn't know my youngest two children, at least the president could.

We would visit every year at Christmastime, around the president's birthday, and often for no particular reason at all. We would always bring Mrs. Reagan an orchid and the president a treat, something chocolate. I could never go wrong with homemade chocolate chip cookies, banana bread with chocolate chips in it, or a chocolate birthday cake, complete with candles that the kids would help him blow out and presents they would help him open. The kids would draw pictures for the president and make him little crafts at school. They would get excited to bring him their special creations. I'm sure their preschool and elementary schools never had any idea they would be creating a project for the former president of the United States.

Over the next five years a few visits to the residence in particular stood out.

One time in 2003 I went to visit the president alone. Mrs. Reagan was out, so the Secret Service agents let me in. The house was quiet and still, but sun filled the entryway with light and warmth. I was told that the president was outside waiting for me.

As I entered the back patio I stopped for a moment to admire the breathtaking view of the Los Angeles skyline. There was another view, though, that was even more beautiful to me. There on the patio I could see the backs of two men sitting side by side in two chairs. One was the president. The other was a Secret Service agent who, in years past, would have been posted at the sliding glass door. However, during these final years of the president's life, the agents also took on the roles of comforter and friend. Instead of letting the president wait alone for me, the agent had taken my chair. As I approached I realized he was not just sitting there, but he was holding the president's hand. He wasn't just protecting him. He was providing a reassuring hand of friendship.

My eyes started filling with tears, thinking back to all the times in the office when the Secret Service agents had gone far above and beyond their assigned duty. Now they circled around him with love and even friendship at a time when he was no longer able to return it to them. That one small gesture showed how they had stretched themselves beyond their own comfort zones, beyond their job description or duty, beyond the confines of their role, and stepped into the beauty of a relationship with him.

The agent noticed me and abruptly popped up, not quite embarrassed yet not wanting to linger once he realized he was being observed. I thanked him for his kindness to the president and took his seat—my seat. And I also took the president's hand. We sat in silence for a few moments, enjoying the view and just enjoying being in this peaceful and beautiful place. The agent had disappeared again, though I knew he would still be nearby, not to protect the president from me but to be there if he needed anything.

I started talking about the kids and about life and about people we both knew. He was mostly quiet, which helped me relax and slow down from my fast-paced life and join him where he was. I knew he enjoyed the sound of conversation since his world was especially quiet right now. I would talk for a while and then allow the silence to return, enjoying the beauty of the view and the beauty of the moment. I thought back to all the times in the past we had sat in silence and how comfortable that felt. Since he'd been an actor and a politician, the greatest sign of respect and familiarity was the sound of his silence. If he didn't feel the need to entertain you, to engage you or impress you, to earn your vote, a laugh, or your loyalty, then in essence he knew he already had you as part of his team, part of his inner circle. His words were for everyone, but his silence was reserved for a select few. I had always been honored to be among those. And yet now I longed for his voice, but I would have to accept that it was almost gone. I savored every moment that day, even the silence, knowing that not only were the minutes of this visit fleeting, but the window in which to ever visit with him again, even in silence, was slowly but most certainly and surely closing.

*　　*　　*

Another visit that stands out was a beautiful spring day in 2000 when Paige was about a year old and Taylor and Courtney were six and four, respectively. Mrs. Reagan had told me on my last solo visit that she missed the children, so we trudged through the routine required for a visit, packed a bag of snacks and toys, and set off.

Thankfully the weather was warm and beautiful so we could be outside, which was much more conducive to a visit with three small children than indoors. Mrs. Reagan was heading out for a bit just as we were arriving, so she said a quick hello, and after receiving her traditional orchid from Taylor, she told him how much he had grown. She gave Courtney a quick hug and instructed her to keep dancing, and gave little squeezes to the baby rolls on Paige's legs, which no one could ever resist touching.

The Secret Service agent also greeted the kids and walked our little entourage to the back patio. I could see the president seated in the shade. He always looked well groomed, evidence of Mrs. Reagan's loving and fastidious care of him. I set the kids' bag of goodies down by a low outdoor table, and we all walked over to say hello. The kids ran to him simultaneously, each hoping to get the first hug, both getting sweet smiles of acknowledgment but no other recognition from him.

I sat down next to him with the baby on my lap. He looked intently, reaching out to touch her doughy legs, just as Mrs. Reagan had. Paige was squirmy so I put her down and stayed next to the president as she toddled off to explore the yard.

Just sitting with this man soothed my soul in ways that only he could. I had missed him far more than I had anticipated. I always knew that my job had been more than a job. I always knew it was personal, yet I didn't realize that I could never fully be whole in a life that didn't include him. In many ways I had grown up with him—not that he raised me, but I had been forced to grow up through some very fast-paced challenging years that stretched me in ways I never could have anticipated, both personally and professionally. And all of those ways were interwoven with him. He was inseparable from my life story and from that of my kids.

When I looked through our family photo albums, he was always there. He was part of our conversations. Photos of him were on the walls of our home, and when anyone talked with our family you knew he was in our hearts. Forever. Yet we also knew that *he* was not forever and that every visit may very well be our last.

As I sat there with the president and looked around me, there was Paige with her little plastic sippy cup, sitting in the grass in front of us under a tree just taking it all in and enjoying the fresh air of the outdoors and the freedom that came with her newly mastered skill of walking. I looked over my shoulder and saw Taylor and Courtney, coloring quietly, making themselves at home in the Reagans' backyard, crayons askew, acting as if it was an ordinary day and they had to entertain themselves like they did in a restaurant or at their own grandparents' house. Yet this was no ordinary day, and even if they didn't know it, I did. Perhaps they sensed it, though, because one at a time, first Courtney and then Taylor walked over unprompted, drawn to his presence. They each took a turn sitting in the chair beside him, looking up at him sweetly, talking to him softly, holding his hand, touching his arm, feeling comfortable, safe, and at home in his familiar and loving presence. Each looked deeply into his eyes, as if to memorize his features and his profile, and they missed the sound of his voice.

That voice was mostly gone now. That voice had been filled with strength and comfort, challenge and courage, optimism and hope. We had grown accustomed to it. Relied on it. Trusted it. And now, with its absence, its deafening silence, I missed it. Deeply. And knew the world missed it. And my kids missed it, maybe them most of all, as they had never known life without it. Studies show that unborn children become very familiar with the voices around them, so I am certain they knew the voice of the Great Communicator before they were even born. That the cadence and the tone and the clarity and the kindness of his voice was known to them and loved by them before they even took their first breaths. I knew they longed to hear it again, as did I, but it was fading. And it would soon be forever silent.

The visit had gone perfectly thus far, and I decided we would leave before any toddler meltdowns occurred, so I gathered the kids and asked one of the agents to take a picture of us all together.

My mind was in conflict, wanting to believe that there would be other occasions, other opportunities, other beautiful backyard visits to cherish and celebrate and enjoy. Yet the other part of my mind, the side of logic and reason, knew that this was the last visit the kids would have with him and the last time we would take pictures with him. We smiled for a group photo, and then I put Paige down and asked the kids to gather their things. It was just the president and me now, and I asked for one more picture. As I had done with my dad a few years earlier, I feigned a smile for the camera, while trying to disguise the intense pain inside. I wanted to capture one last moment of togetherness, though I was unable to pretend that saying goodbye was ever joyful. We continued to hold hands. His face, which had been fairly absent of emotion the entire visit, suddenly looked a bit more alive. There was a small twinkle in his eye, the hint of a smile. It was as if he, too, knew that this was it, our last and final picture together, and he wanted it to be treasured. And it was.

"Mr. President, thank you for letting us come visit with you today," I said. "It's always special. And today was particularly special, so thank you for that."

His eyes may have been twinkling a bit, but mine were suddenly leaking, so I grabbed my sunglasses, not wanting him to see the pain and grief in my eyes. I would never want him to know that he was the cause of it. But he only caused me pain because he was so wonderful. That was the pain. That was the loss. You never want to let someone like that go. I already had to do it with my dad, and I knew I had to prepare to do it again with him.

When I visited the president around his ninety-third birthday in February 2004, I assumed this would be the last time, and it was. With each visit over the past few years he was less engaged, less himself, and less present. I was always happy to see that he was impeccably cared for in his beautiful cashmere sweaters, which would never see the golf course again. He had defied the odds, defied gravity, and stayed young at heart, robust, and active far longer than most of his peers. He had started the biggest job of his life when others had already given up. He courageously went toe to toe with the greatest foes of our time and beat them, often without firing a single shot. The resolve of his conviction and the power of his words had made him a giant on the world stage and a giant in my mind. All of those things he still was, yet it was clear now that he was mortal like the rest of us. The mind and the body that had been his allies in achieving greatness were now his enemies and were making their final advance toward complete conquest. He was surrendering, finally. There was no fight left in him.

I went to his bedside that day, held his hand, and just sat with him. I had few words to offer up. There was nothing left to be said. I had no unfinished business with this beloved man. I had given him everything I had, and he had given even more to me without even knowing it. He had given me his courage, his strength, his love, and his example, which forever changed my life. He had given me a future I could never imagine and had done so without even meaning to. It was who he was. And he had changed who I was. We sat in silence. I enjoyed just being with him and near him. He was sleeping and looked so peaceful, with surprisingly ruddy cheeks and a beautiful full head of hair, still perfectly styled, still trying to tame the wave in it but not fully successful. The perfectly imperfect smile was gone now, and I looked down at his hand in mine.

It's odd when you know someone so well that you take things for granted. Like his hands. Those hands that previously had been rough and rugged, strong and dexterous, tanned and tough, were now soft, yet so familiar to me—every vein, every line, every muscle and bone. The pads of his fingers hadn't seen work for quite some time. They were warm and smooth, soothing to the touch. I loved just being there, holding his hand and being quiet. He briefly awoke, and those beautiful blue eyes opened for a bit, scanning the room and then locked on me. They stared intently, looking at me vacantly as just another part of his room and his view. I started talking to him, telling him how good he looked and how wonderful it was to see him again.

As I spoke, the fogginess of his eyes seemed to dissipate momentarily. He was still looking at me, but it was different. There was a hint of a sparkle or maybe even a twinkle in his eyes, and with that one look, it was if he was saying that even though he was unsure of exactly who I was, he thought he might know me, and thought I was someone he was fond of.

"I'm fond of you too, Mr. President. And always will be," I said aloud.

He drifted back to sleep, and I sat a while longer, not wanting to leave, knowing that regardless of how long I stayed there, ultimately I would have to say goodbye. And this was it.

I told myself it wasn't true, that I would see him again on another visit, that I would have another chance to sit and to study his features and memorize the lines on his hands and in his face. To watch him sleep, to hear him breathe, and to continue to have him breathe life into me. I wasn't ready to let him go. I had already lost my father, and now I was on the brink of losing him.

I didn't want to grow up. I wasn't ready to. I would resist it with everything I had. Yet ultimately I would have to resign myself to that reality. I had to say goodbye and walk out the door, leaving him forever. Unable to delay the inevitable any longer, I forced myself to stand up. I released his hand and instinctively leaned over, gently kissed his forehead, and then his warm soft cheek. He didn't respond. I patted his hand and kissed my hand, placing one last kiss on his hand. I then said goodbye in the only way I could think of.

"Thank you, Mr. President. For everything."

I paused at the side of his bed, looking one last time at him lovingly and longingly, wanting to imprint the image of this man and his memory forever in my mind. And before I turned to walk out, I straightened myself upright with resolve, slowly raising my right hand to place it over my heart, out of respect, not knowing what else to do—just like the first time I met him.

I gave him one last look. Then I left, unable to look back again, tears streaming down my cheeks, trying to control my emotions, but it was not to be. I walked out the front door and the Secret Service agent who was standing post on the porch knew by my look that I had said my goodbye. Forever. I hugged him tightly, grateful for his friendship over the years, and for his comfort now.

"Keep looking out for my favorite guy," I said.

"I will," he replied. "He's my favorite, too."

I got in my car, turned it around, and drove down the driveway, out the gates of the residence, and down the hill. I pulled over at the park where the president had walked, where I had been so many times with my kids, and I finally let go. Of him. Of my tears. Of my past. And of my unknown future, which I would soon have to face without him.

26

Mourning in America

It was Saturday, June 5, 2004, and I was at a backyard pool party with my family. We were celebrating the conclusion of a winning Little League season for my son's baseball team and later in the day would be heading to my daughter Paige's first dance recital. Although much was on the family agenda, I had taken my own car to this party, just in case I needed to leave early. I had been in touch with the office frequently recently and knew the president was failing rapidly. I had been especially vigilant about keeping my phone near me at all times, never missing a call. On the outside everything appeared normal at the party, but my insides were anxious, worried, and completely preoccupied. I checked my phone often, as I had done 24/7 the past week or so, dreading its ring, yet not wanting to miss it, either. No timeline was given on my last call with the office, just that they wanted me to be on standby and to be prepared, both for the imminent news of his passing and for the whirlwind of activity that would follow. There was no possible way to prepare appropriately for either.

Midway through the party my phone rang and I recognized the number immediately. I felt my heart sink as I stopped midsentence in my conversation and turned away quickly, probably without even excusing myself. I ducked into a bedroom and shut the door. My dear friend Joanne Drake, who had succeeded Fred Ryan as chief of staff, uttered five small words that had a devastating impact: "He's gone. I'm so sorry."

"Thank you for calling," I replied quickly. "I'll be there as soon as I can."

No other conversation was needed, as my role was preplanned and clear.

Not wanting to risk news of his passing leaking before it was officially released publicly, we were guarded, careful, and limited in our words. I grabbed my bag and found Greg. I pulled him aside.

"I need to go," I said.

He knew what that meant and all it entailed. He hugged me tightly, gave me a kiss, and said exactly what I needed to hear: "Go do what you do best. Finish strong. I've got everything covered here. We will miss you but will be okay."

"Thank you. I love you," I said.

I turned to walk away. As I left, he chased me down and gave me one more hug and kiss.

"By the way, I'm proud of you," he said.

I said no other goodbyes, as I wanted to slip out quietly and not make a stir or tip off anyone as to what had happened. Nor could I face my daughter and tell her I would be missing her first dance recital. I couldn't risk questions from the kids or any tearful goodbyes, so I just left, my heart breaking and my mind racing. But there was work to do, and I needed to be at my sharpest and best. I drove home quickly, changed into a dress and heels, added a few things to a bag that I had packed a week ago, just in case, and was out the door within minutes.

The drive toward Century City felt both odd and familiar, but, like riding a bike, when you do something often enough it becomes automatic. That came in handy on this day since my mind was anywhere but on the road. Before I knew it I was at the Office of Ronald Reagan, an office with the same name but at a different address, since it had moved locations once the president was no longer going in. Its new location was in a building primarily occupied by government agencies, including the Secret Service, and it was not far from the old office. Though the office space itself was unfamiliar to me, the faces were well known. I knew even more former staffers would be returning in the next few hours and days. When I arrived there were just two of us in the office—Ethan Baker, who worked for the chief of staff, and me. A few of the staff were up at the residence still and would return to the office later. Others were still en route.

I had spoken with Ethan on the phone often and had met him on a few other occasions during brief office visits but hadn't had the chance to work with him closely until that day, since he had started working there just after I left. He would prove to be a terrific ally and friend not only during that week of the funeral but for years to come. He represented both the Reagans and the office with tact, diplomacy, and the respect that was needed and deserved. Although he wasn't part of the original Office of Ronald Reagan team, he certainly fit right in. The office and the Reagans were fortunate to have him on staff. And I was fortunate to gain him as a friend.

The official announcement of the president's passing hadn't gone out yet, but big stories like this are too hard to keep under wraps for long, so we started getting a few calls asking to confirm the swirling rumors. We took messages and assured them they would be included in any statement that might be forthcoming. Before we could release the public announcement, though, we had to quickly call a list of people who needed to be told by the staff personally about the president's passing rather than hearing through the media. This list included extended family members who lived out of town, board members, close personal friends, and some former staffers who not only had been personally close to the Reagans but had also been waiting for this call so they could join in implementing the weeklong plan. Many would be catching flights to LA and some would be flying to DC, depending on their location and their assigned role.

The timeline that had been established twenty-five years prior and revised every year since then was now being implemented, and in fact had already begun. Although the elements of it were familiar and well known, it was daunting to realize the clock was now ticking. It seemed surreal. And sad. And final. The minute-by-minute timeline was complex, proceeding in two locations that were thousands of miles and three time zones apart.

With each passing hour, another person or two would show up. This little office on Wilshire Boulevard would eventually have about a dozen people to do the heavy lifting of making and fielding calls, implementing the logistics of the president's final interment ceremony in Simi Valley, while also coordinating with the small temporary staff in Washington, DC, the permanent staff at the Reagan Foundation in Simi Valley, as well as working with the Military District of Washington. The MDW, a division of the Army, is in charge of all of the movements, which are guided by protocol and steeped deeply in history and tradition. They are tasked with the difficult but honored ceremonial responsibilities of overseeing state funerals, like President Reagan's.

Joanne was in charge of orchestrating the bulk of the logistics from a staff perspective. We were waiting for her to return from the residence to send out the advisory so we could continue with the rest of the planning once the news was official and made public. In the meantime, we were moving forward with a game plan behind the scenes, but couldn't do much else. We quickly prepared as much as possible, knowing the deluge was coming.

Joanne walked into the office and her face said it all: her personal grief would be great—later—but her game face was on as she was being asked to pull off an immense task while the world watched. She had worked for the Reagan campaign in 1984, then took a job in the Reagan White House Office of Presidential Advance. She moved to LA with the Reagans in 1989 and continued to serve them in the Office of Ronald Reagan and eventually at the Reagan Foundation as well. She faithfully committed herself to the Reagans, in total, more than thirty years. Like her, we all knew our grief would hit later, but were determined to stay strong, work together, and follow the president's wishes to a T. He would have had it no other way. And neither would we.

The release was emailed out to the press advisory list. It was much less dramatic than the feeling of pressing Send on the fax machine as we had done just a few years earlier when we announced to the world the president had Alzheimer's. So much had changed in the office, in the residence, and in my life, too. Yet the bonds of connection, commitment, and devotion to the president and to one another as his staff had not changed and never would.

Within moments of the release being emailed out, the phones began to ring. And they would ring nonstop for the next week. We fielded calls from the press, elected officials across the nation and around the world, foreign dignitaries, friends of the Reagans, former staffers, admirers, mourners, and fans. The calls had to be answered—all of them—because amid the well-meaning people sending their thoughts and prayers to Mrs. Reagan or just wanting to share a memory of the president, tell of their personal feelings of loss, or call just to talk, there was also the important business of the funeral plans to be conducted.

We did our best to keep nonessential calls brief, keeping a list of people who wanted to convey their love to Mrs. Reagan, referring media calls to our press spokesperson, and just listening to people who needed to talk and cry and share. People also started calling to ask how they could attend the services at the National Cathedral in Washington, DC, or at the Reagan Library. Invitations were being sent out exclusively via personal phone calls to people on a pre-established list, so no additional invitees would be added, but there were opportunities to pay respects on both coasts, as the president's body would lie in repose at the Reagan Library and then lie in state in the Capitol Rotunda during the week ahead. It felt as if the entire world was calling for information.

We were on the phones nonstop. Calling to invite people to attend the funeral often brought immediate tears from many of the invitees. "Really? I'm being invited? I'm so honored. Thank you so much. Yes, of course I will be there. I wouldn't miss it for the world!" Others, contemporaries of the president and Mrs. Reagan, would often reply with, "I would love to be there, but I need the assistance of a nurse. And I have a driver. And my wife has a nurse that accompanies her. Can the two of us bring five people?" This was not a young crowd, and it reminded me of how incredibly active and amazingly strong, vigorous, and youthful the Reagans had been for many years.

While these calls needed to be brief due to the sheer volume, many were lengthy and difficult due to the raw emotions involved. These were the people who were closest to the Reagans and had meant the most to them, which is why they were being invited to attend the funeral. Over and over, call after call, we had to relive the news and endure the reality of the truth: the president was gone forever. The words coming out of my mouth sounded impossible, yet with each call it became more and more real. The nation began to mourn. His friends and former staff began to mourn. The world began to mourn. But I couldn't begin to mourn. Not yet. There was much to be done still.

The events of the week could fill a series of books in and of themselves—the sheer scope, volume, and magnitude of the events, coupled with the detailed minutia of each individual element could never be adequately articulated, nor could it ever have been prescribed, despite the myriad of plans and assignments and lists and outlines and previously made decisions. That is why the team, this team, was essential. Regardless of where everyone had gone since they left the president's office, they came back together and fell into their previous roles. In one particular instance, a gentleman who had interned in 1989 when the office first opened had gone on to be a very wealthy, successful CEO of several businesses and lived on the East Coast. When I called and asked him what he was doing this week and his reply was "Whatever you need me to do," I was overwhelmed and grateful. He took the first flight he could to get to LA and worked with our team all week long. Yet since all those years ago he had served as an intern in the office, rather than coming back in to assist in an executive capacity, he willingly and selflessly did any and every task that was asked of him, including many that were well beneath his current status and level of responsibility back home.

That was what the Reagans had created: a family. They inspired a loyalty, a selflessness, a sense of teamwork, and a willingness to assist, regardless of the task. There was nothing above or beneath a Reagan staffer, just as the president had never shied away from jumping in to help, or clean up something he spilled, or carry his own bag. By his example he had enabled, empowered, and built a team around him that was ferociously loyal not only to the Reagans but to each other. Though the occasion was sad and difficult, the camaraderie and the togetherness felt good again. We had each gone our separate ways, and yet now we were reunited and recommitted to a singular purpose. None of us had forgotten how to work—and work hard, and work very long hours—individually and as a team. Once again, a handful of us were going to pull off something heroic.

In the midst of an extraordinarily busy week, there were two small breaks from the office forever etched in my mind. On that first day when the president's body was being moved from the residence to the funeral home, they would be driving right down Wilshire Boulevard and past the office where the team was working. The word had gotten out. Helicopters were circling the property and the media was covering every movement. We knew both the timing and the routing, so once we were certain the motorcade would be passing by shortly, the small staff that had already gathered briefly left the phones unattended and planned to walk down to stand on the corner and watch the hearse drive by, the first of several times that week we would pay our respects. We felt as if we should do something more than just stand there, so we grabbed an American flag from the office, which was full-size and on a very long pole, barely fitting in the elevator. We stood at the corner of a very busy street, holding this flag and waiting for the motorcade to drive by. When it did, we all stood, with hands over our hearts, as if at attention, in tribute to our president and as a sign of respect to him. Each of us individually grateful for all he had done and had meant to us.

Later in the week, the president's body was lying in repose at the Reagan Library. The lines extended for hours, and people were parking offsite and taking shuttles up to the library. Two thousand people per hour filed past his casket at the Reagan Library, more than 108,000 in all. The staff was able to go in through a back door and stay behind the stanchions as long as we wanted to, watching the other mourners file by on the other side of the casket.

As I stood there for about half an hour, reflecting on my own thoughts about the president and taking a few moments to pay tribute to him in a small and silent way, I also was able to observe many of the others who had come to pay tribute as well. These mourners ran the spectrum from very elderly to babies on their parents' hips. Men in suits, women in dresses, and mechanics in their grease-covered shirts. There were members of the military, moms and dads, kids and grandparents, every demographic, every socioeconomic group and nationality. Some paused to offer up prayers, those in uniform stopped and saluted, and others uttered words of thanks or stood silently with tears streaming down their faces. Many wore flag pins, or vintage Reagan/Bush campaign memorabilia, or red, white, and blue shirts. All of them had sacrificed an entire day of their lives for just a moment in his presence, just a minute to remember and celebrate his life, just one last time to thank him and say goodbye. I was overwhelmed by the outpouring, knowing I wasn't alone in my grief and that the sentiments I had were widely held and shared. And that indeed this man was beloved by many, not just me.

As much as we wished the day would never arrive, it did. And we had to say goodbye to our beloved president. Finally. And forever. While we continued last-minute preparations for the interment ceremony at the Reagan Library, we caught glimpses of the ceremonial events taking place on the East Coast earlier that day. The procession down Constitution Avenue was symbolic and historic, using the horse-drawn caisson that had also carried President Kennedy's casket down that very same route and a riderless horse that had President Reagan's own riding boots placed in the stirrups facing backward, a symbol that the rider would never return. Ronald Reagan's was the first state funeral since

Lyndon Johnson's in 1973. President Nixon had passed away in 1994 but had declined a state funeral, choosing instead a more subdued ceremony at his presidential library in Yorba Linda, California, so on this day mourners lined the streets by the tens of thousands to be part of witnessing this historic cortege.

The state funeral service was held on June 11, 2004, at the National Cathedral in Washington, DC, and included four thousand mourners from 165 countries worldwide. There were three dozen world leaders or former heads of state in attendance as well, including the president's longtime dear friend and ally Margaret Thatcher. Though she managed to attend the National Cathedral service, she had feared several months prior that her health may have precluded her from attending or participating in his funeral if he passed away before she did. Always determined to speak her mind, she had specific things she wanted to ensure were said at his service, even if she couldn't be there in person, so she selected ahead of time the outfit she would ultimately wear to the service and taped a video tribute ahead of time. Her eulogy to her dear friend Ron ended with the beautiful words "We here still move in twilight, but we have one beacon to guide us that Ronald Reagan never had. We have his example. Let us give thanks today for a life that achieved so much for all of God's children."

President Gorbachev, while in attendance, did not give remarks, yet Brian Mulroney, another dear friend of the president's, spoke fondly, sharing a few humorous anecdotes and also saying, "Ronald Reagan was a president who inspired his nation—and transformed the world. He possessed a rare and prized gift called leadership, that ineffable and magical quality that sets some men and women apart so that millions will follow them as they conjure up grand visions and invite their countrymen to dream big and exciting dreams."

President George H. W. Bush, through a cracked voice and clearly holding back tears, said, "As his vice president for eight years, I learned more from Ronald Reagan than from anyone I encountered in all my years of public life. I learned kindness; we all did. I also learned courage; the nation did. And then I learned decency; the whole world did." He ended by saying, "God bless you, Ronald Wilson Reagan and the nation you loved and led so well."

And in a fitting and symbolic way, George W. Bush, the sitting president, summed up exactly what many were feeling. "We lost Ronald Reagan only days ago, but we have missed him for a long time. We have missed his kindly presence, that reassuring voice, the happy ending we had wished for him. It has been ten years since he said his own farewell; yet it is still sad and hard to let him go. Ronald Reagan belongs to the ages now but we preferred it when he belonged to us...We know, as he always said, that America's best days are ahead of us, but with Ronald Reagan's passing, some very fine days are behind us, and that is worth our tears."

Following the service at the National Cathedral, the funeral procession left for Andrews Air Force Base, passing through streets lined with thousands of people who came just to see his motorcade pass by and to say their final goodbyes. His casket was loaded onto SAM (Special Air Mission) 28000, one of the two Boeing 747-200s that serves the current president as *Air Force One*, for his final flight west. On the flight, the plane dropped altitude and flew over Tampico, Illinois, tipping a wing as a sign of respect to Ronald Reagan's birthplace and to central Illinois where he spent most of his early life. Just prior to landing at Naval Air Station Point Mugu in Oxnard, California (the same airfield he flew into and out of during his presidency when visiting his California ranch), the plane also flew over the Reagan Library, dropping altitude, circling it, and tipping a wing. The guests who were already seated for the service were understandably moved and teary eyed. The plane then landed, and the slow procession to the Reagan Library began.

Everything was perfectly timed for the evening, down to the minute, yet no one could have anticipated what happened on the twenty-eight-mile drive from the Naval Air Station to the Reagan Library. As in DC, people lined the streets, but unlike DC, people pulled their cars over and parked on the sides of the roads to watch the motorcade drive by. They lined overpasses, waved flags, brought signs of love and support, took photos, and recorded the motorcade driving by, saluting and weeping and waving. It was a remarkable sight. Up on the hill of the library where we were waiting, we were concerned since the anticipated arrival time was getting close but we hadn't yet received word that it was imminent. I called to inquire and was told that I would have to wait until later to see the footage on TV to fully understand and believe what was taking place. Traffic had slowed to a crawl and then had stopped, even on the freeway. People pulled over and got out of their cars to allow the motorcade to pass by as they watched and waved and saluted. As a result of the outpouring, the motorcade was driving half as fast as they had planned because they wanted to show gratitude to all those who had taken time out of their day and their lives and their busy schedules to pay tribute, to see him, to honor him, and to be near him one last time.

On the hill the timeline was adjusted, everything was pushed back by a few minutes as we awaited the arrival. Joanne had been emphatic that once he arrived, his personal staff should be seated, participating in the service itself at that point and beginning to say our own farewells. My seat was next to Greg, just a few rows from the front, and on the end where it would be easy to seat myself at the last minute. But I wanted to wait for him to arrive, to welcome him home once and for all, and to see Mrs. Reagan. He arrived amid fanfare, being lovingly carried by a military unit comprising strong young men from each branch of our armed services. I am certain that for each of them this was the honor of a lifetime, to carry the former commander in chief to his final resting place. Yet I also knew the president was never more proud than when he was surrounded by the brave men and women of our nation's military. Undoubtedly he would have been honored to be flanked by these American heroes.

And then I saw her—Mrs. Reagan. She had traveled to Washington, DC, with the president's casket, so I hadn't seen her that week except on television. She looked so small and frail, especially on the arm of her military escort, who was tall, poised, and unflappable. He was the epitome of strength and courage, and I am certain he had given her both as he had been unfailingly by her side all week long. Though the sadness was in evidence on her face, the determination was even more so. You could see in her a desire to honor her husband with the grace and composure that had always been their hallmark. Her grief was profound, yet there was a peaceful resolution on her face, as if she would not let the Alzheimer's that had robbed her of her husband shake her resolve or steal her ability to honor him with dignity. She had held up amazingly well all week long as the world watched. She had honored her husband in his life and now was continuing to do so even in his death. Her strength had given us all strength, just as her devotion had inspired ours. Once she was seated, I finally seated myself and started to absorb both the significance and the beauty of the evening, a fitting tribute to an individual who had led our country and in many ways had inspired the world. And yet had also been my boss. And had changed my life personally. And had meant the world to me.

Amid the sorrow, the ceremony was truly spectacular, as it should have been. The evening was perfect—the gorgeous sunset, the flag seemingly waving in time as the U.S. Air Force Band played musical honors, followed by a lone bagpiper solemnly playing "Amazing Grace" for the arriving casket. After the invocation, the U.S. Army Chorus sang "Battle Hymn of the Republic," which was followed by words of remembrance and the reading of Psalm 23.

The tributes were eloquent and stately, appropriate for the watching world yet surprisingly personal to me. The president's son Ron, amid his loving tribute, mentioned a funny little anecdote about his father's fondness for earlobes and how he would reach out and touch them on people, especially kids. I smiled when I thought of all the times I had seen the president do that to my kids and the photos we have of him doing that, and I felt intimately connected with this personal story that was now being shared with the world.

During Reverend Wenning's remarks, he recalled one visit to the president's office when he came in to pray with him. The president wasn't having a particularly good day and uncharacteristically didn't get up to greet the pastor or move over to the sitting area where they usually met. He just stayed seated behind his desk. Unbothered, Reverend Wenning pulled up a chair across from him and continued to talk and pray with him from there. The pastor recalled for the crowd that, a few minutes later, I had brought in his wife, Freda, to join them. The moment the president saw her he jumped right out of his chair to greet her. He was always a gentleman—it was embedded in his DNA. Through Reverend Wenning's words, the world was getting a little glimpse into the life of this beloved and faithful man, and with a story that had involved me. It was almost surreal, hearing my own personal experiences being shared so publicly.

When the speakers concluded, the military honor guard moved the president's casket to the memorial site, leading Mrs. Reagan to her husband's final resting place. A twenty-one-Howitzer salute was a powerful and jolting reminder of the loss and finality and gravity of the moment. A bugler played "Taps," and four Navy F-18 fighter jets flew overhead in the missing man formation. While the U.S. Air Force Band sang "America the Beautiful," the flag that had flown over the Capitol during President Reagan's 1981 inauguration and now draped his casket was folded by the military honor guard and presented to Mrs. Reagan by the commanding officer of the USS *Ronald Reagan* aircraft carrier. The audience joined the U.S. Army Chorus in one final song, "God Bless America." On the hillside below, horse-mounted police were patrolling, and intermittently we would hear the whinny of the horses or the clip-clop of their hooves, sounds the president had always loved. The ceremony engulfed the senses from every direction, filling the audience with love for our country and for this beloved man we were honoring and to whom we were reluctantly saying goodbye.

Midway through the service, Greg reached down and handed me the program he had removed from my chair earlier to make room for me to sit down. When he handed it to me, it was as if time came to a complete stop. All of a sudden I was no longer aware of what was being said in the service, I no longer was aware of the VIPs who surrounded me. I was aware of only one thing. I stopped and gasped. There it was, the very program I had been asked to design years earlier. I hadn't seen it since the last time I worked on it with the president. Immediately in my mind I was right back in the office, there on the thirty-fourth floor of Fox Plaza.

I was there at my desk, finishing up the final draft, trying to find the perfect words. But as difficult and awkward as approaching him had been, I had done it. And we had tackled this together, going through several drafts, changing a Scripture here and there, reducing the program from a large format with multiple pages and pictures and lots of text to a more simple design, which he preferred. And I agreed. In my mind I was back there in his office—seeing him, absorbing the sights, sounds, and smells of the office again, standing in his office, admiring the breathtaking view, waiting next to him behind his desk while he read it and reviewed it. It was as if I could hear his voice once again asking my opinion, commenting on this and that, making a little joke, knowing it was an uncomfortable situation for me to be addressing and wanting to put me at ease. It was as if I could still hear him thanking me for my willingness to step outside of my comfort zone and do this for him and with him.

And even more than being back in that place, I was back with that man. In my mind he was suddenly alive and well, larger than life and in charge again. That's how I wanted to picture him and remember him. I wanted to ultimately forget what he looked like when he was sick and failing and thin and quiet and remember him healthy and vigorous and robust and talkative. I wanted to remember him as the world remembered him, and not as I had seen him the past few years. I knew, as with my father, that eventually those memories of sickness and frailty and death would fade, though not immediately. But with time and patience the good would come to the forefront and the bad would retreat, only to be recalled intentionally whenever I wanted to—though even those images would become less graphic, less painful, less prominent, less clear in time.

Yes, these programs to me symbolized something so much more than ink on paper. They symbolized one of our last collaborative efforts together; they captured exactly what he had wanted to be printed on this day and how he wanted to be remembered. To me they symbolized our teamwork, the planning we did, how we were able to accomplish something meaningful and worthwhile in spite of our dissimilar backgrounds, our different life experiences, and our enormous age gap. They represented to me a piece of him and a piece of me, beautifully and forever fused together in this final piece. I thought of all the people who had touched this, seen this, revised this, and then ultimately printed this during the past week. None of them consulted me—none of them probably even knew it was the president and I who had collaborated on and agreed upon this final work. Yet it had been left virtually untouched, just as he had wanted it. And to me it was beautiful in its simplicity and in its symbolism. It represented the perfect blend of formality and familiarity that he represented. The text was minimal, just capturing and commemorating a moment, rather than trying to summarize an entire life.

But even more than all of that, to me, these programs were a part of him, one of the last pieces of work on which he ever commented and contributed. I had been honored to play a very small role, and this was now part of his legacy. In essence I was holding his legacy in my hands, both literally and symbolically. A few tears began to fall, directly from my heart and onto the program, his program. The realization that he was gone was beginning to hit. I didn't want to believe it or accept it. And even more, I didn't want to let him go. He was always there, even as he faded. His presence had given me strength; his life added purpose and meaning to mine. His leadership had inspired me, changed me, taught me, and challenged me.

I wasn't yet ready to think about his legacy, because that would mean that he had departed. Left us. Left me. The thought of his legacy was ominous. How would this man be remembered? And revered? And celebrated? And analyzed? What would history say? What would those who knew him say? And what would *I* say? Indeed, his legacy was in my hands, in part, to tell what I saw, to share what I learned, and to talk about the attributes that made him different and powerful and humble and kind and aware and patriotic and wonderfully revered. The thought of this was too much for me to bear. There was so much to share and recall and give back and live up to. It was too overwhelming and too daunting.

But then, as I looked down the aisle and looked at the people seated in front of me, behind me, and all around me, I realized that they were holding programs in their hands, too. This same program. His program. And though I had been the one to prepare it with him, I was not the only one holding it now. Everyone there was, too. So in essence, everyone was holding a piece of his legacy in their hands and would also have to face the burden, the obligation, the honor, and the privilege of being a caretaker of that legacy and a worthy steward of that which was entrusted to them. We all were unified in paying our tribute to this man and unified now in our unspoken pledge to pick up the torch that he had held high throughout his life and carried on behalf of us all. Now *we* must continue to shine it in a dark world—in every place that needs his light, his toughness, his comfort, his optimism, his faith, his joy, and his love for God, for America, and for us all. We would all leave there, each to our own corner of the world and our own circles of influence, taking with us the charge to share with others that which had changed and touched and inspired each of us and our life stories as a result of his.

As I sat there, I began to think even beyond the people seated there on that beautiful hilltop who were part of the service. I thought of the millions of people who were watching worldwide, who had been drawn to one last opportunity to be touched by this man, to be inspired by his life, and to become part of his legacy. All of those people, too, would now leave with a charge of their own to pass it along, to pay it forward, to give back that which they had received from Ronald Reagan to others.

I realized on the day of the president's funeral that not only were we reluctantly saying goodbye to a man whom many loved and respected, but more than that, we were saying goodbye to a piece of ourselves. We loved Ronald Reagan because we loved ourselves and we loved America when he was president.

We want to be proud of ourselves and proud of our country and now have to make that happen without him. Yet we have all the tools to make that happen. In giving to us first, Ronald Reagan gave us everything we would need to give back to each other, to our country, and to the world.

Ronald Reagan left a piece of himself in each of our lives and in our hearts—a memory from watching a televised speech, perhaps a handshake in person, or an autographed photo in the mail. Maybe it was a wave at an event or a smile into the camera you were certain was just for you, a quote in the newspaper you cut out and stuck to your refrigerator or on your desk at work as inspiration, a joke that made you laugh and that you loved to retell, a change in a regulation that lowered your taxes, an improvement in the economy that helped your family and created a more prosperous and secure future for your children, a chance to innovate that grew your business, or a dose of optimism and faith that drove you to do more, be more, build more. Or maybe he gave you, your family, or your nation of origin the ultimate gift: freedom.

We don't just need that one man, Ronald Reagan, now again in America. We need everyone who was blessed and touched by that one man to bring his legacy in their lives back to their families, their workplace, their community, and the world. These separate little pieces of Ronald Reagan's legacy that are scattered far and wide and have been held in stewardship all around the world now need to be brought back together and reassembled to reveal the beautiful mosaic of Ronald Reagan's legacy, which exists in us and could once again change the nation and inspire the world. Just as the president would have wanted.

Epilogue

When I started out writing this book I anticipated it would be a nice stroll down memory lane, recalling and retelling some memorable and historic years. I thought it would be a sentimental reflection of a decade of my life that paralleled a decade in the life of Ronald Reagan. I would reflect on what an honor it had been to serve him, what a privilege it was to have had a front-row seat to this man's life, and how unique a vantage point I had as a fly on the wall to special meetings with other world leaders. I anticipated that as the years had passed my stories would be pleasant and polite, new but still nostalgic. I never imagined that flipping the pages of my life back twenty-seven years would be so emotionally draining, so gut-wrenching, and so difficult to relive.

I thought I had gotten over the loss of this man—president to the nation, boss to me. I thought I had taken the legacy of my decade with him, gleaned the principles, applied the lessons, shared the takeaways, and matured in my life and in my perspective of what he had meant to me. But as I dug deeper, looked harder, shared more, and pushed myself further into territory I had never fully explored and never really wanted to, I discovered a painful reality—not only had I not yet gotten over this man and his impact on my life, but I never would. And I didn't want to. I never wanted to let him go—in my life, in my memory, and in the very heart of our great nation.

And I realized that my feelings, while unique because of my proximity, were likely symbolic of many in the nation and around the world who have never fully gotten over Ronald Reagan's impact on their life personally or gotten over the positive legacy of impact he left in their homes, their businesses, and their communities. They never would. And they don't want to.

I believe that we as individuals and as Americans not only don't want to get over Ronald Reagan, but want to get back to Ronald Reagan. Obviously not as our president, but as a symbol for what we can be, for the best we can be individually and the best we can be collectively. We want to get back to principled leadership and get back to optimism, vision, faith, civility, and confidence in ourselves and in our united purpose. We want to get back to the place where government works for *We the People*, not against *We the People*, get back to being a beacon of freedom that brings light and direction to dark corners of the globe where oppression still exists, and get back to loving ourselves and loving America as we did when Ronald Reagan was president.

Acknowledgments

Thank you to everyone who is part of the beautiful mosaic of Ronald Reagan's legacy:

Those who supported his rise to the presidency, those who were part of the Reagan Revolution in the 1980s here at home, and those who helped American leadership change the map globally with the expansion of freedom under President Reagan. To the brave men and women in our military who protect and defend this blessed land, you have my undying gratitude. And to the men and women of the United States Secret Service—I admire your commitment and professionalism and applaud your remarkable kindness, especially in Ronald Reagan's final years. You have my utmost respect.

To the unrivaled Office of Ronald Reagan staff from whom I learned so much—and with whom I shared so much. Together we accomplished great things. Even though our numbers were small, our hearts were huge and we made the impossible possible through hard work, creative tenacity, and committed teamwork—with a generous dose of humor along the way! My gratitude to the ORR team of Fred Ryan, Mark Weinberg, Joanne Drake, Cathy Busch, Jon Hall, Sheri Lietzow, Selina Jackson, Lisa Cavelier, Kathy Osborne, Dottie Dellinger, Erik Felten, Ethan Baker, Eileen Foliente, Johanna Afshani, Kerry Perlow, Bernadette Schurz, Kay Paietta, Wren Powell, Libby Brady, Dan Quiggle, Dan Zarraonandia, Keith Redmon, Steve Christiansen, Karen Moore, John Reid, Alison Sparrow, Stefanie Davis, John Lee, Chuck Jelloian, Suzanne Marx, and Dianne Capps. To Laurie Gurley, Ozra Lotfizadeh, and Bel Air Presbyterian Preschool for helping with the kid shuffle all those years—and to

"Miss Patty" Corry, who always said yes to anything I needed during that demanding decade, regardless of the day or the hour. You are truly the best neighbor and friend anyone could ever have!

To my friends at the Reagan Library who, under the leadership of Duke Blackwood, preserve the Reagan legacy for history and for generations to come. Thank you to Steve Branch for reading my mind when I describe what photo I have in my mind, and then sending me exactly what I am looking for—and doing so in the blink of an eye. You're amazing!

To John Heubusch, who keeps the Reagan legacy alive through the work of the Reagan Foundation—and the heroic efforts of your talented and hard-working team.

To other keepers of the Reagan flame—Eureka College and John Morris, the Reagan Ranch and Young America's Foundation, the Friends of Ronald Reagan organization, and the Ronald Reagan Centennial Celebration—each plays an important role in telling the totality of Ronald Reagan's life and legacy. To Morton Blackwell and the Leadership Institute for training the next generation of leaders and allowing me to be part of it. To Americans For Prosperity for their efforts to promote an informed and engaged electorate on important issues. I'm honored to be affiliated with AFP.

To those who made this book happen: From a comment in passing by UVA's Jeff Chidester years ago that stuck with me and I couldn't shake, "If there was a woman who sat right outside Abraham Lincoln's office every day for ten years, don't you think we would want to know what she saw? And wouldn't she owe that to history?" To a providential introduction at an event in New York to RoseMarie Terenzio, former executive assistant to John F. Kennedy Jr. and reading her book, *Fairy Tale Interrupted*, which sparked my imagination for what might be possible, to her bold and unsolicited introduction to her literary agent, Steve Troha of Folio Literary, who believed I had a story to tell before I even told my story—and took initiative to bring it out of me and bring it to life. Steve, I owe this book to your vision for what it could be. To a casual conversation around a cocktail table at a wine bar in NYC (I don't even drink wine!) with Paul Whitlatch of Hachette Books, who I thought was just being courteous and generous with his time, but a life-changing email from him a few weeks later ultimately led to this book. Thank you, Paul, for taking a chance on me—an unknown name with no manuscript, but with passion and drive to honor the man I served. I have worked tirelessly to be worthy of your belief in me and in the value of my point of view. I am proud to bear the Hachette imprint and honored to work with you and your talented team—Lauren, Hallie, Michelle, and Betsy. And to Danelle Morton, who helped me find *my* voice after so many years of writing in the president's voice. You pushed me to get away from the principles and talking points of my years and reveal the heart of my experience. You unleashed the dormant writer in me and tapped into the beauty of storytelling from a place of authenticity and truth. This book wouldn't be what it is without you.

To my mom, Susan Giboney, an amazing matriarch who has held our family together bravely and lovingly, keeping my dad's memory ever present. For Carrie and Andy Wall, Paul and Paula Giboney, and my six beautiful, accomplished nieces—Jenna, Jessica, and Michaela Wall and Amy, Anna, and Ashley Giboney. I am grateful for the fun and the faith that we share—and the memories in the past and those still to be shared. And for my dad's enormous, fun-loving, flag-waving, faith-guided Giboney family, which spans from sea to shining sea—his eight siblings and their spouses, twenty-six cousins and their spouses, eighty-one great-grands and twenty-nine great-great-grands...and counting... everyone should be so blessed to have been raised on your love and your laughter. Your faith, work ethic, optimism, and patriotism are inspiring. Grandma Ruth would be very proud! And to my grandma Archie, who taught me to love our nation and love our flag by her enthusiastic example of patriotism.

For Greg's family, who welcomed me years ago as their very own, not knowing what a tornado of activity would come along with me: John and Virginia Grande, the most loving and supportive in-laws anyone could ever dream of. Thank you for raising your son to be a remarkable husband and father. You are a blessing to me and to our family. For Greg's siblings and their families—Debbie and Allen Polfer; Andrew, Jen, Hazel, and baby Polfer 2017; MJ Grande and Mike, Isaac, and Laurel Stark; Rich, Lysa, Nicole, and Ryan Grande; and Marianne Browning. You tolerate my absence at family gatherings when my travels conflict and show undying support and enthusiasm for each one of my projects and opportunities. I love you all dearly!

Friends galore I'm blessed to share life with: Erik Felten, who is family—"ohana"—from college to the condo, from Sherman Oaks to Century City, from the 91011 to the 5-0, and a world of adventures in between. Thanks for our years as the original "Three's Company" and for showing my family and me the world. I appreciate your always "calling it in" and keeping the bumpers up for me. And for your incredible talent of sending me a five-word email that can make me laugh all day. Love and gratitude to your sweet family as well: Hayley, Gretchen, and Katie. To Stewart McLaurin, the consummate professional and treasured friend—we have worked very hard side by side and had a lot of fun along the way, too. I have learned invaluable lessons by your example and leadership. Ethan Baker, my colleague-at-large, who has read and reread and advised and revised this manuscript. I value your loyal friendship, enthusiasm for this project, and shared commitment to excellence and respect. Your support keeps me sane and breaks the monotony of my days. Governor Scott Walker and Tonette—for your treasured friendship and enthusiastic support of this book project. Dan Quiggle, my longtime friend, you have pushed me out of my comfort zone and encouraged me to be bold in sharing my story. An amazingly talented speaker, you have helped me hone my message and confidently find my own voice. Mark Weinberg for fact checking, checking on my progress, and reminding me "It CAN Be Done," even as you were up to your eyeballs in writing your own book. To Ed Henry, my valued friend, whose simultaneous book project, *42 Faith: The Rest of the Jackie Robinson Story* will certainly be a bestseller. Thank you for inviting me to be part of it. The

Mosaic LA Church community for keeping me connected to God and to amazing people of faith, creativity, and passion; Andrea and our "granny walks" and talks, which help clear my head; Amy, Brandon, and Wunda-Bar Pilates, which keeps me fit, keeps me grounded, and helps me reset after my travels; Juan and JnB for keeping me caffeinated; Bob Rountree and Kacey Rountree for sharing your island homes as I finished writing this book; Matt Robbins, Dan Mason, Bret Peters, Chas Turansky, Erik Ovanespour and Printefex, Ron Bailey, Chad Fears, Aaron Schock, Adam Fidler, Linda Lynch, Kent Strang, Brent Barksdale, Jim Angle, Daryn Iwicki, Tammie Wallace, the Pepperdine community, Al Han, Sally Hogshead, Jon Gordon, Kristina Boyd, Tom at Crestmont, the Ginns family, and Andy Kitchen Photography—each of you played a role that is greatly appreciated. To Paul G. Haaga, Jr. and the LA County Natural History Museum for finding a needle in the haystack—hunting down the president's office painting. And to the global executive assistant community, who serve faithfully behind the scenes day after day, you have my utmost admiration and respect—you play an essential role and I hope you know the value you add.

To Kristen Kilaghbian, whom I have watched grow up in our house from toddler to teen—you're a delight at every age. Ashlyn Adelman, who has been a special part of our family for years—we love you and are so proud of you. Cambri Russell, you bring beauty and grace every time you walk in the door. Julia Kaissling, you have been embraced by our family with open arms and have been brave enough to stick around, blessing us with your smarts and your smile. And to all of our Pancake Party friends new and old, who bless Casa Grande with your friendship, your laughter, and your appetites. I hope you always feel welcomed and loved here—because you are!

To Lola, my loyal four-legged sidekick, who sat by me for hours on end as I wrote, keeping me company and making me happy. And in memory of our sweet Dutchess, whose passing has left a void in our home. Her majestic beauty is missed dearly.

To my husband, Greg, my faithful companion and partner in life and in love, who has experienced many seasons of life with me. I couldn't ask for a more supportive husband and incredible father for our four kids. You're a blessing to me and to us all.

To Taylor, my favorite son, who is a champion for others, just like the president was. Your many talents and your generosity in sharing them are rarities in the world today, and your kind heart draws people to you. Your bright mind and compassionate heart will continue to open doors of opportunity for you. I delight in watching you achieve and succeed. I am proud and blessed to be your mom and am grateful for all the ways you have made my life better.

To Courtney, who constantly reminds me and the whole world that we are loved. You bring grace, joy, love, and support to those around you and have an amazing way of setting a goal and being undeterred in accomplishing it. You ran our household while I wrote this book, and I couldn't have done it without you taking everything else off my plate for those months. I am the luckiest mother in the world to be yours.

To Paige, my junior editor-in-chief, who has an amazing knack for helping me say what I want to say. Your wisdom and insight are far beyond your years, and your enthusiasm for life and your drive in making things happen will take you anywhere you want to go in life—I'll just sit back and marvel. A natural-born leader, you pour your heart and soul into everything you do, and you are an unstoppable force of achievement and passion.

To Jocelyn, you have found your own remarkable place in the midst of a crowded family. No one is more thoughtful and kind than you are. You're intuitive and smart, always ready to be helpful and supportive, volunteering your time to help others less fortunate and graciously serving your family, too. Everyone knows and loves you as you bring beauty and happiness everywhere you go. You completed our family and make my life complete.

To Ronald Reagan, for teaching me everything I will ever need to know about how to live life to the fullest; lead with integrity, excellence, and kindness; and leave a lasting and powerful legacy that is memorable and meaningful. You set the standard. None will ever match you. And Mrs. Reagan, who was faithful and true, bringing out the best in her husband for the world to see and benefit from.

To almighty God, who constantly surprises me with the ways in which He makes His will known to me and chooses to bless me in spite of my inadequacies.

Photo Credits

Interior image credits: (business card) Courtesy of the author; (doodle) Courtesy of the author; (handwritten notecard) Courtesy of the Ronald Reagan Presidential Foundation

Photo insert credits: (page 1) Courtesy of the author; Courtesy of the Ronald Reagan Presidential Foundation; Courtesy of the Ronald Reagan Presidential Foundation; Courtesy of the Ronald Reagan Presidential Foundation; (page 2) All courtesy of the Ronald Reagan Presidential Foundation; (page 3) All courtesy of the Ronald Reagan Presidential Foundation; (page 4) Courtesy of the author; Photo by Mary Anne Fackelman-Miner, courtesy of the Ronald Reagan Presidential Foundation; Photo by Mary Anne Fackelman-Miner, courtesy of the Ronald Reagan Presidential Foundation; Courtesy of the Ronald Reagan Presidential Foundation; (page 5) All courtesy of the Ronald Reagan Presidential Foundation; (page 6) All courtesy of the Ronald Reagan Presidential Foundation; (page 7) All courtesy of the Ronald Reagan Presidential Foundation; (page 8) Courtesy of the Ronald Reagan Presidential Foundation; Courtesy of the Ronald Reagan Presidential Foundation; Courtesy of the author; Courtesy of the author